Pluralism in Education

Pluralism in Education

CONFLICT, CLARITY, AND COMMITMENT

By

RICHARD PRATTE

Professor of Education
The Ohio State University
Columbus, Ohio

CHARLES C THOMAS • PUBLISHER
Springfield • Illinois • U.S.A.

Published and Distributed Throughout the World by
CHARLES C THOMAS ● PUBLISHER
Bannerstone House
301-327 East Lawrence Avenue, Springfield, Illinois, U.S.A.

© *1979, by* CHARLES C THOMAS ● PUBLISHER

ISBN 0-398-03911-9 (cloth)
ISBN 0-398-03912-7 (paper)
Library of Congress Catalog Card Number: 79-11247

With THOMAS BOOKS *careful attention is given to all details of
manufacturing and design. It is the Publisher's desire to present books that
are satisfactory as to their physical qualities and artistic possibilities and
appropriate for their particular use.* THOMAS BOOKS *will be true to those
laws of quality that assure a good name and good will.*

Printed in the United States of America
V-R-1

Library of Congress Cataloging in Publication Data

Pratte, Richard.
 Pluralism in education.

 Includes bibliographical references and index.
 1. Minorities--Education--United States. 2. In-
tercultural education--United States. 3. Bilingualism
--United States. I. Title.
LC3731.P7   371.9'7'0973   79-11247
ISBN 0-398-03911-9
ISBN 0-398-03912-7 pbk.

PREFACE

THIS book is about cultural pluralism and education. It deals with the conflict that surrounds cultural pluralism and how education is affected, but above all its presupposes the need for clarity before commitment. If this quality is present in this book, it should be counted a success, for the task of clarification is a large onè, and its accomplishment will require all the intelligence and perseverance that can be mustered.

The task then is straightforward. The book is designed to provide the reader with a working knowledge of cultural pluralism, its clarification, and its bearings on education. It is not a book on the history of Americans and their experience with cultural pluralism and education, but deals with what is sadly lacking in the crisis mentality of the present, namely, just what is cultural pluralism? Why is cultural pluralism important for education? Why does cultural pluralism appear so strong today? Why should the schools embrace its doctrines? If the general public and the educationists do not carefully study cultural pluralism and the commitments that have come to enshroud it, then continued conflict is not unlikely.

This book is thus addressed both to educationists and to the so-called lay public. In this day when so many ethnics are "coming out of the closet" it is imperative that we take the message of cultural pluralism seriously. The point is that never was the cultural pluralists' message so clear and urgent as it is today. In establishing a framework and content for grasping the many faces of cultural pluralism, it is hoped that a needed literature has been added.

I am indebted to my wife Janet for all her help. Without her assistance my task would have been immeasurably more difficult. In addition, I also wish to thank Philip L. Smith, a col-

Pluralism in Education

league, for suggesting the idea. Finally, I owe an expression of gratitude to my students whose discussions helped me to clarify my thinking in a great many ways.

R.P.

ACKNOWLEDGMENTS

IN organizing material for this book, I collected five essays that span no more than five years. The earliest of them was published in 1973 and the last in 1978. Three chapters are new and were written to give this work a more balanced, complete perspective. Each chapter was written for a particular purpose, prompted by the need to clarify a problem that seemed particularly pressing in terms of a need for clarification at the time of composition. Thus as a whole, the work lies within a very short span of time and reflects a class of unified emphases despite the fact that the earliest were not written entirely with that purpose in mind.

I am grateful to the following publishers for permission to reprint my previously published works:

"Cultural Diversity and Education," reprinted from *Ethics and Educational Policy*, Kenneth A. Strike and Kieran Egan eds. (London, Routledge & Kegan Paul, 1978).

"Ideology and Cultural Diversity," reprinted from *Ideology and Education* (New York, David McKay, 1977).

"Cultural Pluralism and the Public School Movement," reprinted from *The Public School Movement: A Critical Study* (New York, David McKay, 1973).

"Cultural Pluralism and Its Relativistic Component," reprinted from *Review Journal of Philosophy and Social Science*, 1 (1, 2), 1976.

"Bilingualism and Pluralism: Between a Rock and a Hard Place," reprinted from *Current Issues in Education* (Glassboro, N. J., John Dewey Society, 1976).

R.P.

CONTENTS

INTRODUCTION

THERE is growing interest in cultural diversity and the ideology of cultural pluralism that sanctifies it. This book rests on the conviction that critical thought is of the first importance in coming to understand the nature of these two volatile phenomena in American education, especially as they form some fresh, and some not so fresh, visions for those who wish to reform American schools and schooling.

Two Objections

Anyone writing a book devoted to the clarification of the relationship among cultural diversity, pluralism, and education must try to answer two sorts of objections, for both contain a partial truth:

1. Cultural diversity is not a phenomenon which has significant importance for education.
2. Cultural pluralism is not an ideology which has significant importance for education.

First Objection

In relation to the first point, it must certainly be admitted that there is no exact correspondence between cultural diversity and education. In passing from the experiential world of racial, religious, and ethnic groups to literature, the concept commonly degenerates into a slogan. This is obviously true to some extent of the relationship of any cultural idea to any organized endeavor such as the institution of formal education: school. But it is also true that in a general phenomenon such as cultural diversity, based on conflicting, often antagonistic, informal and formal groupings, the role of many competing groups influencing schooling will tend to be difficult to ascertain.

The conclusion derived from the above, however, need not be depressing. Cultural diversity as a movement in American life has been and continues to be ubiquitous, although its legitimacy and place in American life is not always recognized and respected. It is thus not remarkable that it may be viewed as either a blessing or a curse. And it is even less remarkable that it cannot be easily ignored. For many decades, cultural diversity was seen as a curse, something to be negated. The continued maintenance of subcultures and subgroups based on racial, religious, or ethnic lines was regarded as antithetical to a truly democratic society. The viewing of cultural diversity as a blessing is a somewhat more contemporary view, brought about in part by blacks and other non-European ethnic groups who wished to achieve political and social gains in America.

As a phenomenon in American life, cultural diversity has helped shape educational policies and practices as well as educational beliefs in a number of generations of Americans, although all these beliefs have not always been compatible. On the positive side, for example, it is instructive to observe that the teaching of foreign languages has been encouraged by ethnic groups. Ethnic studies, multiethnic education, multicultural education, and international education are but a few of the curricular programs supported by second- and third-generation immigrants as well as the non-European minorities.

This is not the place to specify the total educational effort of those who support a positive cultural diversity. Suffice it to say that considerable effort is given to encouraging schools to avoid the tokenism of a Columbus Day, Martin Luther King, Jr., Day, or a Black America Week. Proponents of cultural diversity are asking, exhorting, encouraging, cajoling, and threatening educators in order to get them to recognize that cultural diversity exists, that it is legitimate, and that an education that discounts the value of cultural diversity by ascribing to cultural differences a negative connotation — "culturally deficient," "culturally disadvantaged" — is itself not legitimate. It is no longer acceptable or tolerable. The new-found pride of blacks,

Native Americans, Hispanics, and European minorities is more than evidenced in a growing assertiveness aimed at reforming educational policies and practices along the lines of a positive cultural diversity.

In response to this assertiveness, educational functionaries are hastily developing new curricula designed to engage students in activities aimed at achieving intergroup understanding, particularly in terms of stressing the values that diversity is good as an end in itself, and it is better to have a society with a varied population since this adds to the vitality, interest, and possible range of human interaction. Students are encouraged to learn the roots of prejudice and its function in society, the nature and consequences of discrimination, the strengths of subgroups, and the need to search for personal identity within a culturally diverse society. Other school programs are being designed to help minority group members become facile and productive within the dominant culture without, at the same time, devaluing the worth of their own subgroup values.

It can be legitimately argued, however, that one of the weaknesses of cultural diversity is the lack of a completely articulated defense against the charge that it promotes divisiveness in society. The long history of failure to promote human rights, the lack of tolerance regarding others, bigotry, and overweening ethnocentrism are alleged to be the evils of cultural diversity insofar as it encourages a vulgar and unscrupulous narrowness of group aims and purposes in society. Encouraging narrow group interest, cultural diversity makes it impossible for citizens to find common areas of interest and agreement and to promote tolerance not only of groups but also of individuals. It is then not hard to understand, according to some, that Americans find it next to impossible to reconcile interests and negate traditional antagonisms toward one another. In other words, cultural diversity must be suppressed, for it presents a false and distorted picture in which every group is the equivalent of every other group and in which our common heritage as a nation is either defamed or negated.

At this point an objection can be raised. Some political theorists would agree that cultural diversity has made a valuable contribution to American democracy. The importance of competition between rival organized groups and major social associations, especially organized interest groups, involves a balancing process which operates largely outside the government. Government acts more as an umpire than as participant in setting rules for conflict resolution and moving in to redress the imbalance when one group goes too far. All of this is basic to what many would call "participatory democracy." Thus as a movement in American life, cultural diversity has done much to enrich and propagate democratic processes and, in turn, improve the quality of life.

If cultural diversity is ubiquitous, it is also ambiguous. It has meant many things to different people. Like some primitive native god, cultural diversity has many faces but few clear meanings. It has reflected different racial, religious, and ethnic traditions, and its influence has been discontinuous, for different phases of cultural diversity have required different ideological justifications. This leads to the second objection.

Second Objection

It hardly seems that one can pick up a newspaper, a popular or academic journal, or listen to the evening news without being bombarded with reports of the splintering of traditional economic classes along racial or ethnic lines. In their stead we find ethnic combinations that have considerable influence and clout at the present time, particularly in the education arena. It is the strength and cohesiveness of these groups — the degree to which the group acts as one — which determines their success in the competition for society's goods and services, including public education. Indeed, it seems to be the case that the most pressing issues of education today assume ethnic or racial form. Witness the desegregation/busing issue as well as the "quota" and "reverse discrimination" issues in higher education.

The full flavor of what is happening in formal education, and not only in America, can be gained only by recognizing that ethnicity, reduced to its essentials, is embedded in cultural diversity, and the ideology most commonly promotive of cultural diversity is cultural pluralism. In other words, cultural pluralism is the ideology that glories and revels in cultural diversity (some might say *rationalizes* it). The cultural pluralist assumes that diversity is a virtue from the standpoint of ourselves as well as from that of others. Diversity is a good, and cultural pluralism is protective of the rights of individuals to be different. In this view, there is no necessity to invoke theological or metaphysical beliefs to shore up cultural diversity. One need only imagine a society without it. What comes to mind is a society overtly or subtly totalitarian, requiring a pervasive sameness of its citizens along with a lack of tolerance of others. The suicidal nature of such a promenade of "imagined horribles" as found in such a society is at the heart of a defense of cultural pluralism.

It is misleading in the extreme, in my judgment, to refer to cultural diversity as ideology; this simply is not the case. Moreover, it is equally misleading to believe that we always aspired to the ideology of cultural pluralism. We did not march steadily toward it; we merely stumbled into it. We got cultural diversity — racial, religious, and ethnic groupings — because of historical factors: immigration and multiplication. The building of a new nation in the New World is an old story now. It began with an extraordinarily heterogeneous population, and this phenomenon never has been arrested, despite changes in immigration laws. The fact is, old groupings remain viable and new ones continue to form in America. Hence, the old groups multiplied and were added to by new arrivals until there was nothing anyone could do about them. Thus, through no great design or plan, we settled on giving the diverse cultural groups permission to exist, and we now call the ideal state of culturally diverse groups living together "cultural pluralism." To a considerable degree, then, we found, to our vast delight, that by default in some instances, and by positively proclaiming the virtue of cultural diversity in other instances, we could congratulate ourselves on having achieved a democratic public ideology of cultural diversity: cultural pluralism.

There is, however, a curious fact to observe about cultural

pluralism. Its status, even in its most mature phase, has always been precarious at best. There are other attractive ideologies of cultural diversity — assimilation, amalgamation, and the open society — and these have successfully competed and occasionally overwhelmed cultural pluralism, although the mystique of cultural pluralism, its belief that diversity is good and tolerance is the most desirable of all virtues, has an enduring fascination and attraction for many Americans.

What this sketch so far fails to offer is the deep sense of kinship between cultural diversity and cultural pluralism. The belief that the true value of a society can be realized only in situations promotive of subsocietal groups living together in the polity, but separated in order to guarantee the freedom of ethnic or religious communality and traditions without at the same time interfering with the carrying out of standard responsibilities to the general American civic life, is certainly the defining characteristic of cultural pluralism. In this ideology, subgroup affiliation is ennobling because it provides the human spirit with its proper communal nourishment and *raison d'etre*. All other social orders are somehow lacking, at least in this view. Society must acknowledge the prior and absolute claim of the subgroup entity to obedience, values, and attitudes of which the individual forms a part. What is left, therefore, of the nation-state is a federation of loosely allied groups working together in the secondary relations areas of political action, economic life, and civic responsibility.

It is obvious that cultural pluralism conceives of freedom through diversity. In simple terms, the ethnic, racial, and religious enclaves of America are not its weakness but its strength. Minority group membership is not to be viewed so much as a marginal existence removed from the larger society but, rather, a positive form of social identity, a way of knowing who you are, what your "roots" are within the larger, often depersonalized, society. Moreover, freedom is had because the various groups represent political interest groups. Each group is, in its own time and place, organized in order to acquire its share of society's rewards.

It is not often enough noticed by either cultural pluralists or its opponents that, ideologically, cultural pluralism is celebrated not because it actually achieves or performs any single function perfectly, but because it is said to promote, more effectively than any other ideology of cultural diversity, a belief in freedom of association, implying the further belief that a democratic society must afford room for many competing life-styles, and that no one of them is superior to the others. Herein lies a very powerful belief employed to justify and legitimize actions. Those who embrace the ideology of cultural pluralism do not think of it as arbitrary or unwarranted. On the contrary, they claim that their view is valid. They think of its as "self evident," "what any rational person will hold," "realistic," or "based on what human nature really is." Cultural pluralism is assumed to combine the best features of conjoint associated living, group participatory democracy, and its logical conclusion is the allowing of each individual to develop a sense of purpose which makes up a fully developed and integrated personality.

Moreover, according to the cultural pluralist, society as a whole benefits from cultural pluralism, for its offers a reasonable assurance that the involvement of individuals in society through group association will give most citizens a stake in the society and will help generate loyalties needed to maintain political and cultural stability with a minimum of coercion. And if this were not enough to convince the skeptic of the value of cultural pluralism, it is further claimed that new groups can articulate their perspectives and preferences in society which will eventually enter the decision-making process, affecting the direction of conflict issue resolution.

If the celebration of diversity is the central characteristic of cultural pluralism, then the proposing of an unachievable purpose, an ideal state, is a close competitor. Cultural pluralism embraces the belief that a particular state of affairs — group participatory democracy — is its goal or purpose. Obviously, no matter how much a society moves in the direction of this state of affairs, there is a sense in which it fails to achieve the ideal. In other words, only a fool would consider such a state of affairs achievable, and the wise person would be content to bring about progressively a more perfect state of affairs, even though it falls short of realizing the ideal.

The fact that cultural pluralism posits a utopia of sorts is significant, because the attempt to specify a single univocal set of criteria as a basis for distinguishing the ideal society from what is not has been one of the most obsessive and futile preoccupations of modern and ancient thought. The lesson to be learned is not how difficult and complex it is to achieve an ideal state, but rather, is the ideal state, by definition unachievable, serving its purpose if it leads citizens to effect a state that progressively resembles more closely the ideal state.

But the unity of cultural pluralism, even in its most basic premises, always has been precarious. Not all cultural pluralists are agreed about how the ideal state of affairs is to be progressively approached. Their differences turn on the degree of segregation or isolation needed to achieve group participatory democracy. Some espouse an insular pattern, proclaiming the virtue of groups living as much apart and having as little contact with one another as possible, except, of course, on the level of polity. In this view, each group would restrict both primary and secondary relations to members of that group, and intergroup contact, always minimal, would be limited solely to contact on the level of polity or civic association. Other cultural pluralists opt for a less insular pattern, claiming that primary relations should be restricted to ingroup members, but secondary relations or associations must be carried on with other groups and outgroup individuals.

The difference in style as well as substance between the two forms of cultural pluralism is not easily explained. It may help to understand that all ideologies are identified, at least in part, by the fact that they are carefully wrought systems of belief designed to do battle with opposing ideas. Cultural pluralism was elaborated after the great waves of immigration had come to America and after earlier groups continued to multiply and maintain themselves in the face of the majority ideology of assimilation in the form of Anglo-conformity. Grasping this point, we can understand that cultural pluralism was employed to refute and negate other ideologies aimed at defining the "real meaning" of American democracy. Hence, for some cultural pluralists, insular as opposed to broadened pluralism is the proper means for achieving group participatory democracy. To others, including some cultural pluralists, insular pluralism is an anti-democratic ideology, for, taken literally, its acceptance on a widespread scale would mean the end of the United States of America. Instead, we would have a Federated Union with each state representing a large grouping of interests along racial, religious, or ethnic lines.

One more element can be added as a capstone to an objection to the ideology of cultural pluralism. Intellectually, some see it as containing a basic fallacy. Orlando Patterson claimed to have detected a fundamental contradiction at the heart of this ideology. He argued that cultural pluralism neglects individuality insofar as an emphasis on group diversity and group tolerance works against a respect for individuality. He called this the "pluralist fallacy":

> [Cultural pluralism] . . . protects the rights of individuals to be different. . . . For it turns out that this defense centers wholly on social groups rather than on individuals. When liberals talk about a diverse society, they mean a diversity of ethnic groups; and when tolerance is mentioned, it refers to tolerance not of other individuals but of the groups to which they belong.
>
> This defense of pluralism not only neglects individuality; much worse, an emphasis on group diversity and group tolerance works against a respect for individuality. This is what I call the pluralist fallacy, which originates in the failure to recognize a basic paradox in human interaction: the greater the diversity and cohesiveness of groups in a society, the smaller the diversity and personal autonomy of individuals in that society.[1]

Patterson's conclusion is inescapable: "Group diversity, in short, is antagonistic to individual diversity and autonomy."[2]

Hence, while numerous theorists have taken a critical stance toward the ideology of cultural pluralism, the cumulative result has not been wholly negative. On the contrary, if cultural pluralism is not wholly accepted, it has acquired during its

---

[1]Orlando Patterson, "Ethnicity and the Pluralist Fallacy," *Change*, March 1975, p. 10-11.

[2]Patterson, "Ethnicity and Pluralist Fallacy," p. ii.

history strong support. One reason for this is due to the fact that over the years cultural pluralism has acquired rather precise aims. They were first and foremost of a negative or defensive kind. One can, of course, argue that there is nothing negative about a sincere commitment to cultural diversity and to the preservation and greatness of traditional beliefs and attitudes brought by immigrant groups. It is a positive value, and cultural pluralism would be inexplicable without the force of such subgroup sentiment. However, not all supporters of cultural diversity are cultural pluralists, but the reverse is quite true. For cultural diversity to be converted into cultural pluralism, love of ethnic communality and religious diversity must be transmuted into a particular ideological force promotive of primary group relationships following racial, ethnic, or religious lines. *Desegregation*, for example, may be supported by cultural pluralism because it refers to the elimination of racial criteria in the operation of public or quasi-public facilities, services, and institutions, to which the individual is entitled as a functioning member of the public, as a citizen of the local or national community equal in legal status to other citizens. *Integration*, on the other hand, is not supported by cultural pluralists because it implies much more than desegregation, namely the elimination of hard and fast barriers in the primary group relations and communal life of the various ethnic groups of the nation. Specifically, integration presupposes an easy and fluid mixture of people of diverse racial, religious, and ethnic backgrounds in social cliques, families (intermarriage), private organizations, and intimate friendships. The presupposition, obviously, is anathema to cultural pluralists.

A corollary is that for school to play an important role in society, it must be viewed as "legitimate"; that is, the people who are served by school must believe that it serves their interests and needs. A great deal of heat has been generated in recent years by cultural groups who dispute the schools' claim to legitimacy. For some, the present day school experience is not legitimate because it demeans, denies, denigrates, or ignores ("benign neglect," perhaps) the brute fact of cultural diversity. *Inequality* is a label used by these groups to refer to disparities between groups defined not in terms of social class, occupational status, or income level, but to refer to disparities between racial or ethnic groups and the dominant majority. Inequalities which for moral/political/economic reasons are found unacceptable, hence not legitimate, are regarded as forms of discrimination to be removed or at least modified through political measures. This is somewhat of a recent phenomenon in the United States since previous definitions of disparities referred not to racial or ethnic disparity but to social class, occupational status, or income level.

Obviously, what is regarded as discrimination changes over time and in terms of geography. In other countries differences between racial, cultural, ethnic, or religious subgroups traditionally have been in the forefront of the inequality discussion, but until recently, inequalities in the United States were not identified with anything but social status, and to many this remains the case. But today it seems safe to say that beliefs about what is discrimination in the relationships among racial and/or ethnic groups have become solidified. For one thing, the question of inequality may relate less to attainment than to control over what is being attained. Offering an ethnic group equal opportunity to attain something to which the group attaches little value, but denying it services to which it really attaches great value, may be viewed as discriminating as any inequality measured along the lines of quantitative attainment.

This work suggests that educational policy and practice must respect the ideology of cultural pluralism. Whatever may be the consensus regarding cultural pluralism as normative theory, even its sharpest critics agree that in practice its effects are seen practically everywhere; it is a highly visible set of social, political, and moral beliefs which informs an individual's (or group's) interpretation of the world and shapes his actions. Hence, those who are centrally concerned with educational policy making, lay persons and school personnel, cannot ignore or be blind to cultural pluralism. Respect, however, does not necessarily mean blind acceptance, an uncritical, compulsive readiness to "get on the bandwagon" in promoting educational policy and practice in compliance with cultural

pluralism. The acquisition of facts without a theoretical framework, pat answers without questioning, commitment before
clarity, and programs without direction are not part of what is
meant here by respect. What is needed is a grasp of underlying
concepts and principles — a knowledge of why the pluralist
interpretation is not so much wrong as it is systematically
misleading, and a working knowledge of why the ongoing
controversy over cultural pluralism ideology is linked to fundamental questions about the nature and proper functions of
political pluralism. Such a respect will enable decision makers
to develop their own critical judgment of the pros and cons of
the short- and long-range effects of cultural pluralism in education and thus make ready the arena in which rational discussion may take place.

Plan of the Book

This is a practical book. It attempts to explicate what we
should and must grasp if we are to understand the dominant
ideologies of cultural diversity in American life today. It is
assumed that the quality of our decisions can be no greater
than the quality of our understandings. But what counts as
"practicality" to one may not necessarily count to another. To
some, it may seem that the book does not offer definitive answers to specific issues or questions. Others may see the book as
sufficiently clarifying conceptual and logical problems but
lacking in specific directions to teachers, administrators, coun-
selors, and other interested individuals. Still others may find
the work deficient in terms of having no direct practical application to the methodological or curricular decisions classroom
teachers have to make each day.

The problem of practicality is solved when we consider that
this book does not present in serial fashion pat answers to
questions, a cookbook approach, but concentrates on examining questions and developing answers that are defensible
ones; that is, arguments are given and the reader is encouraged
to analyze the reasons that constitute the arguments. The point
is to provide a clarification of the problems generally associated

with cultural diversity and pluralism in education by making clear the tangled roots and by showing how these are embedded in many of the methodological, curricular, resource, and distributive decisions that provide the context, content, process, and purpose of today's schooling.

Hence, written in a hopefully objective vein, the book does not soar into the broad, normative dimensions that have characterized most works dealing with cultural diversity and pluralism. It has been my goal for several years to give an in-depth treatment to the concepts of cultural diversity and pluralism and their implications for American education, but without taking sides or pushing a point of veiw. Hence, the peculiarities of my method of procedure, partly historical, partly analytical, partly critical, are to be explained by the fact that I do not write out of a sense of deeply committed passion for either cultural diversity or pluralism, but I do write out of a sense of alarm, but an alarm which is double-edged. The normative, passionate literature strongly supportive of cultural diversity and pluralism fully convinces me, so far as personal observation goes, that men and women cannot ignore these two phenomena. But I find no less alarming the suggestion that education and society will be better served only by forgetting what it has so gradually learned, by easily reverting to attitudes and modes of thought which it only recently shook off.

The present intellectual mood on which cultural pluralists thrive is antihistorical, and I do not share it. The ideology of cultural pluralism has been promoted by the argument that American society has always been pluralistic. We must note that this argument is more ideological than sound. Karl Popper has warned us of the problem of "historicism," that it can often be misleading and inaccurate to explain or understand a phenomenon in terms of its origins alone.[3] It is not enough to justify cultural pluralism by a resort to its origins in the United States. There have been many historical phenomena (slavery, for example) that have been wholly despotic, totally irresponsible, in its attitudes fostered. If one's argument begins in his-

---

[3]Karl R. Popper, *The Poverty of Historicism* (New York, Harper & Row, 1964).

tory, it is a start, but it is not sufficient. Other considerations, such as moral, economic, political, and social factors, must be viewed as contributing to the justification of the phenomenon.

So far as this work treats cultural diversity and pluralism and their implications for education, it underscores the belief that to separate the social from education is detrimental to all concerned, whereas to bring the social into communication with education is to enrich and illuminate both the former and the latter.

This does not mean, of course, that a superior social vision implies the principles or purposes of schooling in any exact correspondence. As a social phenomenon, cultural diversity comes up short in terms of yielding clear, even good, visions. Nor does cultural diversity yield directives to educational policy in a univocal manner, fashioning what is to be considered a clear and legitimate direction policy is to take. One suspects, as has already been suggested, that these considerations are not completely decisive. Ideologies have been wrought in order to take up the causes for or against the phenomenon of cultural diversity. Hence, it simply is not true to believe that cultural diversity is irrelevant to educational purpose or policy making. If we hope to understand the forces swirling about successfully and unsuccessfully influencing educational policy and practice, then we ought to attempt to try to grasp the spirit and the form of cultural diversity and be prepared to make a judgment about whether it is worthy of preserving and maintaining. No one with any knowledge of American history could have any illusions about it, how the best and the worst have so often gone together, as the history of Chicago or New York City vividly exemplifies. We should think of ourselves as having a duty to examine and make a judgment for ourselves and posterity and why it matters when ethnicity is destroyed. I will ask how we can determine whether political pluralism is viable in American society and what moral objections there are to attempts to change it, all the while retaining my overarching intention: to consider whether cultural diversity demands a political, moral, or metaphysical understanding.

These preliminary remarks may, in the long run, help to

guide the reader through the twists and turnings of the analysis. But in every case the arguments must speak for themselves.

The Central Questions

Thus far, the purpose and plan of the book, as well as some
of the major assumptions that guide it, have been discussed.
Each chapter may be viewed as raising a particular question.
Chapter 1, for example, deals with the concept of cultural diversity and its relationship to education. We look closely at the
concept to show its nature and function. Such an examination
will, hopefully, provide the basic framework for further analysis and attempts to locate some key problems or issues within
education. After examining the necessary conditions for cultural diversity, it is argued that cultural diversity represents to
some a social ideal insofar as it demands that different groups
coexist with one another, and that such contact will not limit
or endanger but will enrich the diversity.

In Chapter 2 the relationship between cultural diversity and
ideology is critiqued in order to elucidate the significance of
ethnicity in American life. The major point at issue is just how
fundamental ethnicity is to the life we wish to lead. The evidence in its favor is strong. The traditional group lines of race,
religion, and national origin continue to maintain themselves
despite great efforts to eradicate them from society. Moreover,
they are being joined by blacks, females, homosexuals, "ug-
lies," Gray Panthers, and consumers, who are seeking to protect a way of life by forming "ethnic" interest groups. What
these and other groups have in common is they were created for
ad hoc protection against threats regarded as quite real. As
different groups coalesced in order to secure greater freedom,
goods, and services, they have stressed that they are "oppressed," "victimized," "denigrated," and presently experience
the shortcomings of the earlier, traditional ethnic groups in
American society. This claim to "being oppressed" carries considerable force today, as most people do not want to be called
"oppressors." This is what the new ethnicity is all about. Every
group that has suffered some discrimination or oppression feels

it is justified in seeking and gaining redress of grievances —
not just traditional minority groups, but new groups as well.
This condition is the basic one that the school is asked to take
up today.

Chapter 3 provides us with an understanding of the ideological bias of curricular reform today. The bias is this: Today's
reform is based on five ideologies of cultural diversity — assimilation, amalgamation, insular cultural pluralism, modified
cultural pluralism, and the open society. The five ideologies
make no attempt at exhaustiveness but aim to show that
ideology, which may seem remote when encountered in print,
has a practical bearing on vital curricular reform issues.

For each ideology a curricular reform is given as well as its
hoped-for results. A framework is provided for understanding
the bias of those who favor cultural diversity as opposed to
those who wish it eliminated, why ethnic studies are favored
over multiethnic and multicultural education, and what we
may reasonably expect to happen with regard to cultural diversity and curricular reform.

In Chapter 4 the analysis teases out what constitutes the
presuppositions of political pluralism. The result, which appears to be paradoxical, is that although the theory of political
pluralism itself does not foster the use of a hidden-hand explanation to justify certain decisions or choices of, say, educational
policy, the politics of political pluralism does. Hence, two
images of contemporary political pluralism result. In some
instances it appears as the surest, best form of participatory
democracy, favorable to all groups and citizens and most efficient. In other instances it appears as a predatory creature — all
cunning, deceptive, and lethal. Together the two images capture the essence of contemporary political pluralism.

It is my hope that political pluralism will be completely
discarded, along with a number of other intellectual burdens of
the past several decades — ideologies of cultural diversity other
than the open society. We need to consider such questions as
what kind of society, what ends of society, and what forms of
human relationships are appropriate for our time and for the
future. Until we address such questions, alternative ideologies

will continue to elude us.

Chapter 5 deals with an issue more central to the problems of education, namely, the intimate relationship between cultural pluralism and the Public School Movement in the United States. The analysis shows cultural pluralism to be lacking in conceptual clarity, and great pains are taken to explicate the concept. It is shown that, as an ideology, cultural pluralism has the potential to encourage a deep commitment to participatory democracy — for groups, that is — but this is as far as it goes. It remains pregnant with possibilities for what might be. Hence, in its stead a theory of dynamic pluralism is offered.

In Chapter 6 cultural pluralism is depicted as the ideology employed by cultural self-interest groups to justify their obtaining a share of society's goods and services. The exposition centers around an explication of how cultural pluralism, ideologically, is intimately connected to ethnicity, and how both cultural pluralism and ethnicity have a relativistic component. This component, in other words, in its main outline takes the form "X is good because the society in which I live agrees that it is or approves of it." The confusion of pluralism, of the proper tolerance for diversity of ideas, with relativism, the doctrine that there are no right or wrong answers in ethics or religion, is central to how cultural self-interest groups seek, demand, and justify a greater role in society. Much of the force of justifying ethnic demands today, particularly in education, stems from relativism, particularly the claim that "What is right for you is not always right for me." Hence, ethnic demands couched in the terms of relativism are quite powerful and may be presented in uncompromising terms.

Quite properly, this work concludes in Chapter 7 with an educational issue: The ramifications of equating bilingual education with bicultural education are examined. This essay explores the problem of identifying bilingual education with a kit bag of slogans, definitions, hyperbole, and the like. For some, present-day indications in the form of protests and militancy, black and white, are the outward signs of decaying respect for the public school and destroyed trust in the legitimacy of its efforts. The cry for bilingual education is seen as a

viable response to those outcries, especially in terms of legitimizing the public schools. The phoenix of bilingual education
arises out of the ashes of the cry for participation, decentralization, and relevant education. Whether bilingual education is a
viable response is questionable. The problem goes much deeper
than touched by the efforts of bilingual education.

In conclusion, then, the reader is encouraged to consider
what is central to every chapter, and this is what is the most
important issue of all, the influence of ideologies and the insid-
iousness of ideologies that mask outmoded, dangerous educational policy and practice. But it would be wrong to leave the
impression that ideology is not needed. Ideologies are systemat-
ized and propagated out of the need for a coherent set of beliefs
to order one's experience. In the United States the history of
cultural diversity has resided with ideologues of various stripes,
but need the future of cultural diversity lie there too? A society
that can make of cultural diversity an evil or a good can also
unmake it. Up until the present we have not chosen to do so,
thus we are surrounded in suspense: Is or is not public education in the United States in good hands?

Pluralism in Education

Chapter One

CULTURAL DIVERSITY AND EDUCATION*

INTRODUCTION

THE general purpose of this chapter is to examine the phenomenon of cultural diversity with a view to drawing out the relevance and significance for educational policy and public education.

Today, as perhaps never before, there is an expanded interest in cultural diversity and ethnicity. This is true not only of the United States but of many developed and undeveloped countries of the world. Both have asserted themselves forcefully, and demands related to them are among the most persistent and troublesome for educational policymakers. Many ethnics are particularly sensitive to what they regard as their changing status resulting from recent social revolutions, and the result has been a demand for greater expectations and outcomes to be had primarily through schooling. Educational authorities have been pressured on many fronts either to take greater account of cultural diversity or to suppress it altogether. In most cases, administrators, school board members, teachers, and others have been reluctant to institute changes because the content of their training has left them unprepared for an intelligent appraisal of the situation. The basic issues remain unarticulated, the forum of understanding not made ready. This chapter, then, is an attempt to contribute to the articulation and the making. And although its main focus is the United States, the issues and problems are applicable to other countries as well.

It is important, moreover, to note that this effort is neither an attempt to justify ethnicity nor an attempt to make capital

*Adapted from *Ethics and Educational Policy*, Kenneth A. Strike and Kieran Egan, eds. (London, Routledge & Kegan Paul, 1978).

of the problems of culturally diverse societies. Rather, it is an attempt to explore the fundamental question, What is called for regarding the making of educational policy and the functioning of public education in a culturally diverse society?

CULTURAL DIVERSITY

The initial question I wish to pose is, Just what is cultural diversity? *Cultural diversity* is a much bandied-about term that bears examination, for it is central to many present-day discussions concerning the role and future of public education. What is less obvious, although closely related, is the term *diversity* itself. In what situations, under what conditions, is the term *diverse* or its cognate *diversity* used? Oftentimes there is great variability rather then sameness exhibited in employing these terms.

To explain how different human groups were originally distinguished is beyond the scope of this work; such an undertaking would require an extensive historical/sociological/anthropological study. Suffice it to say that two facts do stand out. First, it is clear that "human groups do not exist in nature, or rather, the part of difference that exists because of nature is unimportant."[1] Whenever distinctions are made and groupings result, it is we who make them. Second, the distinctions that we make to create groups or factions may be drawn along regional, economic, ideological, political, occupational, and other such lines, and among the most persuasive distinctions that divide mankind are those which we designate as "ethnic," that is, those distinctions based on race, religion, or national origin.[2]

---

[1]Nathan Glazer and Daniel P. Moynihan, *Beyond the Melting Pot*, 2nd ed. (Cambridge, Mass., MIT Press, 1970), p. xiv.

[2]Perhaps the most common use of the term *ethnic* connotes a group or person. Historically, this use was restricted to nationalities (French, Greek, Poles, Germans, Irish, and others), and then it was broadened to include religious affiliation as well — as, for example, German-Lutheran or Irish-Catholic. Recently, however, the term has been applied much more broadly and includes Latin Americans, blacks, and others as ethnic groups. This is an important, but often unnoticed, observation that I owe to Mary Anne Raywid, "Pluralism as a Basis for Educational Policy: Some Second Thoughts," presented to the Lyndon B. Johnson Memorial Symposium on Education Policy, Glassboro, N. J., May 25, 1973.

There seems to be no end to human ingenuity in thinking of characteristics that can set groups apart. Hence, we are all familiar with the realization that diversity may and does take different forms. But what is claimed here? And what does it mean to say that some group is diverse? At rockbottom we would say that the decision to regard any group as diverse signifies a decision on somebody's part to single out different factors in the group — such as skin color, beliefs, ancestral heritage, or language — and establish these as criteria for the basis of the so-called diversity.

The point is, of course, that diversity of some sort exists everywhere and is visible everywhere. Every society is diverse in some respects, but this observation can only be made from a certain point of view. It could be made only by someone who looks at a number of people and because of some reason or other finds it important to observe that some members are different. While seeing that every society is diverse in some respect, it should not go unrecognized that we make certain criteria count in establishing differences. To turn the coin over, when we say that a particular group is homogeneous, we mean simply that the ways in which the members differ are unimportant or irrelevant to any practical concerns. However, we do not suggest that there are no differences. When we say that a society is diverse, we are saying that from a particular vantage point we find something relevant, interesting, and for some reason important to mark off a group or groups as different. Thus, we may identify differences of exclusiveness along the lines of cultural difference, and group identity may be ordered along the lines of ritual, dietary habits, beliefs, folk tales, and language pattern. One or a combination of these aspects generally is regarded as necessary for identifying a group as culturally diverse.

But is this sufficient for establishing cultural diversity? No analysis of cultural diversity is complete without a recognition that the selected differences between groups must be viewed as fundamental enough to be capable of producing values and dispositions that contribute to significantly different outlooks on the world. The variety or variegation of unlikeness among groups must be capable of making a difference. The difference must have reality in the minds of men, not just in the eye of the beholder. The point to be observed is that cultural diversity within society must have a concrete social reality; it must be made incarnate within the behaviors of the people. It must be expressed in a concrete situation which bears on political, economic, and social policy. Hence, the second condition that must be met for a society to be culturally diverse is that diversity go beyond being merely visible; diversity must be exhibited in the social behavior of groups who wish to embody their views in choosing among the various social arrangements which determine the division of advantages for underwriting an agreement on the proper distribution of goods and services.

But even this is not sufficient: Diversity is not a matter of genetics; it is a matter of cultural transmission across generations. Hence, a third condition of cultural diversity would require that a sense of historical and participational identity and the selected traits which mark the identity must be transmitted from generation to generation if the group is to continue to maintain its identity. It is doubtful that any group could long maintain its peculiar features if it did not jealously guard them and limit the members' sphere of relations, particularly in the decisive period of formation, namely, childhood.[3]

With these three conditions in mind, we may further identify what *cultural diversity* expresses. We can start with its descriptive use. As a descriptive term, at the very least cultural diversity refers to the co-existence of unlike or variegated groups in a common social system. It makes no judgments about this situation, for it is employed simply to record the fact that different groups are able to live together in such a way that allows the society to accomplish the basic functions of producing and distributing goods, defining social arrangements and institutions which determine collective goals, and providing security.

But *cultural diversity* may be also used normatively to express a social ideal. As a social value, the phrase goes beyond

---

[3]It would be wrong to assume that explicit sanctions would be needed to enforce expression of cultural diversity. Nothing more than a carefully nurtured sense of historical identity and well-defined and available satisfying participational roles within the group and the larger society are needed.

the descriptive sense to emphasize the value of freedom of association, the so-called "democratic ideal." That is, a culturally diverse society is commonly portrayed as a cooperative venture for mutual advantage, everyone profits from a plurality of groups expressing different values and interests. Thomas F. Green expressed this point most eloquently:

> The view is that any society is richer if it will allow a thousand flowers to blossom. The assumption is that no man's culture or way of life is so rich that it may not be further enriched by contact with other points of view. The conviction is that diversity is enriching because no man has a monopoly on the truth about the good life. There are many ways. Diversity is further valued because it provides any society with a richer pool of leadership from which to draw in times of crisis.[4]

Green develops this position by observing that the value of diversity entails two further assumptions:

> In the first place it means that there must be contact between the divergent groups in society. A household may be richer for including persons of different aspirations, values, dispositions, and points of view. But these differences will not be enriching to any particular individual unless he talks with, eats with, or in some way he has an exchange of views with those who are different. The value of diversity implies contact between persons, and not simply incidental, temporary, and casual contacts. Secondly this fundamental value implies that the diversity which is enriching is not itself endangered by the contact which is valued. The diversity must be sustained through contact.[5]

If Green is right, and there is good reason for thinking he is, then it seems that cultural diversity as a social ideal includes certain fundamental values or beliefs. It demands that different groups coexist with one another, having more than mere fleeting or casual contact, and it presumes that such contact will not limit or endanger but will enrich the diversity.

Cultural diversity as a social ideal is immensely significant

---

[4]Thomas F. Green, "Education and Pluralism: Ideal and Reality" (Twenty-Sixth Annual J. Richard Street Lecture, Syracuse University School of Education, 1966), p. 10.

[5]Green, "Education and Pluralism," p. 11.

for public education. Our understanding of the ideal could influence the positions we take on the issue of informal or casual education versus formal education or schooling as well as determining the flexibility we allow to public education in accommodating religious and language differences. But if the ideal of cultural diversity is to have any influence in determining practical educational issues, it will do so to the extent that the ideal is embodied in and expressed through the decision making of individuals voting their various agendas of politics. In other words, the ideal of cultural diversity will or will not be expressed in no other terms than in the reality of American social structure.

From the view of social structure, American society has had difficulty in accepting cultural diversity. There is strong evidence that cultural diversity has been viewed as potentially divisive. The point is that the United States has been seen as a congeries of culturally diverse (and potentially divisive) groups, most with distinctive social, economic, and political concerns, who prefer living with other members of their group and take pride in efforts to sustain and build up group self-confidence and self-assertiveness. The divisive tendencies of cultural diversity have been seen as promoting a view of politics which makes of local and state government a federation of groups, with protected and excluded turfs.

Reasons for the lack of congruence between cultural diversity as social ideal and as realized in social institutions are found in the hard core of the American experience. Since most Americans have no ethnic roots in past millennia, as do so many other peoples of the world, the Americanization process has taken on a central role in the formation of a national identity and self-concept. What is unique in the American experience is not the fact that the naturalization of immigrants has taken place, but rather that we have the example of a new nation starting from scratch, as it were. In fact, to question the wisdom of the necessity for engaging in the Americanization of immigrants has struck many as questioning the very possibility of America's continued well-being. Both the explanation and the fact of Americanization have affected the nature and function of cultural diversity, and both have done so in a cumulative and accelerating fashion.

Nevertheless, a double anomaly is hidden in this phenomenon. The first anomaly is that so many could be de-ethnicized so easily. The second is that having apparently been de-ethnicized, they have not become more indistinguishable than they are.

TWO ANOMALIES

The first anomaly has received much attention. The Americanization of immigrants has been explained by scholars and laymen alike in terms of one or another combination of the following: (1) the destruction of immigrant family patterns under the impact of rapid industrialization and urbanization; (2) the American emphasis given to childhood and youth, and the outdating of adult values and patterns; (3) the attractiveness of American culture coupled to an Old World weariness which immigrants wished to be rid of; (4) the openness and ampleness of the American reward system gained primarily through public education; and, finally, (5) American nationalism was nonethnic from the very first, and to become the "ideal" American, immigrants were encouraged to repudiate their older lifestyles, customs, and language.[6]

The fact of the matter is that any immigrants who thought moving to the United States made them masters of their own

---

[6]For early documents on the immigrant problem and a workable bibliography of this aspect of the Americanization movement, *see* Edith Abbott, ed., *Historical Aspects of the Immigrant Problem: Select Documents* (University of Chicago Press, 1926). *See* also Andrew M. Greeley, *Why Can't They Be Like Us?* (New York, Dutton, 1971); Marcus Lee Hansen, *The Atlantic Migration, 1607-1860* (Cambridge, Mass., Harvard University Press, 1940); Edward Hartmann, *The Movement to Americanize the Immigrant* (New York, University of Columbia Press, 1948); John Higham, *Strangers in the Land: Patterns of American Nativism, 1860-1925* (New York, Randon House, 1970); Dwight Macdonald, *Against the American Grain* (New York, Random House, 1962); Roger Portal, *The Slavs* (New York, Harper & Row, 1969); Richard Scammon and Ben J. Wattenberg, *The Real Majority* (New York, Coward-McCann, 1970); George M. Stephenson, *A History of American Immigration, 1920-1924* (New York, Russell & Russell, 1964); Rudolph S. Veceli, "European Americans: From Immigrants to Ethnics," in William H. Cartwright and Richard L. Watson, eds., *Reinterpretation of American History and Culture* (Washington, D.C., National Council for the Social Studies, 1973).

fate — or of their economic well-being — were in for a rude
shock. In the United States, as in Europe, power flowed from
above. And power — the capacity to get other people to do
what you want them to do — was found at the level of management and ownership of the industrial-corporate order or being
a politician on practically any level. Moreover, patterns of
ethnic stereotypes dictated a clear pecking order for immigrants
from eastern, central and southern Europe. Many Americans
thought that such immigrants were plodding but industrious,
and that, because they had brought little cash from the old
country, they had to work or starve; particularly they would
work in menial occupations which were spurned by nonimmi-
grants. In short, the immigrants were considered mentally and
socially inferior. They were seen as a group to be basically
uneducated, ignorant, and easily misled by labor agitators and
by politicians. Above all, immigrants were considered unfit for
the industrial discipline needed in the factory or workshop.[7]

The net result was the de-ethnicization of the immigrant. Its
story is largely a tale of transforming the immigrant and his
children into a stable, quiescent labor force. The process, where
effective, conceded very little to racial or national diversity.
Many immigrants, almost as soon as they had established resi-
dence in America, took for their own the slogan "Americanize
the immigrant." The years from 1880 to 1923 witnessed a great
deal of unanimity in the shaping of the American ideal of
nationhood. First- and second-generation immigrants collabo-
rated with the descendants of earlier, more respectable, and
more prosperous immigrants to define "100 percent Ameri-
canism."

Lest the reader be misled, it must be remembered that the
immigrants had come to America to gain freedom and opportunity, and most were willing to sacrifice, to shift, to change,
both personally and culturally, in order to acquire the benefits
of being in America. America was regarded as a land of great
opportunity, and the immigrant visualized his children becoming American. Hence, while the first generation themselves

---

[7]Gerd Korman, *Industrialization, Immigrants, and Americanizers* (Madison, Wis., The
State Historical Society of Wisconsin, 1967).

might be called Hungarians, for example, and their sons and daughters would be called Hungarian-Americans, they dreamed of the day when their children's children would be called American. Most immigrants appeared to be willing to cast their lot with a new land, a new culture, and a new image.

But it is significant that over fifty years after mass immigration from Europe to this country ended, the culturally diverse pattern is still so strong. Thus, we come to the second anomaly.

The second anomaly is indeed a curious one. Ethnic groups and ethnicity, language loyalty and language maintenance abound on the present American scene. Many Americans of today, the progeny of the immigrant folk of decades ago, wear lapel buttons that say "Irish Power," "Kiss me, I'm Italian," "Viva la Raza." In addition, some Navajos these days drive cars with bumper stickers proclaiming "Dine Bizell" ("Navajo Power"), and there are Sioux headbands and Afro hairdos. Comedians rejoice in the fact that ethnic jokes and dialects of yesteryear are no longer regarded as vices to be indulged in behind closed curtains in discretely defined neighborhoods. Even some Americans of northern and western European origin, including German, French, Norwegian, and Swede, recognize their ancestry and partially define themselves in accord with it. For reasons that seem to be little understood, many American groups have not lost themselves entirely within their American surroundings even after three, four, and more generations, although there have been coercion and opportunity enough to do so. Hence, cultural diversity is a constituent part of American life and politics.

Is it the case that industrialization and the much-touted economic and social mobility of America contains limits which non-Anglo-Saxon ethnics cannot transcend? Have recurring anti-foreigner sentiments elicited protective withdrawal and insularity in their threatened targets? Is the threat of de-ethnicization in America so conducive to anomie and alienation that the retention of cultural diversity of some kind is called for to perform an orienting and stabilizing function?

These questions, according to Michael Novak — who celebrates ethnicity as a basic attribute of men which, when suppressed, will always rise again — have yet to be answered.[8] His contention is that the resurgence of ethnicity today is a fact all too well ignored by most. American society, although paying lip-service to the ideal of the melting pot, maintains or permits ethnicity beyond the point of cultural assimilation. The surprise, according to Novak, is not that cultural diversity is still alive and kicking, but rather that all of a sudden a great many people are rediscovering this.

There is, however, a curious fact to observe about the phrase *resurgent ethnicity*. *Ethnicity, as a concept, suggests a movement of affection and identity, enriched perhaps by the subtle, provocative ways in which one differs from others, and reinforced by a strong attachment to family and relatives.* Resurgent ethnicity lends itself to an interpretation of ethnicity which suggests that the immigrants' experiences in America were those of continuous pressure to conform to an alien culture, but, paradoxically, the immigrant and his children's ways were never accepted. Despite enormous pressure to "Americanize," the Americanization process, although outwardly successful for a period of time, could not ultimately succeed due to some sort of ethnic "unmeltableness." This rather awkward term catches precisely Novak's claim that human nature demands ethnic identity, and many Americans today are simply exhibiting the remarkable recuperative power of individuals, who in the face of serious social and psychological adversity, seek a return to their most basic and rewarding source of identity. According to Novak, "The new ethnicity is a form of historical consciousness. Who are you? What history do you come from? And where next? These are its questions."[9]

At the core of the slogan "resurgent ethnicity" lies an extremely seductive line of thinking, particularly when the phase is given Novak's metaphysical formulation. It is seductive insofar as its unquestioned acceptance points us to the conclusion that the immigrants' experiences in America were those of

---

[8]*See* Michael Novak, "One Species, Many Cultures," *The American Scholar*, Winter, 1973-74; "The New Ethnicity," *The Humanist*, May/June 1973; *The Rise of the Unmeltable Ethnics* (New York, Macmillan, 1971). For a variation on this theme, *see* Peter Schrag, *The Decline of the WASP* (New York, Simon & Schuster, 1970).
[9]Novak, *Rise of the Unmeltable Ethnic*, xviii.

facing discrimination and privation, and ultimately the immigrants' children and their children could not repudiate their ancestral past, at least not without doing a disservice to their basic humanness.

Novak paints in broad outline the dimensions of resurgent ethnicity. He contends that ethnics have proved themselves to be a dynamic force in American politics and culture, and he claims that the 1970s is the "decade of the ethnics." But on the periphery of Novak's works lies a relatively unexamined assumption that a "crisis of identity" exists in America today and this crisis is the cause of resurgent ethnicity. Novak claims that "the new ethnicity . . . [is] a movement primarily of personal and social identity."[10]

How does this explanation compare with others? It seems that Novak's position is parallel to the view advanced by the historian Marcus Lee Hansen in his study *The Problem of the Third Generation Immigrant*. In this work, Hansen suggested that "What the son wishes to forget, the grandson wishes to remember."[11] Hansen's Law stipulates that assimilation characterizes the second generation, but when the second generation throws off its immigrant skin, the third generation suffers an identity crisis. That is, Hansen's Law contends that changes in the attitudes of social groups correspond to generational changes. Put in other terms, in a truly diverse society it is not enough to be just an American. The question becomes "What kind of American are you?" According to Hansen, the third generation falls back upon the social identity of its grandfathers.

Glazer and Moynihan, in a pioneering study of ethnicity and politics in New York City (1963), said, "We have precious few studies of ethnic identity, despite the increasing prominence of its role in the mass media in recent years . . . ."[12] They do, however, suggest the following reasons for the revival of ethnicity:

1. Ethnic identities have taken over some of the task of self-

---

[10]Novak, *Rise of the Unmeltable Ethnic*, xxiv.

[11]Marcus L. Hansen, *The Problem of the Third Generation Immigrant* (Rock Island, Ill., The Augustana Historical Society, 1937), p. 15.

[12]Glazer and Moynihan, *Beyond the Melting Pot*, p. xxxiv.

definition that occupational identities, particularly working-class occupational identities, have formerly given. The status of the worker is downgraded; as a result, apparently, the status of being an ethnic, a member of an ethnic group, has been upgraded.

2. International events have declined as a source of feeling of ethnic identity, except for Jews. Identification with homelands (involvement in and concern for) declines, and more and more the sources of ethnic identification are to be found in American experiences, on American soil.

3. Along with occupation and homeland, religion has declined as a focus of ethnic identification, particularly in the Catholic Church. For the first time, the Catholic Church does not complement the conservative tendencies of Catholic ethnic groups.[13]

Glazer and Moynihan offer some basic insights into the nature of the problem of cultural diversity. Their hypothesis is best stated in their own words: "The assimilating power of American society and culture operated on immigrant groups in different ways, to make them, it is true, something distinct and identifiable . . . . The ethnic group in American society became not a survival from the age of mass immigration but a new social form."[14]

According to the authors, ethnic differences remain with us but they also assume new social meanings and functions. Such membership is a form of social identity, a way of knowing who you are, within the larger society. Moreover, each of the so-called hyphenated-American minorities (such as Irish-American or Italian-American) represents a political interest group. Each group, in New York City has become politically organized in order to reap its share of the goals and services of society.

In short, it has been argued, both explicitly and implicitly, that a "crisis of identity" is sufficient to account for resurgent ethnicity. Novak, Hansen, Glazer and Moynihan, and others are in agreement that resurgent ethnicity today is merely a response to an identity crisis. But to establish this as the reason

---

[13]Glazer and Moynihan, *Beyond the Melting Pot*, p. xxiv, xxv, xxvi.
[14]Glazer and Moynihan, *Beyond the Melting Pot*, p. 13-14, 16.

why is perhaps to accept a too facile explanation. While it is not denied that identity is connected in some way to the phenomenon of resurgent ethnicity, it may be unwarranted to claim that a "crisis of identity" is a sufficient condition (or even a necessary one?) for the phenomenon. It may be the case that a too ready acceptance of the identity factor as the only or even the most plausible explanation of resurgent ethnicity is unfounded.

For example, it may be granted that the identity factor is connected in some way to the phenomenon of resurgent ethnicity, but to what extent this needs to be connected to a historical identity (ethnicity) is a moot question. If we limit the sources of identity to those rooted in race, religion, or national state, have we in effect excluded a great many categories of identity commonly known to operate in today's society? Does such a limitation exclude, for example, the identification of someone with a "reform" political candidate, some political action group, an Archibald Cox, a Henry Kissinger, Martin Luther King Jr., Ralph Nader, or the Beatles? In short, it seems to be the case that the single path of personal identification with the traditional ethnic sources commits us to too narrow an explanation of resurgent ethnicity.

There is another possible explanation to be considered. Our first step is to ask a prior question, namely, Just what is resurgent ethnicity? Resurgent ethnicity may be explained in part by noting that the term *ethnic* has been broadened to include *lifestyle*. Mary Anne Raywid has pointed out that the phrase *ethnic group* was "previously restricted to national groups, often in religious combination (as, for example, in Irish Catholic)" but "the term has recently come prominently to apply to blacks as well."[15] She contends:

> We've not given much attention to the considerable switch this represents in identifying cultural difference or ethnicity: from acquired or learned difference like nationality, to biological differences such as race. According to current usage, blacks are an ethnic group, and at least some women have

[15]Mary Anne Raywid, "Pluralism as a Basis for Educational Policy: Some Second Thoughts," presented to the Lyndon B. Johnson Memorial Symposium on Education Policy, Glassboro, N.J., May 25, 1973, p. 6.

acquired that particular consciousness of kind entitling them to ethnic group status, too. And this, of course, represents an even further extension of ethnicity, from a racial to a sexual basis.[16]

I agree with Raywid that a broadening of ethnicity has occurred. Indeed it is a "considerable switch . . . in identifying cultural difference or ethnicity . . . from acquired or learned difference like nationality, to biological differences such as race." However, what is important in this shift is the fact that certain subcultural groups have "asserted" their fundamental claim to ethnicity. What is indicated here is that some blacks and women have asserted that they have a distinct subculture or life-style that is sufficiently different to warrant their having ethnic group status.

What can we say about such a shift?[17] If we recall the three criteria for cultural diversity established earlier [(1) we make certain criteria count in establishing differences; (2) the selected differences between groups must be viewed as fundamental enough to produce values and dispositions of a significant sort; and (3) there must exist a sense of historical and participatory identity capable of being transmitted across generations,] then we see that the inclusion of blacks and other minority groups as well as women as "new ethnics" is permitted.

But what needs clarifying here is that the locus of the first criterion has shifted. Previously in the Americanization movement culturally diverse groups were labeled as such by the older established Americans who claimed a cultural superiority. Immigrants were told explicitly and implicitly to become aware of how much they differed from the host or dominant culture. Such a labeling rarely accommodated ethnic identification and dignity marching hand in hand. Although dignity could be

---

[16]Raywid, "Pluralism as a Basis for Educational Policy," p. 6.

[17]Although the precise import of the shift is notoriously difficult to characterize, it is caught in part in the following: "Nowadays, it appears a cultural demand can no longer be weighed on the scales of seriousness and depth. Eventually all demands are to be taken seriously. Indeed, the point about ethnicity and ethnic consciousness is that no group submits to the judgment of others. By their very nature ethnic claims do not allow of a universal scale against which they can be measured." *See* Norman Glazer, "Ethnicity and the Schools," *Commentary,* 58:58, 1974.

had from bearing insult and assault without rancor, it was rarely granted the ethnic through a show of acceptance and kindness. The labeling process easily descended into a squalid form of cultural debasement and gross prejudice.

In this shift from a group being labeled ethnic to a group asserting its fundamental ethnicity is the fact that today's ethnics themselves elect to make certain criteria count in establishing differences; but the criteria are not necessarily nationality, culture, language, and religion. Rather they are of the ascriptive sort, and should be recognized as such. Ethnicity appeals to and is fast taking hold among many Americans who know that they cannot shake or be rid of certain identifying characteristics such as skin color or sex. Thus, the phenomenon of broadened ethnicity is indicative of more than resurgent ethnicity; something larger is taking place. It is caught, in part, by what Ralf Dahrendorf has referred to as the "refeudalization" of society — the return to ascriptive rather than achieved characteristics as determinants of social stratification.[18] Moreover, as Daniel Bell put it, "Ethnicity has become more salient (than class) because it can combine an interest with an affective tie . . . . "[19] Apparently, the strategic efficacy of ethnicity is seen as a major focus for the mobilization of group interests. It is a strategy for asserting claims against the institutions of society, for any oppressed group has a good chance of changing the system if it raises the communal consciousness of its individual members.

It is important, therefore, to recognize that broadened ethnicity suggests the past experiences of oppressed minorities as merely the starting point of a strategy calculated to cash in on today's rapidly changing political situation. The common elements fashioning broadened ethnicity are the crucial considerations of deprivation, powerlessness, alienation, frustration, and the like. In the not too distant past, such conditions were viewed largely in terms of individual-personal discontent, and help was sought from relatives and friends. But today

---

[18]*See* Nathan Glazer and Daniel P. Moynihan, "Why Ethnicity?" *Commentary,* 58 (October): 36, 1974.
[19]Glazer and Moynihan, "Why Ethnicity?" p. 36.

individual-personal discontent has been replaced with collective-political discontent, and the new organizations of broadened ethnicity seek significant power to harness the sources of discontent and to establish a political and a moral base under the emotive slogan of cultural pluralism. (Curiously, the political interest-defined group is now behaving as an ethnic group, whereas in the past the ethnic group behaved as a political interest-defined group.)

The second factor challenging the thesis that "resurgent ethnicity is caused by a crisis of identity" has to do with the fact that many of America's ethnic whites belong to America's working class. In the mid-1960s, the working class discovered that the old rules of the game through which they would supposedly share in the bounty of America were suddenly changed. Welfare, for some, had become an acceptable way of life; police officers were called "pigs", those who flounted the law were not punished, and flag burning and draft evasion were condoned by some. By the late 1960s rampant inflation caused an economic squeeze, and many family breadwinners were hard put to meet the family budget. Inflation made it next to impossible for the average family to save, and it appeared that only the children of the very rich or the very poor (scholarship grants and aid) were able to meet the problem of spiraling costs of a college education. Labeled or characterized as racist pigs, honkies, bigots, the Silent Majority, and hardhats, many white ethnics felt that there was little hope that any foreseeable change in American life would likely benefit them. To them, the social revolution of the 1960s had changed the rules of the game, and the change was largely made at their expense.

Hence, today's white working-class ethnic wants it known that his ancestors' early experiences were not easy ones; that they had to work tremendously hard to "make it" in America; that they were oppressed and exploited; and, in addition, they, too, were the targets of pseudo-scientific racial theories. It is apparent that the message of the third- and fourth-generation offspring is this: Whatever progress or success they have achieved, it was due to hard work, struggle, and self-sacrifice, and no one gave their forebears and themselves anything "on a silver platter."

Finally, the "crisis of identity" cause of resurgent ethnicity can be challenged in terms of yet another phenomenon, namely, the collapse of accommodative politics — that curious blend of ethnic groups and local and state-elected officials — has changed significantly the political and social mobility of white ethnic groups, such as the Irish, Jewish, and Italian. The long-term contribution of accommodative politics was its providing of political stability facilitating the mobility of white ethnic groups within a permissive political environment. For example, accommodative politics is reflected in the Irish-Catholic transition from a despised and feared outgroup to one for whom the traditional American holders of institutional power had to make room or accommodate. Indeed in Boston they became a despised and feared ingroup — the Irish Mafia! The primary political benefactors of accommodative politics shaped public policy in the Democratic party coalition and, to a lesser extent, through the labor unions and fraternal associations of America.

Accommodative politics was largely ethnic, with political candidates showing up at, say, a local picnic, attempting to enjoy an athletic feat or perhaps a polka, and attempting to say a few words in another tongue. But this was changed in the 1960s. The "new politics," made up of groups representing the "new" minorities (ethnics?) — women, blacks, Chicanos, Native Americans, Puerto Ricans, and others — displaced the white ethnic coalitions and claimed for themselves the political rewards of exercising power.

My major point is that Novak and others, who stress the importance of significance of a resurgent ethnicity, also justify it in terms of its being caused by a mass society type of social order inimical to identity stability. Now it is true that ethnicity and its accouterments are current news at present, but it is not necessarily true that the phenomenon is caused by a crisis of identity; other factors also appear as possible causes. A minor point, but an important one, is, What counts as resurgent ethnicity? This is not just a nit-picking question, but one which is crucial if we are to make judgments about cultural diversity, particularly in the schools. The question is not whether cultural diversity in the form of multiethnicity is undesirable. It is rather that since many, perhaps most, Americans desire some sort of subcultural identity or life-style, we should not necessarily connect this phenomenon to the historic past of racial, religious, and national groups. My concern here is that we ought not be too quick to join those who insist that no separation of the older and traditional view of ethnicity and today's so-called resurgent ethnicity is necessary.

EDUCATIONAL POLICY AND CULTURAL DIVERSITY

To see public policy as a product that authorizes the distribution of benefits and prerogatives in society and educational policy as performing the function of ensuring the acceptance and maintenance of such policy is to appreciate the instrumental function of public education in providing stability to a society. Thus, to consider public education apart from policy making is to run the risk of confusing the cart with the horse. This is the reality: Public education is, and always has been, inseparable from broader social, political, and economic goals.

We must now consider some points which, if recognized, might have the positive effect of creating public education within the parameters of a democratically conceived culturally diverse society.

First, the bulk of evidence is in and it indicates that most Americans desire some sort of group affiliation tie or ties. If my analysis is correct, we are in the presence of more than simply a renascent ethnicity. The pattern of cultural diversity emergent in our society is both broader and deeper. It incompasses sex, occupation, race, and age. People are rejecting the goal of a monolithic American culture and are discovering themselves to be members of groups distinguished by interest-defined concerns. Since the goal of a monolithic American culture is no longer acceptable to the many self-identified subgroups or to the dominant core culture itself, public education should attempt to secure some workable expression of cultural diversity, although not necessarily as a response to Novak's (et al.) claim that it is a resurgent ethnicity.

My objection is not to the notion that an ethnic factor remains with us, although colored by assimilation, for Glazer and Moynihan's observation that ethnic groups assimilate but remain distinct is a most important one for us to remember. But in discussions concerning the role of public education in a culturally diverse society we should note the brute fact that for some Americans today acceptance of the notion of a resurgent ethnicity requires no more than the politicalization of passions along black-white lines to fan the flames of a latent racism. In a word, the need is for stability, particularly in the area of race relations, because for some ethnics, white and black, the resurgence of ethnicity is simply a cover for racism.

My point is a simple one. The need for stability in a society dominated by a broadened ethnicity may turn into a mockery of a great society. We may note a pragmatic folly in easy accommodation to the "new ethnic consciousness" celebrated by Michael Novak. For the poor and the victimized it could be nothing more than a cruel hoax, since it could be made to exploit the reactionary potential of the not so recent American past. Stability, at any cost, however, might lend support to the glorification of racial and religious peculiarities offering as a viable alternative a federation of races — each with its own territory or elected representative. Such a proposal would assure freedom for the group, but not for the individual. The individual's fate would be predetermined on the basis of his cultural identity.

A system of public education sympathetic to a legitimate cultural diversity demands standards drawn from more than one culture. In this context, the curriculum requires that due recognition be given to all who contributed to our national heritage. The tokenism of Black America Week or Columbus Day simply will not suffice. Public education must deny the position that has consistently refused to recognize that a legitimate cultural diversity exists, or even that it should exist. Implied here is the notion that schooling that discounts cultural diversity by ascribing to cultural differences all kind of demeaning terms — culturally deficient, culturally deprived (culturally depraved?) — is no longer acceptable; it simply cannot be tolerated any longer. But neither can we substitute a new kind of advocacy which emphasizes the racist and the ethnocentric aspects of American life.

The revival of ethnicity is growing and will continue for some time to come. The new-found pride and economic power of Native Americans, blacks, Chicanos, Puerto Ricans, women, and others will result in a growing assertiveness aimed at reshaping occupational, housing, and educational patterns. In particular, the positive aspects of ethnicity will call into question the failure of the neighborhood school to prepare children for successful roles in adult life. Hopefully, the realization of the inadequacy of the old accommodation model of politics to deal meaningfully with this problem should be seen as the starting point of most discussions of educational policy. But the search for something more adequate in shaping public education based on the recognition of cultural diversity should not encourage exclusivist tendencies. Divisive groups who wish to achieve separation should be recognized but not encouraged.

My contention is that the ethnic factor remains with us, although colored by cultural assimilation and the "broadening effect." If ethnicity is honest and is viewed as a source of cultural strength rather than of personal deprivation, then public education may help develop a cultural stability rooted in youths who are open to change, who are flexible, adaptive, and receptive. This means introducing the student to many life-styles, not superficially, but in depth. Students should study the variety and richness of America's multicultural history. Hopefully, such an education would defuse a latent racism and provide a solid, stronger type of social stability.

Resurgent ethnicity, minority group assertiveness, and the need for stability are directly related to two further consequences for public education. We can see this as follows: For one thing, the problem may produce a willingness to compromise on vital matters. This practice was defended in the accommodation model as not only a necessity of politics and white ethnicity, but also as the supreme virtue. As previously mentioned, the long-term contribution of the model was that it provided stability facilitating the mobility of white ethnic groups within a somewhat adaptive political environment. But it is entirely conceivable that the very broadening of passions and cultural issues in current "ethnic politics" makes such facile pragmatic accommodation, even if one is willing, all but impossible to achieve. That is to say, the policy at present is too broad, too involved in scope to make possible easy accommodation of all interests involved. As John Dewey foresaw in the late 1920s, the sentiments and symbols of shared cultural attachments are themselves too varied, disparate, and incomplete. He said, "The social situation has been so changed . . . that traditional general principles have little practical meaning."[20] Further on he commented, "Symbols control thought, and the new age has no symbols consonant with its activities,"[21] and "Our Babel is not one of tongues but one of signs and symbols without which shared experience is impossible."[22]

The essential point here is that the newer collective strategies and methods — such as the use of skyjacking commercial aircraft, political assassination and kidnapping, and economic sanctions against supermarkets — have outrun mere mediation and negotiation efforts aimed at a compromise. This points toward major reconsiderations which involve educational policy conceived primarily as a function of informative criticism, inquiry, and publicity. The need, in other words, is the improvement of the methods and conditions of discussion and debate. There being no universal arbiter who decides which ethnic demands are just and which are not, relevant data must penetrate the whole system of decision making, and policies must be developed which reflect the bearing of knowledge supplied by the various groups.

Second, the implementation of cultural diversity studies as part of the curriculum of public education would involve, minimally, a school setting in which programs are designed to help students learn about and possibly appreciate the many diverse

---

[20]John Dewey, *The Public and Its Problems* (Chicago, Swallow Press, 1927), p. 133.
[21]Dewey, *Public and Its Problems*, p. 142.
[22]Dewey, *Public and Its Problems*, p. 142.

American life-styles as well as learning to interact productively with people from different backgrounds. Teachers would teach students not to stereotype others and how to prevent alienation in social intercourse.

Hopefully, teachers would engage students in a number of learning activities designed to accomplish intergroup understanding. The curriculum would in part be derived from the many cultures and problems of a culturally diverse society and would be related to academic subjects of study such as language arts, social studies, and the physical sciences. Projects involving in- and out-of-school activities would be utilized to help students better understand the roots of prejudice, the consequences of ethnocentrism, the strengths and weaknesses of local ethnic groups, the search for individual identity within a multiculture, and how to become resourceful in the dominant culture as well as in the subculture.

There is, however, a need for a cautionary note. I am not advocating a multicultural education per se. Rather, I wish to suggest that schools can be utilized as vehicles for fostering tolerance and understanding among culturally diverse groups. But if this is to be accomplished, teachers must conduct a careful assessment of the impact of their work and their knowledge of the political as well as the self-serving purpose of schooling.

Chapter Two

IDEOLOGY AND
CULTURAL DIVERSITY*

IT is more than passing interest to note that
the phenomenon of cultural diversity in the United States has
been commonly wrapped up in the language of a seductive
metaphor, the *melting pot,* which emphasizes a social situation
in which various different elements are transformed through a
heating process into a new amalgam. Society, the bubbling
cauldron, eventually creates a new and better social-cultural
product. Moreover, zealous proponents of this ideology reasoned that the new amalgam would not be merely representative of all aspects of the different elements — the bad as well as
the good — for somehow, through magical alchemy, only the
best qualities of the different elements would blend to constitute the new social-cultural type. In this regard, then, it was
believed that all groups offer unique contributions to the new
cultural stock, and many different cultures would produce a
new and somehow better America.

In an important sense, then, the cultural diversity factor in
the United States has been given a particular slant by the
ideology of the melting pot. By tying cultural diversity to the
melting pot, the basic direction given was that the immigrants
were to intermarry on a large scale, repudiate their Old World
heritage by changing cultural patterns to those of the dominant
or majority group, and impart positive meaning to an otherwise chaotic and highly fluid social situation. Thus, to the
immigrant and the established American, the ideology of the
melting pot gave support to the belief that the American experience was a new historical epoch for humanity; human history
was being given an entirely new direction by the melting pot of

*Adapted from *Ideology and Education* by Richard Pratte. Copyright © 1977 by
Longman Inc. Reprinted by permission of Longman.

America.

It mattered not that the metaphor of the melting pot provided for two different interpretations by its employers. First, it was believed that the process called for was totally a biological one, the fusion of races by interbreeding and intermarriage. Second, it was believed that the melting pot meant a process by which persons or groups who are unlike in their social heritage somehow come to share and cherish the same body of tradition, loyalties, and attitudes. The first belief is commonly referred to as amalgamation; the second as assimilation. Some ideologists of the melting pot looked at both of these as called for, and many older Americans as well shared this view. The melting pot was thus an ambiguous ideology for shaping thought and action regarding cultural diversity, but the ambiguity was no obstacle and allowed for a number of groups to work together to direct social change in a particular way.

If we concentrate our attention on the metaphor, we see that the ideology relied heavily on the ambiguity of a "melting pot" to organize and persuade thinking regarding the future direction of the American experience. Rather than being used to *clarify* the situation, the metaphor was employed to *change* the situation. By claiming that society was "as if" a great bubbling cauldron in which particular elements were melted down into a new amalgam, it was assumed that certain consequences of a moral or normative character necessarily followed. For instance, there are similar relations between elements in a melting pot and immigrants and American society. If the ingredient in the pot fails to melt at a particular temperature, we simply turn up the heat to the necessary melting point of that element. Similarly, if any particular group defies amalgamation or assimilation by certain known and accepted processes, it is only necessary that we "turn up" the social heat — using injunction, punishments, coercion, and so forth — until that element melts. In short, this particular use of metaphor helped organize and support a coercive American view toward cultural diversity, and subsequent unthinking behavior involving coercion of immigrants was the consequence.

Of course, the ideology of the melting pot needed a slogan as well as a metaphor to relate belief to action. The slogans varied from "America: the great crucible," or merely "the crucible," to "a new American type." Use of the phrase *the crucible* conveyed a sense of coercion and pressure that had the effect of advancing the priority of established American culture over that of the immigrant's. The slogan "the crucible" advanced and gave legitimacy to the notion that the culture of the dominant group was in some prima facie sense superior to all others; conversely, the immigrants' cultures were decidely inferior. The slogan helped to make fashionable, if ever it was not, a kind of discrimination. That is, morally and socially sloganized rhetoric gave direction to immigrant and older American alike insofar as ethnicity and ethnic identity were downplayed. The many white ethnic groups were encouraged to develop new economic, political, and cultural patterns and to discriminate against their distinctive historical experiences, cultures, and attitudes.

But, of course, this is not the whole story. What was to identify which groups were and were not to be assimilated? The matter was quite simple. No one really expected a man to change his faith, but he could be expected to give up his language and his nationality and adopt new ways. Within very narrow limits, race, above all else, would identify the groups to be assimilated.[1] Indeed, much of the appeal of the ideology of the melting pot stemmed from a dislike and fear of the racial other. Racial superiority was evidenced in terms of denigrating the immigrants from Southern and Eastern Europe (Slavs, Greeks, Syrians, Hungarians, Russian Jews, Italians, Poles, and others). The ideologues of the melting pot never doubted the correctness of interpreting the slogan in terms of a view of racial superiority.

Thus, in the context of examining the phenomenon of cultural diversity and the ideology of the melting pot, it is important to distinguish among at least three different aspects. First is the ideal of the melting pot, which is simply the viewpoint of a "melting process" producing a somehow new and uniquely

---

[1]The point is, of course, that the ideology of the melting pot was not considered to apply in any great numbers to the black American, the Native American, and the Latin-American minorities, only a few of whom were allowed to become assimilated and as groups have been refused complete assimilation in the United States.

American biological and cultural phenomenon envisioned as being superior to any individual ingredient before melting. Second is the myth of the melting pot, which is the social fiction that the melting pot has been realized in the society as a whole. Third is the reality of the melting pot, which is the actual extent to which the melting pot ideal has been realized, apart from exaggerations and myths about it.

IDEAL OF THE MELTING POT. The idealistic vision of various racial and religiocultural groups living together side by side, intermarrying in successive generations, and ultimately fusing and producing a new American and America has been an *idée fixe* for almost 200 years. For example, in 1792, the French-born farmer Jean Hector St. John de Crèvecoeur observed, "I could point out to you a family whose grandfather was an Englishman, whose wife was Dutch, whose son married a French woman, and whose present four sons have now four wives of different nations. He is an American who leaving behind him all his ancient prejudices and manners, receives new ones from the new mode of life he has embraced. . . . Here individuals of all nations are melted into a new race of men. . . . "[2]

The broad and unique appeal of a nation "melted into a new race of men" was sustained over subsequent decades by the ideology of the melting pot. Milton M. Gordon, in an analytical study of the roles of race, religion, and ethnicity in the United States, argued that " . . . the melting pot hypothesis found its way into the rarefied air of historical scholarship and interpretation."[3] Supporting this ideal were America's seemingly endless stream of immigrants, the informal voluntary associations that helped the immigrants make the called-for political and economic adjustments, and the formal system of checks and balances.

The ideal presumed that no deliberately adopted measures of assimilation could have accomplished what was happening. The ideologists of the melting pot were perhaps correct in talking about a continuing and increasing racial fusion among

---

[2]J. Hector St. John de Crèvecoeur (Michel Guillaume St. Jean de Crèvecoeur), *Letters from an American Farmer* (New York, Fox, Duffield, 1904), pp. 54-55.
[3]Milton M. Gordon, *Assimilation in American Life* (New York, Oxford University Press, 1964), p. 117.

the American people, but the ideal included an absence of prejudice and discrimination in American life vis-à-vis language, religion, and national origin. Such a view is a fine example of what Karl Mannheim has called a utopia.[4] He defined a utopia as a social reality that departs from the actual state of affairs in a new way. In other words, a utopian doctrine describes a situation that has as yet not happened. This description accurately accords with the ideal of the melting pot, for it projected a new future for the United States and, particularly, for the immigrants who had severed their connections with the past.

MYTH OF THE MELTING POT. When a metaphor is no longer believed to be an "as if" vehicle for organizing our thinking and is taken to be a literal statement, a myth has been born. The most important kind of myth is a myth that becomes the official doctrine of something — in this case, the official doctrine of the ideology of the melting pot.

The beginning of the twentieth century marks the turning point at which the ideal became the myth. To a British-born Jew, Israel Zangwill, the "melting pot" seemed to be an ideal worthy of his best efforts. In his 1908 play, *The Melting Pot*,[5] Zangwill bequeathed to America more than the ideal; his legacy was the cherished myth, the official doctrine of the ideology of the melting pot. The play, a popular success, ran for months on Broadway; its title was considered a concise statement of a profoundly significant American fact of life, not an ideal by which we might judge our attempts to achieve a very difficult goal.

In the play, Vera Revendal, a beautiful Gentile, calls at the home of the violinist David Quixano to invite him to entertain the immigrants down at the settlement. To her amazement she learns that David is a Russian Jewish immigrant, a "pogrom orphan," escaped to New York. She hears him refer to America as "the crucible." "The crucible," she says, "I don't understand." David answers:

---

[4]Karl Mannheim, *Ideology and Utopia* (New York, Harcourt Brace Jovanovich, 1936, paperback ed.). Mannheim's work was a pioneering effort in the sociology of knowledge.
[5]Israel Zangwill, *The Melting-Pot* (New York, Macmillan, 1923).

You, the spirit of the Settlement! Not understand that
America is God's crucible, the great Melting-pot where all the
races of Europe are melting and re-forming? Here you stand,
good folk, think I, when I see them at Ellis Island, here you
stand in your fifty groups with your fifty languages and histories, and your fifty blood hatreds and rivalries. But you
won't be long like that, brothers, for these are the fires of
God. A fig for your feuds and vendettas! German and
Frenchmen, Irishmen and Englishmen, Jews and Russians —
into the Crucible with you all! God is making the American
— the real American has not yet arrived. He is only in the
Crucible, I tell you — he will be the fusion of all the races,
the coming superman.[6]

Zangwill's hero enters the amalgam process with the greatest
of zeal, and the play ends with the approaching marriage of
Vera and David. All concerned have been reconciled to a homogeneous future, emphasizing the fact that, for Zangwill, the
play was no myth, no fiction, but was an accurate description
of a real event writ large in American life.

Glazer and Moynihan, in their pioneering study of ethnicity
and politics in New York City (1963), have this to say about the
play:

Yet the play seems but little involved with American reality.
It is a drama about Jewish separatism and Russian anti-
Semitism, with a German concertmaster and an Irish maid
thrown in for comic relief. Both protagonists are New Model
Europeans of the time. Free thinkers and revolutionaries, it
was doubtless in the power of such to merge. But neither of
these doctrines was out of their mold, but the groups remained. The experience of Zangwill's hero and heroine was
not general. The point about the melting pot is that it did not
happen.[7]

It is significant that Glazer and Moynihan emphasize the
mythic nature of the melting pot: "The point about the
melting pot is that it did not happen." But it is of greater

---

[6]Zangwill, *The Melting-Pot*, pp. 33-34.
[7]Nathan Glazer and Daniel P. Moynihan, *Beyond the Melting Pot*, 2nd ed. (Cambridge,
Mass., MIT Press, 1970), p. 290 (italics deleted).

significance that the myth had become a doctrine people swore by. In expending their energies upon a mythic belief, the enthusiasts of the melting pot did not see that the myth was overlaid with ambiguity and its core altogether obscured by metaphors and sloganizing. The myth, however, retained an aura of being true because of continuous and increasing racial fusion among Americans, but this racial mixture through intermarriage was not general and indiscriminate but largely channeled along certain restrictive lines. Moreover, the myth supported a cultural "contributionism" in making the new American, and this was seen to be a fact in terms of America's developing cultural cuisine.

The fact remains, however, that the myth was a passionate belief by which people lived. The broad name for this type of venture is fantasy. Will Herberg, an observer of the assimilative process, claims that the ideologues of the melting pot were wrong in regard to the cultural aspect of the assimilative process.

> They looked forward to a genuine blending of cultures, to which ethnic strain would makes its own contribution and out of which would emerge a new cultural synthesis, no more English than German or Italian and yet in some sense transcending and embracing them all. In certain respects this has indeed become the case: our American cuisine includes antipasto and spaghetti, frankfurters and pumpernickel, filet mignon and french fried potatoes, borsch, sour cream, and gefilte fish, on a perfect equality with fried chicken, ham and eggs, and pork and beans. But it would be a mistake to infer from this that the American's image of himself — and that means the ethnic group member's image of himself as he becomes American — is a composite or synthesis of the ethnic elements that have gone into the making of the American. It is nothing of the kind: the American's image of himself is still the Anglo-American ideal it was at the beginning of our independent existence. The "national type" as ideal has always been, and remains, pretty well fixed. . . . Our cultural assimilation has taken place not in a "melting pot," but rather in a [citing Stewart] "transmuting pot" in which all ingredients have been transformed and assimilated to an

idealized "Anglo-Saxon model."[8]

A combination of rhetoric, abstruseness, and persuasion more or less sums up the myth of the melting pot. Instead of introducing clarity and sanity, the myth encouraged varied fantasies and a fascination with the "wretched refuse," the Statue of Liberty's "poetic" inscription. The opportunity for all immigrants to begin afresh in America carried with it a powerful impetus to renounce the past. They soon discovered that America, as the land of opportunity, seemed to exact a price — that of becoming an American — which all had to pay. The ideal was that all were to pay and be rewarded equally. The reality is that some were more equal than others. The myth was that no one had to pay, and all would be rewarded. The reality is that the American was not a mixture of many ethnicities — comparable in an analogic way to America's cuisine — rather, the reality is that the American was paradigmatically a white Anglo-Saxon Protestant or one trying his or her best to become as WASP-like as possible.

REALITY OF THE MELTING POT. One can emphasize the extent to which immigrants and their descendants have melted into a new American mixture only by overlooking the great diversity of customs, subcommunity enclaves, and minority group ties that still exist. The reality of American society today is that while many ethnics have been acculturated — that is, have adopted many mainstream cultural tastes in music, clothes, entertainment, food, the WASP ethic, and so forth — all have not been totally assimilated into the mainstream social system. Many disparate ethnic groups are at different stages of the assimilative process.

But like the beat, "the myth goes on." Swallowing the myth, Herberg was led to predict in *Protestant-Catholic-Jew* the impending disappearance of all or most ethnic groups in the United States in what was not, as had hitherto been generally assumed, a single but rather a "triple melting pot."[9] Herberg's hypothesis was that new identities based on religion were

---

[8]Will Herberg, *Protestant-Catholic-Jew* (New York, Doubleday, 1955), pp. 33-34.
[9]Herberg, *Protestant-Catholic-Jew* (*see* Ch. 3, "From the Land of Immigrants to the Triple Melting Pot: The Third Generation and the Religious Community").

taking over from disappearing ethnic identities.

Few prophecies have ever been so quickly and thoroughly confounded. The role of religion as a primary identity for Americans was weakened. Protestant and Catholic black Americans have ignored religious differences in behalf of their common liberation; Puerto Ricans, Chicanos, and Native Americans are following their example. "Catholicism no longer confirms as fully as it did some years ago the conservative tendencies of Italians and Irish."[10] Today the ironic climax of Herberg's theological perspective is that even third-generation "middle America" is discovering "ethnicities" that were thought to have been socialized out of existence a number of decades ago. The fate of Herberg's prophecy might well give us some second thoughts about the social fiction called the melting pot.

In attempting to deal knowledgeably with the ideology of the melting pot, we should not overlook the problem of assimilation. Into what, if at any time in American life group X was involved in the process of becoming an American, was the group assimilating? The answer given by Herberg, Gordon, Glazer and Moynihan, and others is into the host or core culture, namely, the dominant English society — English institutions, English language, and English-oriented cultural patterns — as modified in the American experience. In effect, the core culture pattern in America was comprised essentially of WASP values, life-styles, and identifications to which the ethnic cultures were seen as subordinate.

The implications of the core culture concept have been widely circulated. But less evident is that core culture assimilation has been for many less of a reality than a slogan. Under this persuasive slogan the perpetuation of cultural diversity was viewed as divisive and inimical to the best interest of a homogeneous, chauvinistic society organized around the WASP ethic. But the reality of ethnic identity and the significance of ethnic identity in American life continue to exist. Edgar Litt, an astute student of this phenomenon in American politics, says, "Although the American political culture is highly inclu-

[10]Glazer and Moynihan, *Beyond the Melting Pot, p. xxxvii.*

sive, ethnic forces play a surprisingly persistent role in our politics."[11] Litt contends that the persistence of ethnic politics in America is no little achievement: "The persistence of unassimilated and/or unacculturated ethnic groups provides a source of American politics tinged with ethnic components. The American melting pot never steamed away the layers of group sentiment and symbols that underlie ethnic identification. Herein lies the durable base for the varieties of racial and religious politics within the ongoing system."[12]

Glazer and Moynihan, although their concern is more narrow than Litt's, express a similar point in the Introduction to their second edition:

> Have ethnic identity and the significance of ethnic identity declined in the city [of] New York since the early 1960's? The long-expected and predicted decline of ethnicity, the fuller acculturation and the assimilation of the white ethnic groups, seems once again delayed — as it was by World War I, World War II, and the cold war — and by now one suspects, if something expected keeps on failing to happen, that there may be more reasons than accident that explain why ethnicity and ethnic identity continue to persist. In *Beyond the Melting Pot*, we suggested that ethnic groups, owing to their distinctive historical experiences, their cultures and skills, the times of their arrival and the economic situation they met, developed distinctive economic, political, and cultural patterns. As the old culture fell away — and it did rapidly enough — a new one, shaped by the distinctive experiences of life in America, was formed and a new identity was created. Italian-Americans might share precious little with Italians in Italy, but in America they were a distinctive group that maintained itself, was identifiable, and gave something to those who were identified with it, just as it also gave burdens that those in the group had to bear.[13]

The purpose here is not so much to account for the differences between the author's quotes as it is to bring their agree-

---

[11]Edgar Litt, *Ethnic Politics in America* (Glenview, Ill., Scott, Foresman & Co., 1970), p. 2.

[12]Litt, *Ethnic Politics in America*, p. 15.

[13]Glazer and Moynihan, *Beyond the Melting Pot*, p. xxxiii.

ment into focus. Both claim that ethnic identity and significance have not been eliminated by the pressure of the melting pot. Indeed, the melting-pot reality is that both culturally and structurally the ideology of the melting pot has been illusory — a too naive illusion, one we can no longer afford. Of course, in one sense it is not difficult to understand why the ideal was unrealizable. The ideal advanced the view that the new American type, made up of the tired, the poor, the "wasted refuse," "the huddled masses yearning to be free," was to be fused to the older elements by the magical twin efforts of amalgamation and assimilation. But it was never terribly clear as to whether the new type was to be a culturally new indigenous American, one in whom ethnic differences had been eradicated, or whether the melting-pot magic was to produce a biological merger of the older Anglo-Saxon peoples with the newer immigrants, thus achieving a blending of their respective genes into a new American type. The myth emphasized that the blending was not only desirable but also actually taking place. The myth thus functioned to give relief and affirmation to the ideal, as much a matter of reassurance that what was taking place would somehow turn out all right as encouragement to carry on in the same direction. In any case, the pot bubbled slowly. Indeed, the final smelting was never complete. Unassimilated ethnic identification remained. "In 1822 the Chinese were excluded, and the first general immigration law was enacted. In a steady succession thereafter, new and more selective barriers were raised until, by the National Origins Act of 1924, the nation formally adopted the policy of using immigration to reinforce, rather than further dilute, the racial stock of early America."[14]

In conclusion, the burden of this section should be quite clear. American society has been given a particular direction by the ideology of the melting pot. Yet, the melting pot, either as ideal or as myth, may well be an absurdity and a mockery of America today. It is a too facile metaphor for those who wish to understand the deferral of the final smelting of the different

---

[14]Glazer and Moynihan, *Beyond the Melting Pot,* p. 289.

ingredients into a new amalgam in the United States. The ideology does not give the general causes for this American pattern of ethnic subgroups.

It is striking and perplexing that today, over fifty years after mass immigration from Europe to this country ended, the ethnic pattern is still strong. American society is composed of a number of ethnic groups, or "pots"; some are racial and are not allowed to melt, and others reflect substantial remnants of those who chose not to melt.

THE PUBLIC SCHOOL LEGEND

But what of schooling? What role, if any, did the schools play in the ideology of the melting pot? The mixture of myth and reality in America has produced numerous legends, not the least of which is found in public education. If one were to ask the so-called man on the street what role, if any, did schooling play in the success of the melting pot, the answer would most likely be that public school was the prime factor. Indeed, many Americans look on schooling as the chief vehicle of assimilation. This belief is an interesting one, but the fact is the myth of the melting pot produced the public school legend. It goes like this: The success or miracle of the melting pot was accomplished with schooling serving as the prime agent in the process. The legend has it that an enlightened body of teachers and administrators led the immigrants in establishing themselves as 100 percent Americans. The school, without hesitation, did its best for the immigrants and the country by making a new American out of the "wretched refuse." For some, the public school legend makes of schooling the primary means of Americanization.

While a core of reality lies behind the legend (myths usually have some basic connection with reality), the legend, as it stands, simply is not true. The twin elements of melting-pot magic and public schooling alchemy are largely pseudo-historical, tending to ignore the fact that the school was, after all, only one institution that stood ready to meet the melting pot's demands for amalgamation. Moreover, the schools were not supported on a grand scale, and in large cities where the crush of immigrant children was heaviest, teachers were hard put to teach the basic three Rs, let alone socialize the students in terms of the melting-pot ideal. If ethnics were Americanized, the school did so in terms of imposition of WASP values and standards, not the ideal of the melting pot.

The main point is that although most Americans have assumed that schooling was essential to the success of the melting pot, the fact is that immigrants were not inculcated with the melting-pot ideal at all — they were indoctrinated in the schools with the values of the dominant WASP culture. Moreover, other institutions, the factory, the union of the labor movement, the ethnic settlement itself, alongside the school, served as Americanization agencies. These institutions were in no better position than the school to promote the melting-pot ideal. Hence the reality is that a great many social agencies played a decisive role as instruments of assimilation. David Tyack described this emphasis in terms of schooling: "Despite the usual reverence expressed toward the family in the textbooks and in the official culture of the school, teachers were in effect telling children that they must change their ways and not emulate their parents. The public schools became a wedge splitting immigrant children from their parents."[15]

It can be argued, of course, that even if the school had taken seriously the melting-pot ideal and had wished to consider appropriate ways of guiding and directing students in that ideal, it would not have gotten very far. The ideal of the melting pot was normative, not descriptive, and the immigrants themselves made demands that the schools could not ignore. The reality was that the immigrant was quite isolated from his European past and sought to make adjustments in America. Oscar Handlin has argued,

> "Wherever the immigrants went, there was one common experience they shared: nowhere could they transplant the European village. . . . The pressure of. . . strangeness exerted a

[15]David B. Tyack, *Turning Points in American Educational History* (Waltham, Mass., Blaisdell, 1967), pp. 229-30.

deep influence... upon the usual forms of behavior, and
upon the modes of communal action that emerged as immigrants became Americans."[16]

This last point is further explicated by Timothy L. Smith:

Quite as much as any coercion from compulsory education
acts or any pressure from professional Americanizers, the immigrant's own hopes for his children account for the im-
mense success of the public school system, particularly at the
secondary level, in drawing the mass of working class
children into its embrace. By their presence, and by their
commitment to these several ambitions, the first generation of
immigrant children prompted educators, in administrative
offices as well as classrooms, to a thousand pragmatic experi-
ments geared to the interests and the needs of their students.
Self-styled patriots and scholars devoted to the special value
of the liberal arts later found the results displeasing, though
for different reasons of course.[17]

Smith also points out:

Statistics for literacy and school attendance in the federal
census of 1910 suggest that immigrant families showed as
much or more zeal for education as those in which the parents were native Americans. Not just in the South, where the
school system was weak and the former slave population
large, but in every section of the country, the percentage of
children of foreign or mixed percentage aged six to fourteen
who were enrolled in school closely approximated that for
children of native Americans. And the literacy of the immigrant's offspring was uniformly higher, even in the populous
Middle Atlantic and North Central states, where newcomers
from central and southern Europe were many, and traditions
of education among the Yankee population strong.[18]

But be this as it may, it is an old story now,[19] and yet it bears
remembering: *Economic stability for any ethnic group must*

---

[16]Oscar Handlin, *The Uprooted* (Boston, Little, Brown, 1951), p. 144.
[17]Timothy L. Smith, "Immigrant Social Aspirations and American Education, 1880-
1930, "*American Quarterly 21*(3): 543, 1969.
[18]Smith, "Immigrant Social Aspirations and American Education," p. 523.
[19]It is not without justice that this understanding appreared largely thanks to the
militancy of the black American civil rights movement of the 1960s.

precede its entry into the broader middle class stage via public education. In other words, an ethnic middle class must be established before the school can work its so-called alchemy. The failure to recognize and appreciate this fact is the most astonishing feature of the public school legend. Seen from this perspective, the school legend is best understood as a myth about a myth.

Today it is, of course, impossible not to recognize that a variety of institutions sought to integrate the newcomer. Gerd Korman described the schooling of immigrants in the company schools of the Harvester Company plants:

> By the eve of World War I, the company's schools had several purposes. They supplemented the education of their young male employees, many of whom came from immigrant families and had little or no formal schooling. The schools were open to all young men with a speaking knowledge of English, but only apprentices were required to attend. The curriculum stressed technical subjects taught in close relationship to actual production. Mechanical training was given in the shops and was supervised by foremen. The schools provided a "real opportunity for moulding character and influencing life," claimed a company spokesman. They promoted responsible citizenship by giving instruction in hygiene, history, and civics. The company maintained that every "effort is being made to stimulate the ambition" of the students "and to develop in them an interest in their work and to fit them for most of the responsible positions in the company's employ."[20]

The immigrant workers learned English through such lessons as the following:

> I hear the whistle. I must hurry.
> I hear the five minute whistle.
> It is time to go into the shop. . . .
> I change my clothes and get ready to work.
> I work until the whistle blows to quit.
> I leave my place nice and clean.[21]

---

[20]Gerd Korman, *Industrialization, Immigrants, and Americanizers* (Madison, Wis., The State Historical Society of Wisconsin, 1967), p. 104.
[21]Korman, *Industrialization, Immigrants, and Americanizers*, pp. 144-145.

Labor's reaction to "the need for educating the immigrant in regard to American institutions and ways of life and in a knowledge of the English language was universal."[22] "That through the Americanization movement nothing but possible advantage could accrue to the cause of labor, seems to have become the dominant attitude of labor in regard to the movement. . . . "[23]

Perhaps no group of Americanizers had a greater impact on the immigrants than certain private groups who took the initiative in an active campaign to educate the immigrant to a better appreciation of his environment and the good "old-fashioned" American ideals. Space does not allow for a full coverage of this element, but passing reference can be made to the Educational Alliance of New York City, the Hebrew Free School Association, the Aguilar Free Library, the Young Men's Christian Association, National Society of Colonial Dames, Committee on Information for Aliens, and the North American Civil League for Immigrants. Believing wholeheartedly in the need for a campaign of education for the immigrant, these societies advertised and sponsored night school programs and lectures for the adult, and public school authorities were asked to open more classes for immigrants and to keep such classes as were already in existence open for a longer period during the year.

Similarly, mutual aid societies flourished in immigrant communities. Workingmen and small shopkeepers exhibited a capacity to cooperate in the days before workingman's compensation and social insurance. The B'nai B'rith, the Croatian and Slovenian benefit societies, the National Order of the Sons of Italy, the American Jewish Congress, and the Anti-Defamation League all served to ease the process of assimilation.

In addition, the effort of the social settlement was a major one in the Americanization movement. Because the large majority of the immigrants were ill educated, unfamiliar with democratic practices, plagued with a language barrier, and were urban tenement dwellers, one major thrust of American-

---

[22]Edward George Hartmann, *The Movement to Americanize the Immigrant* (New York, Columbia University Press, 1948), pp. 140-141.
[23]Hartmann, *Movement to Americanize the Immigrant*, p. 261.

ization came from settlement workers and nurses who talked in terms of neighborhood regeneration and human betterment. The settlement approach was to teach and, if possible, heal the social sores of the nation's immigrants.

In capsule form, the settlement idea was the ideal of the melting pot. Workers stressed the value of immigrant traditions and customs to Americans, and they attempted to make immigrants feel proud of their heritage. During the Americanization crusade of the second decade of this century, the social settlement response to the inhuman conditions of life in urban industrial America was in some measure a humanitarian response. For example, settlement literature, particularly works such as *Americans in Process*,[24] helped mold the contributions concept of immigrants by suggesting that assimilation was a "two-edged sword." But in another sense it was also a middle-class response, where middle class means remedies in terms of individual-personal adjustment to the existing social order.

To comprehend this last point we see no less a reformer than Jane Addams suggesting that native Americans adopt an evolutionary viewpoint of the progress of human society. By acquiring a historical perspective and a "trained imagination," Americans could enjoy the "sweetness and charm" of immigrant customs.[25] Addams plumped for an enlightened understanding of the immigrant and hoped that the result would be elimination of the roadblocks hampering greater urban social integration. She speculated about an imaginary evening in an ideal public night school: "We could imagine the business man teaching the immigrant his much needed English and receiving in return lessons in the handling of tools and materials, so that they should assume in his mind a totally different significance from that the factory gives them, as the resulting produce would possess for him the delicacy and charm which the self expression of the work always implies."[26]

Other settlement workers emphasized the practical import of setting up first-aid centers and clinics that gave not only much needed medicine but also information ranging from child care

---

[24]Robert Woods, ed., *American in Process* (Boston, Houghton, Mifflin, 1903).
[25]Jane Addams, *Newer Ideals of Peace* (New York, Macmillan, 1907), pp. 64-65.
[26]Jane Addams, "The Humanizing Tendency of Industrial Education," *Chautauquan* *34*(May): 271, 1904.

to preventive medicine. The workers taught adults to read, introduced nurseries, and established playgrounds. Generally speaking, the programs developed were aimed at human betterment and were successful insofar as they were developed in response to requests from the immigrants themselves.

Another factor that facilitated the Americanization of immigrants was the effort of local and state government. In the years immediately following World War I, state government legislation was passed in support of Americanization and the need to school the adult immigrant. Many states acted as a consequence of the wave of hysteria that swept the nation resulting from the actions of the Department of Justice in conducting its crusade against the alien radical.

For example, the General Assembly of Connecticut in 1919 established a Department of Americanization and appropriated the sum of $50,000 to carry out a statewide Americanization crusade for a two-year period. A law required "Classes for Non-English Speaking Adults" in all towns of 10,000 population and above (repealed in 1921).[27] Evening school teachers were trained by the State Department of Education and were admonished to "give full evening's instruction during the first session. It is a serious mistake to use the first meeting for formal registration of pupils and 'get acquainted.' "[28] Teachers of immigrant adults were further advised that classification of students on the basis of nationality or racial types might be justified but never beyond the elementary grade level if ". . . we are to teach ideas of democracy and to prevent growth of clanishness."[29]

A special speakers' bureau with a corps of thirty foreign-language speakers was established, and a series of bulletins and circular letters was issued and spread throughout the state. Approximately 10,000 posters in seven different languages were also distributed. The Connecticut Department of Americanization also produced a special movie dealing with Americaniza-

[27]State of Connecticut, *Public Acts of Connecticut*, 1919, Chapter 286 (Approved May 21, 1919).
[28]State of Connecticut, "Classes for Foreign-Born Adults: Organization and Maintenance," Americanization Bulletin no. 1, Series 1920-21 (Hartford, Conn., State Board of Education, 1920), p. 33.
[29]State of Connecticut, "Classes for Foreign-Born Adults," p. 14.

tion efforts. The department remained in existence until 1926 when it merged with the division of adult education of the State Department of Education. But interest in immigrant education was evident throughout the decade of the 1920s.

The foregoing account has made the point that the school was not the only vehicle of Americanization. But it would be sheer nonsense to assume that schooling played little or no role in educating the immigrant. This is not the case. Smith's data regarding "Immigrant Social Aspirations and American Education" support this claim. But it must be understood that the Americanization drive to educate the adult immigrant and formally inculcate him with American ideals and the American language definitely came to an end in the 1920s. The process of Americanization, however, that subtle, often peculiar force, remained ever at work in transforming the foreign-born into so-called average Americans.

In summary, the common view offered with regard to cultural diversity is that American schooling was a highly effective vehicle in achieving the success of the melting pot. But whether we recognize the fact or not, most immigrants and their children experienced little of the melting-pot ideal. The myth continues, but the reality is that schooling promoted an Anglo-conformism that virtually denigrated the ancestral heritage of immigrants. Moreover, some groups were never allowed to "melt" into the American "pot." And it is largely the latter groups who are now determined to be more self-assured and proud of themselves as well as being prepared to be more self-determining about their own destinies.

POLICY AND CULTURAL DIVERSITY

From one point of view of social structure, a society may be seen as marked by a conflict of interests as well as an identity of interests, but is a cooperative undertaking for mutual advantage. An identity of interests exists because social cooperation is needed to make possible a more productive life for all than any would have if each were to face the world solely alone. But there is a conflict of interests since individuals and groups are not always agreed about the methods of cooperation and how the benefits of such cooperation are to be distributed. Thus one of the basic considerations of any society is the age-old problem of "stability."[30] This is particularly the case when dealing with a culturally diverse society.

Public policy may be regarded as the search for the various social arrangements that help determine the division of advantages and for underwriting an agreement on the proper distribution of goods and services in society. Hence the consideration of public policy making raises one of the most fundamental social problems we can consider.

It is reasonable to assume that in any society coercive powers are to some degree necessary for the stability of social cooperation and the maintenance of identity of interests. Granting that groups need to be allowed to function so that their activities are not necessarily compatible with one another, the scheme of social organization is more or less regularly compiled with and its basic rules more or less willingly acted upon. Further granting that various groups in society share a common sense of fair play and that each wants to promote the common interest, they may nevertheless lack full confidence in one another. They may suspect, and with good reason, that some are not working to achieve social cooperation, that some are "easy riders" within the system, not pulling their own weight. The establishment of some sort of coercion makes sense — that is, is rational — insofar as in both economic and political activity people must behave within the general spirit of the institutions if those institutions are to survive. But it is rational only if the disadvantages are less than the losses accruing from instability. Thus, while some sort of coercive socializing mechanisms are necessary, it is obviously essential to define precisely the limits of their operation.

---

[30]A society is stable if there are adequate and appropriate methods for inducting the youth into society to enable them to live up to the publicly recognized standards required of them. In one view, the publicly recognized standards required of youth are not supported by a high or massive level of coercion in terms of use of secret police to inspire fear and obedience, or a demand for compliance with the law, with no exceptions permitted, and death, quick or protracted, as the penalty for heresy. From another view, coercion and the like are acceptable means to ensure stability.

The crucial point here is that in any society, culturally diverse or not, principles of social coordination are necessary and must be agreed upon. Properly understood, then, the important question here is whether public policy will exhibit a greater or lesser degree of coercion vis-à-vis the fact that the United States is a culturally diverse society. Will group or ethnic parity be recognized? What position will the following groups be forced into: the Amish and certain Black Muslims who wish to preserve their subcultures by resorting to an insular position, but who wish to participate significantly in the polity but not in the "general culture"; some Polish, French, Greek, Hungarians, Armenians, Portuguese, Irish, Norwegians, Swedes, Italians, and Germans who freely choose to perpetuate as a culture the old country heritage as modified by three or four generations in America; Native Americans, the original settlers, whose original general culture was reduced to a subculture, but who wish to preserve their ancestral heritage; and Jews who wish to maintain a group identity, even in the conditions of a more fully secular American society?

As we have seen, American society, experiencing the problem of instability as a result of rapid industrialization, booming urbanization, and mass immigration, required that the stability occur within controlled social structures in order to channel it in directions favorable to social unity. The type of public policy advocated championed controlled cultural diversity within the boundaries of ethnicity and politics. We can call this policy the accommodation model of policy making.

Accommodation policy reflects the legacy of the efforts of certain white immigrant groups in America who successfully challenged the host or dominant Anglo-Saxon group in wrestling for themselves more specific advantages (goods and benefits). Political party and white ethnic communities, so basic to the accommodation model, served as effective instruments for determining the distribution of goods. In short, in its emphasis on divisible benefits and on the awarding of particular prerogatives the accommodation model served as the principle vehicle of stability and helped America achieve a large measure of social unity.

However, the accomplishment of long-term stability has not

been realized without cost. For many assimilated ethnics, the cost was the loss of their ancestral heritage. The accommodation model was never well suited to anything but white ethnic community claims to society's goods and benefits, a relationship that necessarily called for ethnic identity within a particular political party. Accommodation politics, in other words, did not take seriously the distinction between persons, although it did for most groups. It could never handle with any ease the principle of "everyman's" claim to equality of educational opportunity. Moreover, this model has not been considered to apply in any great numbers to the black American, the Native American, and the Latin American minorities, only a few of whom were allowed to be "accommodated" and as groups have been refused complete acceptance in American society. In brief, the accommodation model was incapable of coping with the recent expansive changes in public thought and institutions.

Clearly, there is a great and pressing need today for a reinterpretation of public policy. The recent issue of Vietnam merely brought into focus a realization of the failure of the accommodation model. Accommodation policy has failed to define current American problems created by the emergence of new political organizations, many specifically wrought out of the "problem areas" of minorities. The accommodation model is dysfunctional in dealing with radically new approaches to moral values; a black consciousness and pride; a feminist attack on masculine domination; a rejection by many young people of exclusively economic goals; an insistence on economic and educational opportunity for all; and the view that suggests that the natural environment is more important than commercial profit.

The search for something more viable and satisfying than the old accommodation model represents more than the need for new public policy capable of responding to public claims made by the revival of ethnicity. It also calls into being the prospect of new ideologies that will give support to actions determining the division of advantages and agreements on the proper distribution of goods and benefits in American society. The revival of ethnicity has as its significance the matter of calling forth ideologies congruent with reassessing the entire American value system and the supports on which it is based.

The quest for a new public policy must be set within the arena of cultural diversity, this much is clear. The question raised, however, is, What system of predominant values is most appropriate for a culturally diverse society? It seems painfully obvious that public policy necessarily, and educational policy for the most part, must be formed not on the basis of what is good for a particular group, but on the basis of what is fair for people in general, for people on the whole. This is to say that one requirement for public policy is that it must be democratically conceived. Part of what is meant by this is that public policy of a culturally diverse society appears to involve the mutual exchange of and respect for the individuals that comprise the social order. Another part of what is meant is that the diverse groups must approximate equal political, economic, and educational opportunity. Finally, there must be a behavioral commitment on the part of the groups to the social ideal of cultural diversity. Falling short of these conditions, any culturally diverse society will have inherent tensions that will inevitably produce instability. Stability then can only be had by a resort to massive coercive means.

Hence, if we are serious about giving priority to cultural diversity in American society today, it is not a question that some restraint in the pursuit of group interest is necessary for the satisfactory operation of policy making. On the contrary, group activity and public interest will be enhanced insofar as the rivalry between group interests brings about a concern for the "common interest," or what is fair for people in general. The public interest is usually advanced by the search for the "common interest."

In conclusion, to see public policy as a product that authorizes the distribution of benefits and prerogatives in society and educational policy as performing the function of ensuring the acceptance and maintenance of such policy is to appreciate the instrumental function of public schooling in providing stability to a society. Moreover, to consider public schooling apart from policy making is to run the risk of confusing the cart with the horse. Public schooling is, and always has been, inseparable from broader social, political, and economic policy making.

SUMMARY

There is, obviously, little similarity between the ideology of the melting pot and the reality of the American historical experience. The melting pot ideology made two assumptions: first, that immigrant groups in American society were unwilling to pay the price of Americanization and did not want to "make it" on WASP terms; second, that the American culture was accepting and tolerant enough of "foreign ways" to allow for the fusion and emergence of a "new" American. Both assumptions, on the whole, proved faulty. Most of the immigrants — the large ethnic groups of Poles, Russians, Italians, Irish, Germans, and others — were quite willing to pay the price that the dominant culture demanded for acceptance, and that price was an unyielding conformity to the values of the dominant or host culture. Moreover, for many immigrants tolerance was a myth. Up until quite recently, ethnicity was frowned upon, even ridiculed, in American society. This was true in literature and the arts as well as in public schools. About the only exception is in the area of cuisine. So-called "foreign accents," — Yiddish, Russian, Italian, German, Polish, to name a few — were the butt of humor on the stage, on radio, and in magazines.

Clearly, the system of American education we call the public schools and the evening schools, along with the settlement houses, voluntary associations, and the factory workplace, all played an important role in the Americanization of millions of immigrants. We remember that throughout the fifty years of heaviest immigration the immigrants came almost entirely from the lower social and economic strata of society and that they had to take the most menial jobs offered them, and most were willing to pay the price of admission to the dominant or core culture. For the children of immigrants, the schooling they obtained represented the "open sesame" to job and culture opportunity. But students were expected to turn their backs on the cultural values of their parents. In this, teachers were aided by parents who were determined to see to it that their children did not suffer from the same disadvantage. Hence, public schooling was asked to transform or melt the immigrant's child into an acceptable, respectable American.

One can argue that the evidence is not yet in as to whether or not the public school succeeded or failed miserably in assuring the upward mobility of immigrant children, even though they were expected to "pay the price." But in either case, most of the children experienced little of the melting pot ideal, and most were willing and even eager to become Americanized.

Today's revival of ethnicity, as mentioned in the preceding chapter, along with the demand for the inclusion of ethnic materials and ethnic cultures, bilingual and multicultural education, represents a celebration of cultural diversity and may indeed enrich the common American culture. But if enrichment is to occur, the demands and materials must be couched within the framework of a positive view of cultural diversity, not an ideological one. If cultural diversity is to be a strength in the sense of committing ethnic groups more strongly to the total American society, then cultural diversity should be studied and understood as the study of cultural values and contributions of the many cultures to the common good. It is worth repeating a point made earlier. Students should be exposed in depth to the variety and richness of America's multicultural history; such an education might help defuse a latent racism and provide a solid foundation for social stability.

Melting pot theorists were adamant, however, in promoting the ideology of cultural diversity. They openly deplored the atavistic hatreds and feuds that the immigrants brought with them from their homelands, all the while asserting that the "new" and "better" American culture would be built on the values and mores of the immigrant groups and their fusion with the existing American culture. But the fact remains that millions of immigrants and their children were forced by insensitive teachers, factory co-workers, supervisory personnel, settlement workers, and the like to turn their backs on their historical cultural values. Thus for many Americans today, their ethnic culture has been obliterated by the humbling experience of Americanization.

This is not to say that all groups in American society were willing to or did pay the price of Americanization, at least in humbling terms. For example, almost one million French-speaking Cajuns in Louisiana adhere to their own cultural values and appear to be growing in power and influence in the state. Others, notably Chinese-Americans and the Amish, preserve their separateness by maintaining an insular position against the general society as a whole. They seem determined that their children will not suffer from the same disadvantages that other ethnic groups have experienced. Following their lead, other groups, mainly non-European minorities such as Native-Americans, Hispanics, and blacks, have asked the public school systems to inaugurate bilingual and multicultural programs. Each group is resolute in its celebration of cultural diversity and the need to promote an education which fosters positive self-concepts stemming from cultural diversity.

Chapter Three

CULTURAL DIVERSITY AND
CURRICULAR REFORM

INTRODUCTION

AT present there is an expanded interest in cultural diversity and education. This is true not only of the United States but of many nations of the world. In the United States, for example, ethnic groups are particularly sensitive to their changing status resulting from recent social upheavals, and they have forcefully asserted themselves with regard to curricular reform. Following the lead of non-European minorities, ethnics have encouraged, pressured, cajoled, and demanded educational institutions at all levels to take greater account of cultural diversity in general and ethnicity in particular. In many cases, administrators, school board members, and teachers have been ill-prepared to deal with such pressure and reluctant or inefficient in making changes due to their inability to make an intelligent assessment of the situation. Consequently, the emerging programs have varied widely in scope and purpose as well as reflecting, in greater or lesser degree, an inconsistency, incompatibility, or impracticability.

It is a consequence of this consideration that there is a wide range of educational programs aimed at highlighting and illuminating cultural diversity in American society. Programs such as multicultural education, multiculturalism, multiethnic education, ethnic education, ethnic studies, ethnic pluralism, cultural pluralism, bilingual education, and bicultural education are cited as illustrative of this wide-ranging effort.

It is also clear, however, that the programs are not as demarcated as one might hope. What is needed is an effort at clarification of those in order to delineate the assumptions basic to the position as well as the policies and strategies involved. What is at issue, then, is a deeper problem: a failure to understand how the demands of ethnics and non-European minorities for curricula reform are inextricably tied to ideology.

Thus in this chapter I shall attempt to demarcate the parameters of five ideologies that purport to characterize the most salient features of cultural diversity. Having illuminated these features, I will show how they are related to curricular reform. In this regard, then, it is important that we first clarify the question, "What is ideology?"

IDEOLOGY

The question, "What is ideology?" is important because ideologies function not only to explain and legitimate social arrangements, structures of power, or ways of life; they also serve to link up or relate belief to action.[1] Ideology therefore amounts to a very sophisticated system of thought, requiring for its understanding all the intelligence we can muster. Moreover, ideology can only be clarified if we begin to distinguish its assumptions or presuppositions. That is, the test of strength of any ideology is the extent to which its basic assumptions remain not merely unquestioned but literally unrecognized. The more such assumptions appear to be simply a part of the fabric of fact, the stronger the intellectual hold of the ideology they support and the greater the difficulty of changing the practices and policies arising out of it.[2]

In order to better understand ideology, we will employ a particular conceptual strategy which is called the "structural" approach. This tactic is not only common but also desirable insofar as it serves as an appropriate methodological tool in

---

[1] The analysis of ideology in this section is based upon some ideas from another source, *Ideology and Education* (New York, David McKay, 1977), by the author. Those familiar with that work will recognize the general ideas here as condensed and, hopefully, improved.

[2] Lorenne M.G. Clark, "The Rights of Women: The Theory and Practice of the Ideology of Male Supremacy," in William R. Shea and John King-Farlow, eds., *Contemporary Issues in Political Philosophy* (New York, Science History Publications, 1976), p. 49.

many fields of study, including most social sciences. In brief, the structural approach involves explaining phenomena by portraying the structures of the process which gave rise to them.

Turning to the question of how does an ideology originate, we may consider first the circumstances involved. It is postulated that individuals wish to secure for themselves fundamental rights and advantages within the institutions of society. Or more exactly, they wish to participate in the basic structure of society by being part of the major social institutions distributing fundamental rights and duties as well as determining the division of advantages. The intuitive notion here is that individuals, wishing to secure certain benefits in society, hoping to better their lot in life, come together, either because of real or imagined threat or because of a sense of merit, need, or inequality, form an interest group, thereby striking an alliance to bring about certain desired results (results intended).

Since some measure of agreement, cooperation, identity, and the like is necessary if the interest group is to become an organized interest group, it is not surprising that in the course of open discussion empirical claims and observations are made, taken account of, and along with these a historical context or limiting class of conditions is judged to apply. In this way, through discussion, either rational or irrational, the basic elements of the ideological structure (results intended, empirical premises, limiting conditions) are hammered out. But in order to achieve interest group unity — functional coordination, harmony, stability, meaningful identity, definition of oneself, etc. — individual disagreements involving metaphysical, axiological, and epistemological beliefs are overlooked or downplayed, resulting in most cases, but not all, in such disagreements being temporarily "buried" in order for the interest group to realize a political alliance and hence desired results. These factors, then, regulate the choices of the individual and show how an ideology depends upon a person or a circle of persons who take on themselves the task of articulation and codification of the broad areas of agreement. This is an empirical condition of conflict group formation, and it is a necessary, but not a sufficient, condition of organization.

It has been argued that some measure of agreement in conceptions is necessary for a viable interest group. But there are other fundamental problems, in particular those of coordination, stability, efficiency, and identity. Thus the interests of individuals need to be fitted together so that their activities are compatible with one another and they can all be carried through without anyone's legitimate expectations being severely abused or disappointed. Moreover, the execution of these activities should lead to the achievement of social ends in ways that are efficient and effective. And finally, the strategies and tactics must be regularly compiled with and basic directives willingly acted upon.

It is evident that in the absence of a certain measure of agreement, it is more difficult for individuals to coordinate their strategies and tactics in order to ensure that results intended become results actual. Distrust and resentment corrode the ties of action, and suspicion and hostility tempt individuals to act in ways they might otherwise avoid. So while the distinctive role of beliefs is to specify basic values, the way in which group unity, stability, and common purpose are achieved is through creation of an emotionally persuasive interpretative component consisting of slogans, subslogans, metaphors, definitions, hyperbole, analogy, and other language "moves" that purport to capture the essence of the broad areas of agreement. These moves rally support for or opposition to results intended or actual. Because of their battle-cry function, such moves surface very early in the heat of discussion encouraging individuals to take sides, rallying them to action, helping to eliminate distrust and suspicion, and identifying the role of the group. The moves single out similarities and differences using sharp lines and contrasts, all the while exaggerating and caricaturing in the fashion of a cartoonist — providing, of course, symbols to rally the group to action.

The more interesting function of the interpretative component emerges when we see that it provides imperatives or rules meant to be helpful, but which offer nothing specific to follow. For example, the early twentieth century slogan of "America:

the great crucible" was aimed at producing a certain response in Americans, namely, that the culture of immigrant groups was to be downplayed in favor of a new Americanized identity, somewhat different from the cultures brought to America by vast waves of immigration. Of course, if some people did not "get the message" suggested by the slogan, further refinement in the form of subslogans could always be given. It is worthwhile to observe that the activity of further refinement is directed toward producing behaviors of specified sorts, and it does so by formulating the "rules of the game" criterion — that is, a congruent constellation of procedural arrangements or behaviors to be followed.

In line with these remarks, we may note that the basic function of a slogan system is to specify the particular behaviors called for by the broad imperatives. The decisive consideration is, of course, that it is a matter of agreement that the "rules of the game" under certain conditions count as defining behaviors in terms of "Do X," or "If Y do X." The slogans, hyperbole, and definition are capable of refinement and interpretation to any level of specificity desired, and specifying the "rules of the game" to any level will depend upon how much is asked for or needed by a person. As long as someone remains unconvinced, hesitant, suspicious, or resentful, the sloganizer must be prepared to offer further refinements, until the specific behavior under which the slogan is said to operate is spelled out; and this is done recognizing that sometimes people's capacity to act for their own good may fail, or be lacking altogether. But it is hoped that the individual in question will accept the directive and agree with us that we did the best thing for him.

In pinning down what an ideology is, then, this account suggests that an ideology commonly begins in an interest group's desire to achieve certain desired results. In order to succeed, an alliance of a political sort is struck wherein disagreements over basic beliefs or principles are skirted. For the resultant agreement to be acceptable or palatable, it must be seen as enabling results to be obtained which could not be obtained otherwise, or not as easily. In other words, the alliance rests on a subscription to sloganized main articles which form the ar-

chitecture of the ideology, and although some might admit
certain theoretical difficulties in it, it is assumed that these are
worth the price of unity and solidarity. Hence, problems that
usually inhere in group factions are side-stepped, and policy
decision (what to do) is disengaged from policy principle (what
to believe).

But, of course, ideology is not applicable to everything in the
world; there are limits of application. Thus, as broad as
ideology may be in scope, there is always some limiting class of
situations within the boundaries of which ideology can be applied, to which it is relevant, although such a class of application limits may not be indicated very clearly in the ideology
itself.

Additionally, ideology contains sizable data components representing empirical claims and evidence. Empirical generalizations, facts, observations about the world, etc., serve as the
data base of the ideology, providing a concrete data base enu-
merating common sense precepts as well as scientific laws.
Occasionally, the defense of an ideology will rest on particular
questions balanced in the light of the general "facts" of the
situation.

Finally, ideology contains aims, goals, and purposes. In our
everyday view it is not always necessary to hold anything very
definite about the problem of what aim to follow, what goals to
pursue. But our everyday views provide little in the way of
giving direction to decisions about society. If so, the main
function of ideology is to give us a far more exact, detailed
specification of justice, fairness to others as well as legitimating
social arrangements, structures of power, and the distribution
of benefits in society. It will provide a relatively concrete principle for questions that our everyday views find unfamiliar and
leave undecided. Reflections upon the ideology may convince
us that it does apply to society by projecting certain beliefs to
new situations in a rather precise way.

Hence, we can distinguish five structural components of
ideology, each measured in terms of different criteria. First,
there are theoretical-normative or core beliefs, which can stand
up to the criterion of internal coherence or consistency; second,

the codification of an interpretative component in which the
core beliefs are interpreted, extended, and carry the individual
toward certain prescribed actions — its test is the test of clarifying interpretation; third, appropriate conditions or concrete
historical situations wherein the ideology applies — the test
here is of prudent decisions; fourth, verifiable empirical data
toward which the beliefs are directed, the test of which is
whether the empirical claims are true statements; and fifth,
tactical or hoped-for results are involved, the test of which is
confidence in the rightness or justice of the goals themselves.

In line with these remarks, we may note that ideology is the
wedding of (1) beliefs to (2) historical conditions, (3) empirical
statements, (4) strategic or tactical results intended, and the
wedding or linking up of belief to action is accomplished by (5)
the interpretative component that projects beliefs or convictions to the others in an enlightening, illuminating, enriching,
or appropriate way.

The formula for the structural elements of ideology is as
follows:

Idy	any given ideology
M	the metaphysical beliefs of the Idy
K	the epistemological beliefs of the Idy
V	the value beliefs of the Idy
I	the interpretation
C	the historical conditions or limiting class of situations. to which the Idy applies
E	the empirical base of the Idy
R_i	the intended results to be achieved

The paradigmatic form is the following:

Idy is an expression of M, K, V as *interpreted* in C which is
assumed to be consistent with E in order to achieve R_i.

Hence, what is distinctive about ideology is not only the
linking up of theoretical beliefs (M-K-V) to historical conditions (C), empirical claims (E), and results (R_i), but also the
formulating of rather explicit priorities, directives, and prescriptions for behavior (I) that seem especially natural for us
and no doubt affect our sense of justice by legitimizing and
justifying what is to be done. To take a somewhat familiar case,

it now seems clear beyond a doubt that American politics, the theory on which it is based and the practices arising out if it, articulates an ideology of "male supremacy" insofar as it serves the interest of the dominant class of males, a dominance which is assumed to be natural. At its very heart, politics assumes that those who are "naturally" stronger, aggressive, freer from reproductive labor, more contemplative, rational, and objective (in short, the male) should participate. The fundamental meaning and importance of politics cannot be had by females.

We can thus distinguish in the case of the ideology of male supremacy (1) the belief that males rather than females are "naturally" the dominant or superior sex; (2) the limiting condition of parliamentary politics, and not the household sphere of organization; (3) empirically, young males do show a superiority over young females on tests involving logic, rationality, "thingness," and interest in things; (4) the intended result that social organizations and institutions ought to be led by males; and this is accomplished by (5) an interpretative component that defines the private, as opposed to the public, sphere as less significant; uses analogies of women and not-serious, flighty, or irrational situations; and employs metaphors such as "She is a doll" and sloganizes "Anatomy is destiny."

In other words, decisions for action — what is to be done — although not established by the interpretation, are justified through the interpretative component. The conduct of individuals is guided by their acceptance of the interpretation, and its publicity ensures that those who embrace the ideology know what conduct to expect of others similarly persuaded and what kinds of action are permissible. The interpretative component, in other words, makes the theoretical-normative beliefs, generally thought to have jurisdiction in the ideology, second-order insofar as they cannot make rules for themselves. The interpretative component has jurisdiction or authority over all, serving as clarifying or simplifying prescriptions and directives, defining the results of agreement. Hence, an ideologue knows what the rules are, what they demand of him and others, and he also knows that others know this and they know that he knows this, and so on. Ideology thus understood intimately involves beliefs, historical conditions, empirical data, schemes and strategies called for, as well as the forms of behavior encouraged. Hence, the conduct of individuals is guided by their ideology and is coordinated as far as possible to achieve results intended, but the strategies and tactics followed are not part of the ideology itself, for there is no logical necessity involved.

Practical reasoning connects ideology to action as follows:

R, as a purpose, is desirable.

S appears to be the best strategy for achieving R.

Therefore, do S.

What is obvious is the desirability of R can be believed with or without some evidence, likewise for the notion of S. The practical reasoning schema is merely a set of statements, and logically there is no necessity to follow the prescribed course of action. What it offers is neither an argument nor a deductive theory, but rather a practical suggestion for action on the basis of some belief or set of beliefs.

We have argued up to this point that a certain basic structure of ideology exists. First, an ideology contains a theoretical-normative base of metaphysical, epistemological, and axiological beliefs. Second, it has an interpretational component of verbal/written techniques expounding the proper relation of belief to action. Third, an ideology is not universal; it has limited applicability, namely to appropriate historical conditions. Fourth, it contains data on matters of fact and on observations. These empirical data act as empirical premises offering potential for verification. Finally, an ideology offers a desirable end in view, often as justification for the adoption or embracing of the ideology.

By way of general comment, the above structural elements taken separately are necessary and together are sufficient for what may be called a "full-blown" ideology. As their formulation suggests, the beliefs are not fallible and self-corrective; they are not open to testing and criteria. Rather, the interpretative component serves as a "protective belt" encircling the core beliefs by calling for new directives and prescriptions when anomalies (counterexamples and inconsistencies) appear in the wake of a drastically changing data base, when the empirical premises prove false, and when results intended are not consistently realized.

The structural model seems well suited to analyzing ideology because it illustrates that the theoretical-normative base not only does not logically imply its particulars (data base and results intended), it cannot possibly do so. The interpretative component, in other words, stands between the theoretical-normative base and the results intended in an arbitrary (in the sense of "not necessary") relationship and is intended to bridge the two. Hence, the theoretical-normative base is "mapped" onto the data base by the interpretative component — a system of slogans, subslogans, metaphors, analogies, and definitions. Moreover, and this is crucial, the interpretative component is used to specify forms of behavior by use of general imperatives and more specific "rules of the game."

CULTURAL DIVERSITY

Earlier the point was made that cultural diversity bears mightily upon the present educational scene insofar as ethnics and other minorities tend to assess educational policies and practices in terms of the background of cultural diversity. But, of course, the issue is broader insofar as it is assumed that a doctrine of political economy must include an interpretation of the public good which is based on a recognition of the legitimacy of demands couched in the terms of cultural diversity. The social system is to be guided by the reflections of public officials alert to aspects of cultural diversity when considering problems of economic, social, and educational policy. It is incumbent upon public officials to take up the perspective of a culturally diverse society when ascertaining how the society is to be advanced, especially in addressing the social justice issues of equality of educational, work, and political opportunity.

The upshot of these considerations is that ideology and cultural diversity are inextricably bound together today. Cultural diversity provides an Archimedean point for people making choices about the social system and ideology provides an effective means whereby convictions can be focused, made congruent, legitimized, and operative. If this point is accepted, we shall now turn to the relationship between ideology and cultural diversity.

IDEOLOGY AND CULTURAL DIVERSITY

Ideology, it was argued, relates belief to action in a way that accords reasonably well with justifying the action. An examination of ideology and cultural diversity is especially illuminating because it so readily demonstrates this phenomenon. Particularly do we see illustrated the significance or force of ideology as a justification of belief and action.

For simplicity's sake, it is assumed that cultural diversity may be symbolized by A, B, C, D, with each letter standing for a cultural group, be it religious, racial, national, etc.[3] Hence, cultural diversity provides the "difference" criterion by which groups are demarcated in society, but we do not need to know what the differences are or the criteria justifying the "difference."

The second condition necessary for an ideology of cultural diversity is that there be a prescription or judgment as to the proper goal or outcome of cultural diversity in society. In effect, the second condition is a judgment about maximizing the "Good Society." What is of primary importance regarding the second condition is that its function is to give a stamp of approval to a particular state of affairs in society, and it need not be, nor is it usually, an existing state of affairs. Most often, but not always, the state of affairs is a hoped for result of changing the present situation.

Thus, briefly, cultural diversity (A, B, C, D) serves a necessary condition for a cultural ideology, but it is not sufficient. There

---

[3] I am indebted to William M. Newman for the formula given here. This is especially true regarding four of the five formuli offered as the ideologies of cultural diversity. Newman's work is a most thoughtful and detailed analysis of majority-minority groups and social theory. It deserves the attention of the thoughtful, scholarly student of education. *See* William M. Newman, *American Pluralism* (New York, Harper & Row, 1973), especially Chapter 3.

must also be a prescription or judgment regarding what should be made possible in terms of realizing the best kind of society. Moreover, although the goals or hoped for results of the various ideologies do differ, each assumes that a commitment to a cultural ideology or its curricular proposals must occur prior to achieving the "Good Society."

We will focus on five different ideologies of cultural diversity in order to better understand the thrust of present educational programs and their curricular import. Figure 1 depicts in summarized form these five ideologies of cultural diversity.

CULTURAL DIVERSITY AND IDEOLOGY

Cultural Diversity		*Goal*	*Ideology*
A, B, C, D	=	A	Assimilation
A, B, C, D	=	E	Amalgamation
A, B, C, D	=	A, B, C, D	Insular Cultural Pluralism
A, B, C, D	=	A_1, B_1, C_1, D_1	Modified Cultural Pluralism
A, B, C, D	=	O	Open Society

Figure 1.

Assimilation: Ideology of Anglo-Conformism

The ideology of assimilation may be expressed in the formula $A + B + C + D = A$, where A, B, C, D represent different social groups and A represents the dominant or core group. The latter, historically in the United States, has been the case of "Anglo-conformity." This position has held that, over time, all groups (those allowed to) will conform to the life-style, values, and mores of the dominant majority.

The ideology of assimilation arose in the late nineteenth and early twentieth centuries largely in response to severe structural changes in the United States. The immigration of many millions, mainly the "new" immigrants from Eastern and Southern Europe, seemed to call for or justify the elimination of differences in favor of the culture of the dominant group. Only members of the Anglo-Saxon (or so-called Aryan or Nordic races) were deemed capable of producing a superior culture, and the chief strategy chosen to keep America vital (pure) was to demand that others become as much like the superior groups as possible, all the while excluding "inferior" groups such as blacks, yellows, and so on.

To reiterate, the schema of practical reasoning connecting ideology to action is the following:

R, as a purpose, is desirable.

S appears to be the best strategy for achieving R.

Therefore, do S.

It now seems possible to shape up the above as follows:

R (newly arrived immigrant groups in American society conforming to the cultural tradition of the dominant majority), as a purpose, is desirable.

S (the concept of race) appears to be the best strategy for achieving R.

Therefore, encourage the view that there are significant racial differences between human populations and teach the need for others, other than the Anglo-Saxon core group, to renounce their ancestral culture.

In other words, the R of assimilationist ideology held that a belief in Anglo-conformity was the desirable goal. In this respect, two important corollaries were involved. First, it was believed that the culture of the dominant majority or Anglo-Saxons was in some *prima facie* sense superior. Second, perhaps conversely, the values and life-styles of immigrant groups were inferior due to alleged dishonesty, uncleanliness, subversive political beliefs including an allegiance of Catholics to the Pope, and other fallacies.

This way of thinking had profound effects. In order to promote Anglo-conformism it was necessary to discredit the other groups, especially the immigrants. A key strategy in creating and enforcing the social norms and archetypes (trait characteristics of the Anglo-Saxon groups) was the employment of the concept of race. It is necessary, however, to emphasize that a belief in the desirability of Anglo-conformity as the desirable goal of assimilation in America cannot be equated with racism. Milton R. Gordon pointed out:

> In actual fact, it would appear that all racists, in so far as they have conceded the right of any of their disfavored groups to be present in America, and not withstanding their pessimism as to the success of the assimilation venture, have been Anglo-conformists; but the converse is not true — all upholders of Anglo-conformity have not been racists. The non-racist Anglo-conformists presumably are either convinced of the *cultural* superiority of Anglo-Saxon institutions as developed in the United States, or believe simply that, regardless of superiority or inferiority, since English culture has constituted the dominant framework for the development of American institutions, newcomers should expect to adjust accordingly.[4]

The concept of race, as a specific form of prejudice and/or discrimination, was employed to help justify such myths as (1) there is such a thing as a pure race; (2) inherited genetic differences do produce cultural differences between groups; (3) there are innate intellectual or emotional differences between human groups; and (4) there is good reason to believe that there are disadvantageous biological consequences resulting from racial mixture. Most importantly, the concept of race helped justify the "in-group" and "out-group" beliefs of Americans and gave direction to various political agenda. For instance, it justified a tidal wave of racial bigotry culminating in the National Origins Quota Act of 1924. The clear purpose of the act was to preserve the "purity" of the Anglo or Aryan "race" in America, since the so-called "lower races," the yellow, the Slavs, the

---

[4]Milton R. Gordon, *Assimilation in American Life* (New York, Oxford University Press, 1964), pp. 103-104.

Poles, and the Jews, were all to be excluded from America.

Amalgamation: Ideology of the Melting Pot

The ideology of amalgamation follows the central proposition expressed in the formula $A + B + C + D = E$, where A, B, C, D represent different social groups and E represents an amalgam, a synthesis of these groups into a distinct new group.

The ideology of assimilation and its slogan, "The Melting Pot," was one way some American minorities, having repudiated an overt and explicit devotion to assimilation ideology, could identify with America and become Americanized, without accepting the idea of assimilation. Americanization was not the embracing of an Anglo-conformism but the fusing of many nationalities and cultures into a new, composite American people, an amalgamation to produce a new, somewhat better, national stock.

We may shape up the schema of practical reasoning of amalgamation ideology as follows:

R (various groups — Englishmen, Germans, Poles, Italians, Russians, Jews, etc. — will, over time, all blend or melt into a new amalgam that is different, and yet superior, to any of the original groups), as a purpose, is desirable.

S (the melting pot or crucible) appears to be the best strategy for achieving R.

Therefore, absorb all groups, mingling them, and wait for a new American.

Any serious inquiry into the ideology of amalgamation must take note of the fact that it is complete with flowery prose and poetry which, however noble its aims, gave minimal direction as to the exact results intended in the manifold spheres of social organization. For instance, it was never entirely clear what exactly was to be the nature of the amalgamation: a cultural or biological mixing.[5] The former, although not easy, was more likely than the latter insofar as it called for immigrants to enter the cliques, clubs, and other primary groups and institutions of

---

[5]The fact is, of course, that the ideology of the melting pot was not considered to apply in any great numbers to the black American, the Native American, and the Hispanic minorities, only a few of whom were allowed to become assimilated and as groups have been denied complete assimilation in the United States.

the core or dominant society and, in addition, to place their own mark on these social structures. If this was to be achieved, prejudice and discrimination must be absent — a hardly likely prospect.[6]

It is perhaps somewhat revealing to note that the ideology of amalgamation was much more psychologically meaningful than politically real for American minorities. Partisans of the ideology of America as one huge melting pot found it easier to accept the reality of the American experience — prejudice, discrimination, poor working conditions, the shock of being uprooted, etc. — as long as they could believe that their experience would be temporary at best.

Cultural Pluralism: Ideology of Insular Pluralism

The ideology of insular pluralism may be expressed in the formula $A + B + C + D = A, B, C, D$, where A, B, C, and D represent different social groups and A, B, C, and D represent these groups that, over time, maintain their own unique identities.

The ideology of insular pluralism is at odds with the two previously discussed ideologies insofar as they envisaged the disappearance of the immigrants' group as a social entity and the absorption of the later arrivals to America and their children into the existing American social structure. The goal of "Americanization," however interpreted, was not altogether shared by the immigrants themselves. Indeed, a situation like insular pluralism was the initial model in the United States during much of the colonial period, at least in terms of the segregated aspects of English-speaking peoples residing in New England and the southern colonies, the Dutch and Swedes in the Hudson and Delaware valleys, the German population almost exclusively located in Pennsylvania, and Norwegian immigrants who settled only in Wisconsin and Minnesota.

It is this pattern that Robert Park metaphorically characterized as "a mosaic of segregated peoples."[7] A segregated mosaic is repeated over and over again in every part of the United

---

[6]Gordon, *Assimilation in American Life*, pp. 110-113.
[7]Robert E. Park, "Foreword," in Louis Wirth's *The Ghetto* (Chicago, University of Chicago Press, 1928), pp. ix-xi.

States even today. That is, certain parts of the country are demographically different as well as geographically different. Wilburt Zelinsky reports that each religious group holds a dominant position in only one part of the country; the pattern of religious affiliation thus is that the United States consists of numerous distinct religious groups.[8] Moreover, one can find both voluntary (Chinese in San Francisco) and forced residential (black ghettos) segregation within the overall pattern of American society.

It is not difficult to shape up the schema of practical reasoning of this ideology:

R (social groups living together in a state of peaceful coexistence), as a purpose, is desirable.

S (either voluntary or forced segregation along the lines of both primary and secondary levels of association) appears to be the best method of achieving R.

Therefore, constrain each individual within the structural and cultural confines of his birthright ethnic group regardless of his or her wishes in the matter.

It is interesting to note that the ideology of insular pluralism establishes an agenda of politics that encourages each group to engage in only one level of interaction with other groups, namely, in the polity. But beyond that, and only to ensure a voice in determining society's allocation of goods and services, no interaction between groups is called for. The ideology justifies individuals subordinating their broader interests to the overriding goal of immersion in their birthright ethnic group. Intermarriage is seen as a threat to ethnic insularity and communality. Indeed, the idea of the legitimation of numerous ethnic communities and their cultures is referred to as the embodiment of cultural democracy.

Cultural Pluralism: Ideology of Modified Pluralism

The meaning of the ideology of modified pluralism may be expressed in the formula $A + B + C + D = A_1, B_1, C_1, D_1$, where A, B, C, and D represent different groups, but A_1, B_1, C_1, and D_1

---

[8]Wilbur Zelinsky, "An Approach to Religious Geography of the United States," *Annals of the Association of American Geographers, 51* (June):139-193, 1951.

represent groups that are distinct from one another and are also
different from A, B, C, and D. We can readily grasp that an
Italian is different from a German, but an Italian-American is
different from an immigrant from Italy. On this account a
black African from Nigeria is different from an Afro-American.
In the formula, each of the hyphenated-American minorities
represent a group that remains distinct but also assumes new
cultural, political, and economic meanings in the context of
the American experience.

Norman Glazer and Daniel Patrick Moynihan, whose study
of Negroes, Puerto Ricans, Jews, Italians, and Irish of New
York City, give us basic insights into this doctrine, state that
"Beyond the accidents of history, one suspects, is the reality
that human groups endure, that they provide some satisfaction
to their members, and that the adoption of a totally new ethnic
identity, by dropping whatever one is to become simply American, is inhibited by strong elements in the social structure of
the United States. . . ."[9]

They go on to explain that "The assimilating power of
American society and culture operated on immigrant groups
in different ways, to make them, it is true, something that
they had not been, but still something distinct and identifiable. . . . "[10] As a concluding note, Glazer and Moynihan
state, *"The ethnic group in American society became not a
survival from the age of mass immigration but a new social
form."*[11]

It may be useful to note that Glazer and Moynihan point to
two aspects in the assimilation of American minorities. They
claim that each minority group becomes an agency of membership, for even after distinctive language, customs, and culture
are lost, the group forms a basis for social identity, a way of
members knowing who they are, as in the case of "I am a
Polish-American." Moreover, each hyphenated-American minority group, in addition to being connected by ties of family

---

[9]Glazer and Moynihan, *Beyond the Melting Pot*, p. xxxiii.
[10]Glazer and Moynihan, *Beyond the Melting Pot*, pp. 13-14.
[11]Glazer and Moynihan, *Beyond the Melting Pot*, p. 16.

and friendship in its own time and place, becomes an interest group, politically and economically organized in order to receive a just distribution of the goods and services of the social order.[12]

We may shape up the schema of practical reasoning of the ideology of modified pluralism as follows:

> R (hyphenated-American minorities), as a purpose, is desirable.

> S (accommodation style politics) is the best means of promoting R.

> Therefore, encourage group associations to form political interest groups to acquire society's rewards.

The above statements suggest that the ideology of modified pluralism not only binds individuals to a group, informing a person where he or she belongs and whom one can trust, it also shapes the group in terms of political determinations. Ideologues of this stripe, ever alert to the persistent gap between the considerable power and benefits enjoyed by the Anglo-Saxon or white majority and what is possessed by less fortunate groups, especially the non-European minorities who were never allowed to assimilate or melt into the power structure of social institutions, assert the need for groups to wrest for themselves more specific advantages by forming political interest groups. Political parties and ethnic communities are basic to the accommodation style of politicking. In short, in its emphasis on divisible benefits and on the awarding of particular goods and services, the accommodation strategy serves as the principle vehicle of political activity, specifying the terms of cooperation between diverse group interests.

The function of the ideology is such that group associations, as modified in the American experience, are basic to the political procedure. It requires that all citizens, as group members, have an equal right to take part in, and to determine the outcome of, the political process that establishes the division of goods and services in society. The ideology of modified plu-

---

[12]Glazer and Moynihan, *Beyond the Melting Pot*, p. 17.

ralism begins with the idea that where group interests intersect and conflict results, the conflicts are to be worked out from the viewpoint of a suitably defined situation in which each group is fairly represented, the public forum is free and open to all groups, and all have the means to be informed about the issues.

Structural Assimilation: Ideology of the Open Society

The meaning of this ideology may be expressed in the formula $A + B + C + D = O$, where A, B, C, and D represent different groups and O represents no relative advantage or disadvantage to be had by anyone in the polity as a result of affiliation with a group.

The starting point of the ideology of the open society is a rejection of ethnicity, religion, or whatever as a basis for group association, particularly as these become political interest groups in the hope of determining the distribution of society's goods and services. The overall assumption is, then, that while factions might be necessary during periods of social transition, ultimately factions polarize society by perpetuating atavistic hatreds and prejudices. Mainstream followers of the open society acknowledge that group association, particularly political factions, has served in the past, but its political salience must give way to a more democratic — that is, individualistic — civic participation together with wide distribution of the fruits of modern economic development. Ethnic attachments are judged "primordial," an attribute of earlier society, in which people's horizons were narrowly circumscribed and economic opportunities unnaturally curtailed. If the nation would conscientiously cultivate widespread and popular civic involvement and rationally plan for continued economic growth, ethnicity and other factionalism would be no more worrisome than it is among assimilated fourth-generation immigrants in America.

The ideologues of the open society contend that if civic democracy were to take on an individualistic rather than a group pattern, then ethnicity would not continue to intrude upon political decisions or to separate citizens from one another. The main argument seems to be that to be ethnic is to be deprived in some way of power, goods, services, and mobility. To eliminate ethnicity we must become more democratic in fact rather than merely in name. One way to do this is to achieve greater popular participation and equal opportunity, the hallmarks of an open society. The fundamental question is, If Americans and their government do wake up to the fact of limited citizen participation in government and that a small minority receives the major proportion of goods and services and do work toward redressing these, then will ethnic and other factions finally disappear? The proposition of the open society is that it will. Hence, the position focuses on political agenda in terms of redefining democracy and democratic participation away from group processes to individualistic patterns and meeting citizens' expectations in a more equitable way. The mobilization of individualism may reflect the traumas of casting off tradition, but, it is argued, it may also portend innovative political forms for the future, beyond the present century.

Thus we may shape up the schema of practical reasoning of the ideology of the open society as follows:

R (a commitment to a secular, individualistic, and common public interest), as a purpose, is desirable.

S (a nonpluralistic basis for organizing the institutions of society) is the best means of achieving R.

Therefore, ensure open access to the political and economic system (equality of opportunity) regardless of "birthright" origins of citizens.

What is assumed in a secular open society — in which traditional ethnic, racial, and religious differences no longer count — is that individuals will enter and engage in the political, economic, and social structures of society without respect to any group tie or affiliation. It is further assumed that, over time, the various cultural differences between groups will become politically irrelevant in determining the distribution of goods and services. That is, groups will no longer delight in their differences and will tend not to mark off "in-groups" and "out-groups" but will live side by side, not finding anything seriously at stake in their cultural backgrounds.

FIVE IDEOLOGIES: CURRICULAR PROGRAMS

It has been shown that assimilation, amalgamation, insular cultural pluralism, modified cultural pluralism, and the open society emerge as alternative ideologies of cultural diversity. It will be helpful to pause here and examine the ways in which these can be used to help us understand various aspects of curricular reform being proposed today. Figure 2 offers in simplified form the five ideologies and their curricular purport.

Ideology of Assimilation: Curricular Program

Of the curricular programs to be considered, none is more easily grasped than the ideology of assimilation. Most of us have had some contact with it in one form or another and know it as a previously dominant American curricular program centered around Anglo-conformism. Overall, it suggests a curriculum concerned with eliminating cultural diversity by making over the various cultural groups in conformity with the dominant majority's attitudes and values.

Nowhere in the teaching of history, for example, will the teacher attempt to put the minorities in touch with their own history; the strategy is to make an American — defined by the dominant majority — out of everybody. Thus literature and even the history books are peopled mainly by the dominant majority. Indeed the whole of schooling hews close to the point that to be human, accepted, and valued is to cherish the attitudes, values, and behaviors of the dominant majority. The definition of values, ideas, and purpose emanating from teachers, from the kindergarten through the university, hums in on one theme: To give up the old — to be modern — is to become better, liberated, more advanced, and more mature. Becoming assimilated, then, is a matter of learning to be something new and better. It is to imagine oneself in a different relationship to the family, the polity, the society, the universe,

THE RELATIONSHIP BETWEEN IDEOLOGIES OF CULTURAL DIVERSITY AND CURRICULA

Ideology	Curriculum Focus	Hoped-For Results
Assimilation	Study of Anglo-Saxon values and attitudes with a nationalistic bias.	Students develop an attachment to Anglo-Saxon attitudes and values.
Amalgamation	Study of intergroup and cultural interaction designed to break down relationships between groups.	Students become culturally and biologically the amalgam of the "new" American type.
Insular Cultural Pluralism	Ethnic Studies — Secular and humanistic study of ethnic groups as people sharing a common ancestry, culture, history, sense of peoplehood, and common experience in American society.	Students learn about the role of ethnic groups and learn how to participate in the polity while remaining ethnically "uncontaminated."
Modified Cultural Pluralism	Multi-ethnic studies — Different ethnic groups and culture studied, with focus given to a wide range of American cultural groups, their common problems and struggle to maintain their distinctiveness.	Students learn about the histories and experiences of ethnic groups in the American experience, clarifying and studying the function of such terms as 'prejudice', 'discrimination', 'identity conflict', etc.
Open Society	Secular and individualistic studies stress that differences of race, religion, national origin, etc. are simply irrelevant in determining the nature of acceptable primary and secondary associations. Human development taught in terms of personal identity occurring in relation to the civic community, the professions, and vocation.	Students learn to form personal identity in the civic community and are indifferent to matters of racial, religious, and ethnic distinction because these distinctions cease to have practical consequences in the society.

Figure 2.

and above all, to others. Being willing to change is assessed as morally higher than wishing to preserve the status quo. And the more willing to change from the old to the new, the more

likely one is to be judged acceptable, and the more likely one is
to become the "most" American.

Hence, in the varied activities of the school — in discussions,
lectures, cooperative ventures, athletics, textbooks, and the reward system — two forms of prejudice and discrimination
stand out and both are aimed at the "out-groups." One is, of
course, "racial," the other "progressive." According to the
former, it is race that constitutes the "out-group's" inferiority.
Classroom teaching thus focuses on the concept of race,
showing, usually through selected empirical evidence, the "natural" superiority of the dominant majority. Teachers and
school personnel are ever on the lookout for the evidence of
"proper" racial attitudes and values and quick to reinforce
them through discrimination. Conversely, "improper" attitudes and values are punished and denigrated. According to the
latter form of discrimination, it is the "out-group's" social and
political backwardness that stamps it. Hence, school personnel
remain ever alert to teaching the virtues of the dominant majority's tradition and are prepared to negate by discrimination the
"out-group's" clannishness, sense of ethnic community, and
family network ties.

In short, a cultural imperialism marks the curricular efforts
of the ideology of assimilation. An arrogance of power is exhibited by the need to "raise the consciousness" of the other
cultural groups and free them from the narrow-minded influences of parents, kin, community, and tradition. This is supposedly for their own good, in order for them to become
functioning members of society.

We might note that the various cultural groups sometimes
ask, Is it ethical or prudent to have our children confronted
with textbooks we regard as blasphemous or pernicious, to
confront our children with teachers regarded as "change
agents" of a change deemed or judged evil? The notion of
cultural imperialism is raised because the curriculum, quite
literally, is a way of telling students that "we have to destroy
your culture in order to save you." People who resist the
school's efforts are commonly regarded as "problems" to be
dealt with, not as having opinions to be respected.

Ideology of Amalgamation: Curricular Program

The curricular effort of this ideology also suggests a type of schooling aimed at eliminating cultural diversity by bringing about a unified or amalgamated citizenry. In principle, the curriculum would promote intergroup schooling concerned with imparting positive meaning to an otherwise judged to be chaotic and unpredictable cultural diversity. A bias toward an order theory of society is revealed in the sense that the curricular focus is that the dominant majority will allow the "outgroups" to integrate or merge with each other, without embracing the attitudes and values of the dominant majority.

Thus the curriculum, especially literature and history, would necessarily focus on the wide range of cultural groups in order to point out or demonstrate the "best" or "preferred" elements that should be kept in the new amalgamated type. Teaching processes would focus on cooperation, cooperative attitude, sharing, submerging one's own interests in the larger, somehow better, group interest. Hence, some form of value-free or methodologically pertinent strategy is necessary in order to effect the strategy of amalgamation. That is, class and group interests must be submerged in the free play of critical inquiry and constructive invention in society through, say, a scientific approach to inquiry, or some publicly common and so-called value-free method which will help break down resistance to change and reform in the deep-seated atavistic pattern of cultural diversity. The crucial point of method — of how, on the one hand, the present system is to be combatted, and how, on the other, the new system is to be instituted in its place — must be given a central position in the curriculum. Therefore, social problems hold forth as central in curriculum planning, offering courses such as "Problems of Democracy."

If communal, kinship, nationalistic, religious, and other particularistic values can be replaced by a common, alleged to be value-free, method for finding the common good or public interest, then a peaceful, nonmanipulative, and nondivisive resolution of the "problems" of cultural diversity can be achieved. In this sense, then, the method of creative intelligence becomes a social value as well as a methodology in schooling. For example, social class conflict and competition would be viewed as instrumentally inimical in schooling. Emphasis on the need to search for the "common interest" by all contending parties in a social conflict as well as the subordination of personal and particularistic interests to it would be absolutely demanded of teaching and learning. Hence, there would be a social side of schooling that would be emphasized. Cooperation, the search for common interest, and good temper in defeat are all happy conditions basic to this position.

The last point is crucial. It not only offers the basis for the curriculum, but more importantly, it raises the importance of schooling to the highest level. It is school and schooling that is to prepare the way for planned social change — the amalgam — and it is intended to exert its educative influence in the strongest defense of the melting pot. Patience and forebearance in the face of cultural diversity is a virtue, but patience may mean defeat in the long run. One cannot be too patient with the amalgamation process. It must be attended to, nurtured at each and every teaching session, and ultimately school and its effort will replace cultural diversity.

Ideology of Insular Cultural Pluralism: Curricular Program

In a society totally committed to insular cultural pluralism the school system would reflect a patchwork of cultural hegemonies. Ideally, each cultural group would have and control its own schools, teachers, and textbooks, all the while reflecting the values and beliefs of the group. The relationship between family, community, and school would be very closely expressed in singleness of purpose and enterprise. At the heart of education would be the fostering of each group's distinctness, values, and fragility if not properly nurtured.

In a society where the ideology of insular cultural pluralism is merely one of many competing for attention and position, then this view must struggle against other positions, particularly in the shaping of curricular programs. That is, if other ideologies and their programs tend to dominate, then the proponents of insular cultural pluralism would opt for the inclusion of ethnic studies, e.g. if Native American, then Indian Studies; if Afro-American, then Black Studies; if Chicano, then Chicano Studies. Ethnic studies are seen as promoting the sharing of a common ancestry, culture, history, tradition, sense of peoplehood, an experience of "out-groupness," and the necessity to form a political and economic interest group.

Ethnic studies thus refers to not only a curricular program — history, literature, psychology, education, sociology, etc. — but to the objectives and methods comprising courses of study. Students are encouraged to develop *positive* concepts, generalizations, and theories about their cultural group. Hence, the curriculum focuses on students understanding prejudice and discrimination as tools of social conflict, but more importantly, as depriving minorities of a positive identity, or conversely, as creating individuals with a negative identity.

At bottom, the ideology of insular cultural pluralism (within a society dominated by other ideologies) celebrates cultural diversity and the unique differences or characteristics of the group. The curriculum is narrow only in the sense that it is examined from the vantage point of the cultural group. Of course, generalizations may be drawn and applied to a wide range of human behavior, with numerous comparative and conceptual considerations examined, but in theory Black Studies, Indian Studies, and Chicano Studies are to serve specialized needs: to help the student gain a clearer and positive perspective regarding his or her cultural group and what is in its best interest.

Ideology of Modified Cultural Pluralism: Curricular Program

This ideology assumes that any attempt to eliminate cultural diversity will prove ineffective at best and destructive at worst. On the positive side, it supports a view of curriculum in which cultural diversity is extolled as a good. But what must be understood is that although many immigrants from various nations of Europe experienced similar injustices in the form of prejudice and discrimination, each cultural group has been modified in the American experience. In other words, although cultural groups have experienced similar problems in the United States, each requires for its study and appreciation unique, specialized analyses and concepts. Hence, the assumption that schooling should lump the problems of diverse groups together — treating American European and non-European minorities as formed along the same general lines — obscures important distinctions between group experiences of a victimized "slave" and a "colonized" pattern and cannot serve the needs of America's minorities.

A generic focus within a curricular reform effort emanating from this ideology would go beyond the level of ethnic studies to multiethnic education, emphasizing the unique cultures of blacks, Hispanics, Native Americans, and other cultural minorities *and* their experience in American society.

Multiethnic education, a rather specific form of multicultural education, forms the decisive backdrop against which cultural groups learn about and come to appreciate, and perhaps understand, the experiences of other groups and how they have been shaped in the American experience. In other words, it is assumed that there are significant distinct differences in the shaping of the various groups, at least in the American experience. Thus it is imperative to base curricular programs on the fact that ethnicity and ethnic identity continue to persist. Students are to be taught that, in terms of people's lives, cultural group association seems to have great appeal, offering a subtle, and highly cooperative, network of kinship ties; there is mutual economic assistance in time of trouble or sickness, help in occupational achievement, or sharing between families, yet the individuality of each conjugal unit is maintained so that a concurrent corporate and family life is possible. Moreover, ethnic groups, owing to their distinctive historical experiences, their cultures and skills, the times of their arrival, and the economic situation they met, developed distinctive economic, political, and cultural patterns. As the old culture (A) fell away — and it did rapidly enough — a new cultural group (A_1), shaped by the distinctive experience of life in America, was formed and a new identity created. Polish-Americans might share precious little with Poles in Warsaw, but in America they are a distinctive group that maintains itself, is identifiable, and gives something to those who are identified with it, just as it also gives burdens which those in the group have to bear (Polish jokes, for example).

The curriculum of modified cultural pluralism, therefore, makes central the study of various ethnic groups for the purpose of distinguishing similarities as well as differences between cultural groups. The goal of multiethnic education is to make students aware of the cost of being Americanized and to extoll the virtues of cultural diversity in terms of groups being modified over time in the United States.

Plainly, both forms of cultural pluralism reject, for different reasons, both the ideology of assimilation and amalgamation; modified cultural pluralists wish to maintain their identity as changed in the United States. What this ideology asserts is that the divisions between cultural groups are as important as their similarities.

Ideology of an Open Society: Curricular Program

This ideology postulates a thoroughly modern, secular society. Ethnicity is seen as a nuisance, even a danger; religious, racial, nationalistic, and kinship ties are viewed as obstacles that must be analyzed so that students can come to understand their negative influence. It is assumed, for example, that when ethnic identity takes over the task of self-definition — "I am an Italian-American" — society is divisive because those entrusted with decision making affecting large numbers exploit self-definitions and play on historical hatreds and fears. Moreover, cultural groups exploit one another, alleging various offenses in defense of ethnic and group turfs and privilege. Or worse still, ethnicity may be used as a cover for racism, meaning that people are encouraged to see the world primarily in limited or narrow categories — in black, white, or yellow — insisting all the while that one should be up and the others down.

In this view, ethnicity and ethnic identity can be used to order society, educational policy, and curricular efforts in the short run, but eventually they curb progress and blind individuals to their full capacities. Groups founded on ethnic allegiance compete with the nation-state. Such competition is intolerable because the nation-state is the principle vehicle of individual growth and development. Accordingly, ethnic groups are not acceptable because allegiance to them obscures the public interest by rendering the individual into the particularistic spheres of kin, group, family, community, and religion.

The concept of a modern, secular society and its curricular program would focus on civic and citizen well-being as opposed to the sheltering and distribution of society's rewards along the lines of ethnic or cultural communality. An essential element in the curriculum would be a study of the political system and its appropriateness in terms of the degree of centralization versus the individual citizen as opposed to, say, a structural formula of politics based on any given majority-minority relationship. Nonethnic demands — for example, citizen well-being in the form of requisites for economic security — would be necessary and fruitfully examined in this view.

The burden of the foregoing is that a conscious civic involvement and plans for economic growth would be central to curriculum development. Strategies for combatting the possibility of alienation of the individual and centralized injustice in the name of rational economic planning, examination of techniques to solve problems in economic, political, and international affairs, and methods for staying informed about the interstices of macro trends in politics and economics would form the heart of curriculum making.

Conversely, the curriculum would stress the belief that symbols and beliefs drawn from, say, traditional religions are no longer adequate for the contemporary world of the open society. Their origin is in a cultural system based on interpersonal and familial loyalty. Extended to include the impersonal structures of the social and physical world, their symbolic message becomes attenuated, if not actually unintelligible. This judgment implies no great disrespect for the world's major religions, but insightful they may be, they are not adequate for interpreting and understanding individual and nation-state commitment and relationship, especially in a context of impersonal structures. The symbolism of religion makes sense, a great deal of sense, in the interpersonal relationships within the family and local neighborhood, but not within the larger institutional structures of nation-state and international corporations.

Hence, the curriculum would consider paramount the teaching, interpreting, and explaining of symbols translatable into economic and political terms by which we ordinarily describe and justify the large-scale, impersonal, secular, corporate structures of modern society. One such symbol is that of "public interest." The new curriculum would suppose a view that the public interest is good insofar as public interest policy will benefit a parent not as a parent but as a member of the public, along with everyone else, and all citizens benefit under the same description — that is, as members of the public. By contrast, a society dominated by ideologies derived from cultural diversity does not opt for strictly public interest policies but what benefits members of the group under different descriptions as, for example, WASP, black, German, or Irish-Catholic.

In sum, the ideology of the open society and the curriculum it favors would center around the attainment of a common good or public interest. The attempt to foster this goal in schooling necessarily involves continuous integration of beliefs-in-relation-to-action centering around the common system of belief that such a society is the best for all concerned.

CONCLUSIONS

Historically, the ideology of assimilation worked quite well because its main fuel was a curriculum of shame. The immigrant and his children were taught to reject themselves: their dress, language, class and familial patterns, histories, and life outlooks. In the school this shame had incredible power, especially when coupled to a high motivation to become American and by so doing come to share in America's goods and services.

But today it is evident to most Americans that a curriculum built on shame and false hope is no reason for accepting a denigration of one's historical and cultural roots. The all-encompassing shadows of racial prejudice and discrimination are too far removed from the ideals of democracy and brotherhood for the ideology of assimilation to be viable today. It must be rejected as an acceptable alternative.

The ideology of amalgamation is now recognized for what it has always been: a sham. Cultural and ethnic minorities were never allowed to melt in a great national pot. Instead, they were treated as inferiors and faced with destruction of their cultural heritage. The attempt to reconcile the ideal and the reality of the melting pot has been tremendous in cost, for emotional conflicts, damaged self-concepts, bitterness, alienation, marginality, and a feeling of anomie are the all too obvious consequences we see about us everywhere. Hence on these grounds, this ideology must be rejected as not viable today.

The ideologies of insular and modified cultural pluralism must be taken seriously because of the decline of the ideology of assimilation and the sham of the ideology of amalgamation. Both ideologies of cultural pluralism, unlike the preceding two, regard cultural diversity as something to be celebrated. Hence, more and more curricular programs as being developed in the schools in response to the demands of minorities who celebrate their cultural distinctness. There are not only black study programs but Indian study programs and Chicano studies. Minorities hope that these curricular reforms will help in developing a sense of cultural pride, and it is assumed that this is the first step in cultural groups taking more responsibility for their own future — a future, according to the insular cultural pluralist, characterized by segregated cultural groups interacting only minimally on the levels of primary and secondary association, but maximally at the level of polity.

Supporters of the ideology of modified cultural pluralism encourage a belief in cultural diversity and positive ethnic identity, but regard ethnicity and cultural group distinctness as modified in the American experience as the portal to the realization of a truly democratic society. In this view multiethnic education affirms America's democratic commitment to the dignity and integrity of cultural groups, and such a curriculum is basic to promoting group understanding so that the United States will not end up fragmented along political, economic, and social lines.

Although the two ideologies of cultural pluralism differ in significant respects, either must be considered as a viable alternative today, supporting political and educational policies that honor cultural diversity as a way of maintaining democratic institutions and, at the same time, supporting a positive self-identity, sense of community, and forming a pattern of response to family, kin, and brotherhood.

But one crucial issue that is neglected and requires hard thought is the fact that although cultural pluralism ensures freedom for groups, it does not necessarily ensure freedom for the individual. That is, children may be imprisoned by strong group enclaves, not having the chance to decide between alternative life-styles available in society. This is especially true of insular cultural pluralism. Moreover, if cultural pluralism is adopted in wholesale fashion, we may see an entire nation-state population split into hostile factions, resulting in the extreme case of insular cultural pluralism in a divided nation.

The ideology of the open society offers a new universal ideal. It suggests pursuing justice and equality by fostering a humane secular nation-state. The ideology rests on the assumption that the key to the future is humane self-consciousness, identity, and self-renewal, free from the restraints of an American past dominated by cultural diversity where majority and minority waged economic, political, and psychological warfare on one another. If ideologues are to develop a new curriculum appropriate to this ideology, they will have to draw on something other than the model of cultural diversity. To acknowledge the poverty of cultural diversity as a starting point, and to avoid the pitfalls inherent in ideologies of cultural diversity, they must consider radically different approaches to our most basic relationships: man's relationship with man, man's relationship with nature, and man's relationship with the nation-state. All need imaginative reconsideration.

However, it is not entirely clear as to what shall serve as the Archimedean point for this effort. The issues are so large, so complex, so difficult that one can do little more than raise them. To what degree is the emancipation of the human spirit inevitably tied up with the group? Can we, even if we were willing, eradicate cultural diversity knowing that it provides ample foundations for strong communities and institutions? Can self-identity be extended to the nation-state without undermining the spirit and force of community? On the face of it, one can reply that the historical connections between identity and group, group and community, and community and the larger society are quite strong.

It may be that the emergence of a modern, secular nation-state complete with impersonal industrial complexes represents a threat to, rather than a necessary condition of, the furthering of a sense of social identity. Hence, one is left a bit uneasy about our capacity, arising out of the negation of cultural diversity, to affect the goals of the open society. This is, of course, not to say that there are no modern ways of creating or recreating shared purposes and identities, but it is to say that the open society may be premature in declaring all forms of group association based on cultural diversity obsolete, transferring all of their faith to an ideal of the citizen and the nation-state. We can laud a position that makes the politics of the future something other than quarrels between functional economic-interest groups rooted in cultural diversity, namely, the concerns of the nation-state, particularly the inclusion of disadvantaged groups identified along class rather than cultural lines. The quarrels will then turn on the issues of instilling a responsible social ethos in leaders, the demand for greater civic participation, for greater beauty and a better quality of life in the arrangement of our cities, an improvement in the character of our culture, and a more differentiated and responsive educational system.

All these are commendable goals. Americans are striving to avoid the narrowness, marked by prejudice and discrimination, of the past. Yet we are divided on how to achieve new aims and ideals as well as how to apportion the cost. A new ideology seems to be called for, but toward this end it is necessary to recognize that an ideal of the citizen and the nation-state can only supplement the older systems of belief, not replace them. Consequently, our best bet may well be a form of cultural pluralism, for it avoids the extremes of the other positions.

Chapter Four

CONSPIRACY AND POLITICAL PLURALISM

INTRODUCTION

THE most delicate and difficult task that faces a person writing a chapter on conspiracy and political pluralism is that of saying something about what is *not* intended.

First, I do not wish to be interpreted as saying that there are no conspiracies in history in general and in the making of policy in particular. This simply is not true. All policy making requires strategy, and it is often the case that strategic acts of a political sort depend for their effect upon a period of secrecy, and anything that is secret is often described, with but a little exaggeration, as conspiratorial (at least from one person's point of view). But secretive acts by themselves do not constitute a conspiracy; more is involved, as is shown in the following sections.

Second, since what is at stake is what kind of political system is most beneficial in a democracy, I wish to stress that I am not supporting a system of political pluralism. The American experience, complete and replete with ethnic and religious divisiveness and conflict, has plainly been reflective of not only political pluralism but of what Richard Hofstadter calls "the paranoid style."[1] The application of the theory of political pluralism arouses the sinister in many of us, encouraging the paranoid style, and the situation is exacerbated by those who have no access to political bargaining or the making of political decisions — those who view themselves as the victims of power. Consequently, we will do well to understand that the theory of political pluralism has the effect of promoting in

---

[1]Richard Hofstadter, *The Age of Reform* (New York, Vintage Books, 1955).

politics the "paranoid style."

What *is* intended here is to focus attention on a disturbing theme in the recent American experience: the tendency of alarmed citizens to view the outcome of policy in conspiratorial terms. Policy making is portrayed not as an open process but as a secret, sinister plot. But as Hofstadter points out, "There is a great difference between locating conspiracies *in* history and saying that history *is*, in effect, a conspiracy, between singling out those conspiratorial acts that do on occasion occur and weaving a vast fabric of social explanation out of nothing but skeins of evil plots."[2]

Thus, in the second section my primary concern is with an attempt to better comprehend the nature of the concept of conspiracy (its use); in the third section my interest is with the force of conspiracy theory argument (its function); in the fourth and fifth sections the focus is on the extent to which conspiracy theory argument is shaped by the politics of pluralism;[3] and in the sixth section is discussed the conspiracy theory argument in education. Perhaps we best prepare for sections four and five by asking, with tongue not entirely in cheek, whether a fiercely competitive system of political pluralism has bred a tendency to be on guard against the machinations of others, commonly ascribing to them sinister policy making. There are really two questions here. First, has our political system of countervailing forces encouraged us to regard policies as issuing from conspiracies? In other words, is the application of pluralistic politics itself promotive of a fear of conspiracy and conspiracy allegations? I shall suggest that the answer is yes. Secondly, is there currently a general malaise in American life that demands simple, *ad hominem* explanations? I shall suggest that the answer is yes.

In seeking to understand the use of the term *conspiracy* and the function of conspiracy theory, I wish to suggest that there are at least two relatively clear and clearly different factors involved: (1) We can ask what sort of thing conspiracy is usu-

---

[2]Hofstadter, *Age of Reform*, p. 71.

[3]I wish to distinguish between the theory of political pluralism and its application or practice, namely, politics. My claim is that conspiracy theory is not necessarily basic to the theory of political pluralism, but it is necessary to its politics.

ally applied to, supposing of course that it is applied to anything, and (2) we can ask what the use or function of conspiracy is, that is, what type of utterance it is.

USE OF CONSPIRACY

Anyone who has grown sensitive to the frequent talk about
the variant forms of conspiracy may have discovered that it is
difficult to assess the validity or accuracy of the claim made. At
least in part, the problem stems from the many conceptual
difficulties associated with the term *conspiracy*; it is obvious
that two people may mean different things in their use of the
term. Equally difficult is the fact that some conspiracy arguments are not always explicitly stated but only implicitly
hinted at, as in the case of gossipy stories or veiled accusations.
Even when the charge of conspiracy is made explicit, what is at
issue is the allegation that the charge is true that an individual
has conspired, and proving this is not always easy. In any case,
the initial question is, What does conspiracy consist of?

If asked, What does conspiracy consist of? It can quickly be
answered that there is no general answer. Some conspiracies
involve obtaining military secrets, others involve actions
leading to business takeovers, others are called "get-rich
schemes" — such as "secret grain deals" — and others involve
entirely different processes and ends. Moreover, some conspiracies involve payment and unpleasantness while others do not.
There appears to be no action going on in one conspiracy
which need be going on in another. Yet, upon reflection, we see
that although people may mean different things as they employ
the term *conspiracy*, it is obvious that some shared meanings
can be identified among the diverse uses.

To answer the question, consider an example from one of
history's better known conspiracies — the plot to assassinate
Julius Caesar. As we know it, a group of senators decided to get
rid of Caesar who, they believed, was about to destroy the
Roman republic. Brutus was so devoted to the republic, as
opposed to a monarchy, that he joined the conspiracy against
his friend and benefactor. And so, on the Ides of March (March

15), 44 BC Caesar was attacked in the Senate, and his greatest surprise was to see Brutus among the conspirators.

Perhaps another example from recent history will help. It is now beyond a reasonable doubt that Richard Nixon lied about his lack of knowledge of the Watergate break-in. Nixon and his aides did a great many things, i.e. lying, breaking the law, abusing authority, and offering bribes, that, when added up, are tantamount to an Executive Department attempt to "cover up" Watergate. Such actions are what we commonly call a conspiracy.

What is important in the two examples? For one thing, use of the term *conspiracy* suggests that two or more people have agreed upon a course of action with intended consequences. That is, the claim that "X is a conspiracy" implies that at least two people have come to an agreement regarding a course of action hoping to effect certain consequences. Indeed, the concept of conspiracy makes little sense except when two or more people are involved. This fact is illustrated in the many books written about the assassination of John F. Kennedy where the primary question has become, Was the assassination a conspiracy? Those who answer affirmatively assume that more than one person was involved; those who answer negatively judge that only Lee Harvey Oswald, the alleged assassin, was involved.

The examples also suggest another point. Is the use of *conspiracy* a value judgment or a statement of fact? It is both. It is a fact that John Ehrlichman lied under oath and Nixon lied about his knowledge of the Watergate break-in, but it is a judgment of value that Nixon and his aides "conspired" to cover up Watergate. What this point brings out is that *conspiracy* is commonly a mixed word; it serves to *describe* a situation involving at least two people who have come to an agreement regarding a course of action, and it may serve to *evaluate* that situation. In most cases the evaluation is one of disapprobation rather than of approval.

It is a necessary condition of the application of *conspiracy*, as a mixed word, that the agent who applies it has made a value judgment. Just as when one weeds one must judge the plants removed to be undesirable or otherwise it is merely "thinning out," so a necessary condition of the application of the term as a mixed word is that the agent applying it makes a value judgment. The evaluation is not of the skill of the performance but rather of the merit or worth of the actions engaged in. Thus, to say that John Doe is a conspirator involves the value judgment that he is acting badly.

Consequently, to call someone a conspirator is commonly to employ emotive language expressing one's disapproval. We reserve the label for our foes, and acceptance of the conspirator label is likely to be limited. In the recognition that *conspiracy* is a mixed word, it is important to keep the description separate from the evaluation. In what follows we shall limit ourselves to the *descriptive* aspects of the term. In other words, what is the specific force of the description *conspiracy* in respect to which it differs from such descriptions as *planning, organizing, meeting, debating, acting,* all the while avoiding other terms such as *plotting, scheming, treachery, treason,* and *intrigue?* The point is not to deal with a question of the form, What does conspiracy consist of? but a question of the form, How do we use descriptions such as "X is a conspiracy"?

When we describe a situation as a conspiracy, what more are we saying than that two or more persons are in agreement regarding a course of action in the hope of realizing certain consequences? We begin by answering that the term *conspiracy* has various uses. For example, it may be used as a task word, signifying activities engaged in. It may be used as an achievement word, signifying the successful achievement of certain activities. Moreover, the term may be seen as an *inference ticket,* i.e. from the fact that a conspiracy involves two persons and a course of action, we infer other aspects.

First, it can be inferred that a conspiracy is a deliberate human action. Not only is a course of action agreed upon, we presume that the agreement is deliberately chosen. A conspiracy, then, is a human action deliberately engaged in to achieve a desired process or end. Hence, a conspirator is considered to be a deliberate taker of a position, as in the case of Brutus and his fellow assassins or Richard Nixon and his aides. We are further inclined to say, perhaps in more general terms, that if one engages in a conspiracy, it will not help a great deal for the accused to say that he was "merely following orders." This is so because "conspiracy" functions as a deliberate human action insofar as it gives awareness to the fact that no situation can be a case of conspiracy if less than two people are involved and if no plan, no human course of action, has not been deliberately chosen. Deliberately chosen human action is not a way of describing the sort of thing those engaged in a conspiracy tend to try to do or bring about but refers to the deliberate agreement binding those involved.

To generalize this point further, the inference that a conspiracy, in the purely descriptive sense, implies a human action suggests that it is as much free as deliberately chosen. *Conspiracy* is a consent word insofar as its meaning is that one does not ordinarily participate unwillingly in a deliberate human action. Of course, there may be some doubt whether a situation should be labeled a conspiracy in the evaluative sense, but descriptively when someone is a part of a conspiracy, *prima facie* he is considered to have freely chosen that course of action. Indeed, we are prone to believe that the burden of proof that one did not freely consent to an agreement or to a course of action is on the conspirator rather than on the accuser. This was a major point of contention in the Patty Hearst trial. The defense tried to establish doubt that Ms. Hearst was a free, consenting member of the Symbionese Liberation Front. Attorneys for the defense argued that Ms. Hearst's behavior was just that: behavior, not a freely chosen action. Her behavior, it was alleged, was a result of being brainwashed and/or fear for her life.

There is a sense of conspiracy where the person involved finds out that he or she was "taken-in" by others. That is, one may conclude that the human action was conspiratorial, in the descriptive sense, but that the individual was but an unsuspecting dupe in the planning, organizing, or some other aspect of the conspiracy. In this sense, consent is not applicable. However, in the descriptive sense of the term, the burden of proof that mutual consent was not evident is on the defendant.

To carry the function of conspiracy yet another step, note an additional inference. We infer that conspiracy is an opportunity word; it presumes a contingent situation open to the possibility, however remote or slight, of change. Conspirators are opportunists as they are alert to seeing and creating opportunities to advance their own cause or to damage another's. Doubtless the absorbed conspirator is watchful to take the opportunity to "do in" the opposition and, conversely, to give it little or no opportunity to better its position. Hence, a successful conspiracy must have at least one creative and inventive member alert to opportunities for advancing the cause.

Such inference tickets are free, deliberate human actions involving opportunity are part of the associated commonplaces inferred from the term *conspiracy*. Terms such as *deal, intrigue,* and *treachery* are commonly employed in the inference that a conspiracy involves some degree of secrecy of membership, intent or purpose, or course of action. We infer from *conspiracy* a surreptitious plan or design, formulated by two or more persons; hence, the further inferences of *plot* and *scheme.* The fact is that a conspiracy, although it may have public consequences, is always surreptitiously conducted. Indeed, it would make little sense to speak of a group of would-be assassins as conspirators if they met openly, agreed upon a plan of action, and announced their decision by publishing the minutes of their meeting in the newspapers. A full disclosure of such information would probably result in calling such a group any number of things — terrorists, liberators, outlaws, anarchists — but surely not "conspirators."

Finally, although we may speak of *conspiracy* in a purely legal sense in which two or more persons act to break the law, it is not necessarily the case that law-breaking is involved. It seems that we may use *conspiracy* to speak of the actions of those in power who do not break the law — indeed, it is claimed that they use the law — but conspire to keep a certain group powerless or disfranchised. Hence, *conspiracy* may be employed for judging an action involving two or more individuals using existing law to bring about a certain end. What seems to make this situation a conspiracy is the judgment that those involved have a secret plan which, although legal, is evil, treacherous, or immoral.

The last observation is the key to an earlier consideration. The judgment of this situation involves the evaluative sense of *conspiracy,* because what is secretly planned is objected to on moral grounds. This is simply to say that Group A labels Group B "conspiratorial" insofar as Group A has judged Group B's actions as illicit or immoral. Group A will choose to call the members of Group B "conspirators" insofar as they are judged as acting in a way calculated to maximize their best interests at the expense of others. Put differently, Group A has chosen to describe and evaluate the members of Group B as persons with certain ambitions, among them the sentiments associated with those who could legally or illegally take something away or give something undesirable to another person or group. Indeed, this sense of conspiracy suggests that we label, simultaneously describing and evaluating, those who secretly operationalize a strategy (description) calculated to bring about some end judged (evaluation) to be illicit or immoral. In short, the element of evaluation of the secrecy aspect, or the fit of means to end as well as the end itself, may enter into the labeling of a situation as a "conspiracy."

Seeing that *conspiracy* has both a descriptive and an evaluative function, we grasp the fact that the term may be used in both a positive and a negative way. The positive sense of *conspiracy* involves a "moral ideal" insofar as it involves abolishing or negating wrongful coercion against persons and institutions. The problem of abolishing wrongful coercion is the problem of conspiring to abolish that power; it is the problem of planning, organizing, mobilizing, and winning. In every society, some have been in a position to determine the conditions of life for others, to wield power and to force compliance on the unwilling. This is a rudimentary fact of human association. The positive sense of *conspiracy* makes much of the point that those with power have no right to that power. The negative sense of *conspiracy* involves the converse; the plan or course of action against those in power is not justified; hence, it is illegal, illicit, evil, or wrong.

Underlying both the positive and negative critique of *conspiracy* is the assumption that conspirators and conspiracies may or may not be justified. The justification of any conspiracy requires morally overriding reasons, and this is true of conspiracy by private persons and by public officials. In this sense, public or diplomatic conspiracy is no more morally privileged than is private conspiracy.

THE FUNCTION OF CONSPIRACY THEORY ARGUMENT

What is conspiracy theory? What *function* does it have? Conspiracy theory is commonly invoked in response to the question, "Why?" Often asked "why" questions are the following: (1) "Why is policy Z not achieving its proposed results; that is, why is another outcome of policy (Y) occurring?" (2) "Why is a certain outcome (Y) pervasive in so many areas of the United Stated today?" In response to either or both questions, it may be, and often is, claimed, "It must be the policy of some group (X) to bring about Y."

The function of an answer to the "why" questions above (such as "Group X conspired to bring about Y," or "X, the conspiracy, is the reason for Y," or "X is a conspiracy to produce Y") is *informative* insofar as it purports to enlighten, allege, or produce understanding. But it does not merely inform since it functions as a particular type of informative statement. It puts the speaker in the position of giving an explanation of the cause of Y in terms of group X. What is significant here is that the *function* of a conspiracy statement of the form "X is causing (or caused) Y" is necessarily distinct from the *purposes* or intentions someone may have when making such a statement. It is part of the function of "X, the conspiracy, is causing (or caused) Y" to put the speaker in the position of having given an explanation, an after the fact causal explanation of Y. But the speaker's purpose in saying what he or she said may be to embarrass, indict, or give grudging credit or some such thing to the alleged conspirators. Hence, the function of this type of statement may or may not coincide with the purpose of the person making the statement, but in many cases it usually does because conspiracy statements used to damn a certain state of affairs or action involve a strategy calculated to suggest a direct threat to persons and/or society in terms of a successfully operating but heretofore unknown or detected causal factor.

Hence, a conspiracy statement in the informative-explanatory mode offers to the purpose of the speaker a very potent and seductive linguistic function that can convey a sense of outrage, betrayal, and injustice vis-à-vis the alleged conspiratorial act. At bottom, then, the function of this type of statement is to suggest to others a threat to them or to the larger society in terms of a direct causal factor, the conspiratorial action. If successful — that is, if accepted — it can create support for doing away with the situation (Y). The following paragraphs show how this is accomplished.

It is important to see that conspiracy theory rests on the claim "X caused Y." This may be formalized: It must be a conspiracy on the part of X to bring about Y, because either (1) "Y is, in fact, as opposed to what is ostensibly proposed in policy (Z), what policy produces," or (2) "Y is, in fact, the policy outcome of schooling whether the policy is written or not."

Although the distinction between (1) and (2) above is clear-cut, for practical purposes the distinction is obliterated in the Conspiracy Theory Allegation (hereafter, CTA). CTA rests on a general causal claim of the form, "X caused Y." It is generally assumed that X (the conspiratorial group) was sufficient to bring about or cause Y. This line of argument gains its force from the idea of "cause" defined as a sufficient condition. CTA is a causal explanation of a particular Y with X as sufficient to produce Y. Moreover, and this is immensely important, the claim holds X responsible for Y.[4]

This last point is notoriously difficult to characterize, but it

---

[4] I acknowledge my indebtedness to the work of Robert H. Ennis. In "The Responsibility of a Cause," Brian C. Crittenden, ed., *Proceedings of the Philosophy of Education Society* (Edwardsville, Ill., Studies in Philosophy and Education, 1973), pp. 86-93, Ennis argued that a responsibility-attribution sufficiency view does accord with causal assertions in a number of contexts.

may be caught, at least in part, by the recognition that CTA seeks to determine the actual, as opposed to intended, consequences of written or "unwritten" policy, and the outcomes are seen as part of a chain originating with Group X. That is, there is a strong tendency in CTA to hold Group X responsible for the consequences of policy by virtue of being judged the originator in the causal chain: Actual outcomes serve as sufficient evidence for the existence of some conspiratorial group responsible for producing the outcomes.

It is now possible to ask the question, "Why would a person pick a conspiracy as the cause of some educational policy outcome?" "Why would someone pick an alleged opportunistic and secretive group as the most plausible explanation for some policy outcome?" It might be more logical to accept other factors such as inadequate resources, inflation, poor administration and/or implementation, improper responses or adaptation to policies that negate their impact, incompatible goals that bring two or more policies into conflict, or that the nature of the problem at which the policy is directed has changed while the policy was in effect. It would seem that a likely candidate for ignoring other possibilities is the fact that it is always initially tempting, and satisfying, to believe that the actual consequences of policy are the result of planned and designed human actions. On this view, Y, or actual outcomes of policy, are much too regular, pervasive, widespread in their effects, and too consistently rewarding to some group (and punishing of another group) not to be accounted for in some causal way that imputes conspiratorial intent.

A second possible explanation is that it is simpler to think conspiracy theory rather than consider ineptness as a possibility. For one thing, people love to gossip about the secret "plots," "schemes," and "intrigue." Some people do not scruple to tell falsehoods to propagate what they believe to be basically true. A person may be a conspiracy theory advocate, imagining all sorts of conspiracies taking place, knowing his view to be false, and yet persevere in it, with the best intentions in the world, for the sake of promoting the cause of conspiracy theory.

A third possible explanation is that it is also easier to think conspiracy theory rather than view policy evaluation as a complex problem involving empirical data gathering and analysis. A fourth, and perhaps equally plausible, explanation is that CTA is an extremely powerful and seductive line of thought offering not only a satisfying explanation, but one that fixes responsibility for some policy outcome. It must be admitted that CTA is employed to do just that — to render an explanation fixing responsibility and blame for Y.

Given these, it seems to be the cast that CTA involves the following: a state of affairs considered to be the outcome of educational policy is judged illicit, immoral, and dangerous; cause and responsibility for that state of affairs are imputed; and secretive, ulterior, and, perhaps, immoral motives are imputed to the alleged causal agents, namely, the conspirators. The fact of the matter is that it is only necessary that the person employing CTA know that Y exists, judge Y to be illicit or immoral, and allege that some group, acting freely, deliberately, opportunistically, and secretively, has conspired to bring about Y. For obvious reasons, CTA may depend upon not being troubled by questions of other possible causal factors, other possible explanations, or questions of logical and empirical consistency. In most cases it is sufficient for conspiracy theorists to know that Y exists and judge Y to be monstrous. The question becomes, What group has conspired to bring about Y?

One major reason for holding CTA suspect is that it rests on an inference. The conspiratorial group is inferred as the originator of the causal chain from the existence of policy outcomes having alleged monstrous effects. Thomas F. Green has questioned this move.

> Such an inference clearly contains a fallacy, and the fallacy is most clearly seen the minute we recognize that no policy can ever be identified by its actual outcome, because if it could, then *it would be logically impossible even to speak of unsuccessful, inefficient, or ineffective policies.* It is useful, of course, to know the outcomes of a certain policy. But that knowledge, no matter how detailed and accurate, will never

suffice to identify the policy unless there is added the intent, the actual statement and the procedures for implementing the policy. Thus, from the fact — if it is a fact — that schools do little to remedy economic inequality, it cannot be inferred that the maintenance of economic inequality is basic educational policy. What needs to be established, in addition, is the intent to do so, and that must be established *independently* of the actual outcomes. Thus, it is important to observe that policy is always formulated with some intent, and that neither the policy nor the intent can be determined from the outcome.[5]

It seems necessary to say here that CTA achieves in misleading fashion precisely what Green says is demanded to identify a policy, i.e. adding "the intent." However, intent in CTA is not Green's "the actual statement and procedures for implementing the policy," if we mean by "actual" actually stated, but is the sense of "actually determined" as opposed to "disguised" or "make-believe."

We can now note that CTA is a causal explanation of a state of affairs judged to be illicit or immoral. One might hasten to add that in an argument of this type it is not necessary to do much beyond embellishing an inference, establishing intent, a secret motive, or purpose, and giving persuasive significance to the state of affairs judged illicit or immoral.

Focusing on the function of CTA, we know that it is not limited to explanation, for it may be employed to predict events that will occur in the future as well as explaining events that have already occurred. These twin aspects of CTA are essentially the same activity except for a difference in temporal perspective. Whether the CTA constitutes an explanation or a prediction depends on if its use occurs at a time subsequent to the time of the *explanandum* (explanation) or earlier than the event described by the *explanandum* (prediction).

However, it is characteristic of CTA that it is more often retro-dictive (explanatory) than pro-dictive (predictive). This follows from its inference-based factor. As an explanation, CTA infers from a Y judged immoral, illicit, destructive, and evil

---

[5]Thomas F. Green, "What is Educational Policy?" in Janice F. Weaver, ed., *Educational Policy* (Danville, Ill., Interstate, 1975) p. 15.

that some group has secretly caused Y. The inference "X caused Y" is proffered to the question, real or rhetorical, What caused Y? Obviously, it is not a necessary condition for the explanation that it be accurate; it need only be satisfying.

CTA not only describes an assumed causal relationship but evaluates it as well, warning people that the explained state of affairs is illicit or immoral. Hence, CTA is potent and seductive because it asserts not merely that a conspiracy exists but that *the conspiracy is successful.* This feature deserves special attention.

The point needs to be made that CTA usually is proffered to explain a situation that is to be accounted for, a situation judged to be operating successfully. The essential point is that CTA focuses our thinking in the direction of a relationship between an established, successful, but venial outcome of, say, educational policy. In other words, CTA judges that at least one educational policy outcome is illicit or immoral and is adversely affecting the quality of students' lives. With that evaluation fixed, CTA explains the problem of why, what caused the injustice, and who is responsible.

The problem, assuming the above to be plausible, is not why a causal explanation is given to account for a successful state of affairs. The problem goes deeper: Why is CYA invoked? The answer is evident. There is no more potent and seductive way to bring to readers a responsibility attribution in the sense of outrage, betrayal, and injustice than to claim that children are the victims of an educational conspiracy, particularly of the free, deliberate, opportunistic, secretive human action called conspiracy that maintains existing inequalities. What is so seductive is that CTA qua retro-dictive explanation invokes moral criteria without exactly implying what those criteria are. Ordinarily, if X is judged to be morally reprehensible, then we are entitled to know on what criteria. What CTA suggests is that no morally reprehensible act is subject to as high a degree of moral condemnation as is the conspiratorial act.

What CTA can guarantee and (so far as I know) few other arguments can, is that a causal explanation (X caused Y) is intimately bound to an emotive and persuasive force — the suppressed conclusion "and Y is immoral." The key to the argument's effectiveness is the last element.

CONSPIRACY THEORY AND POLITICAL PLURALISM

The test of strength of any political theory is the extent to which its basic assumptions remain not merely unquestioned but literally unrecognized. The more that such assumptions appear to be simply a part of the fabric of fact, the stronger the intellectual hold of the theory they support and the greater the difficulty of changing the practices arising out of it.

One such assumption that has not yet reached the light of day is that the application of political pluralism — politics — accepts without question a willingness to hear, give credence to, and accept CTA.

Doubtless many may say, "So what? What is new about that?" This is, of course, merely a polite way of asserting that what is being said is not significant. It certainly is news to no one that many politicians and political aspirants employ CTA in the hope of discrediting rivals. And obviously the claim that virtually all political practice arising out of political pluralism accepts CTA is trivial, if it is assumed to mean only that it just happens because of a particular political background coupled to a reflecting of the prevalent biases of the day; people are exhibiting mere prejudices, and these can be discounted without serious consequences. But this is not what the claim means. Underlying the theory of political pluralism is, of course, the view that the false and the possibly false are incompatible with the truth, that the true must somehow overcome the false (in the arena of politics), and that actions of conspiracy are somehow never candidates for the true, at least those parts of the conspiracy we label "conspiratorial." Thus when we understand the use of *conspiracy*, when we know how CTA functions, then it may be that CTA is stripped of its significance, leaving nothing whatever, except, of course, its truth or falsity.

Hence, the claim that politics is susceptible to the employment of CTA is not trivial because it insists that the use of CTA in politics is not an arbitrary choice but is nested within political pluralism's implementation. If we start from a position of commitment to the theory of political pluralism, then we will have to be cognizant of the function or role CTA plays in its application, and thus exposed CTA is not so "natural" as it was before.

In seeking to assess the extent to which CTA is shaped by political convictions, what should we take as our benchmark? We need not go very far back in time to find what we now regard as the formulation of American political pluralism — probably no further back than *The Federalist Papers*, although the Anglo-American tradition of political pluralism was begun earlier. The most pointed formulation of political pluralism is to be found in *The Federalist Papers*, No. 10, for in that document James Madison argued that although there are problems associated with the growth of "factions," these dangers can be safely risked in order to procure another good, namely, the freedom of association.[6] Power, Madison held, is properly distributed among a variety of factions or groups, and the alignment of these with each other will, of necessity, shift from issue to issue. The result will be, in a union as large as proposed in the *United States Constitution*, a general, if not necessarily a static, balance of diffused power in which no single set of interests is dominant, at least not for a significant period of time. Hence, according to Madison, it is unlikely that the limited and perhaps self-interest of any one group will long remain unopposed.[7]

Madison's confidence in the theory of political pluralism, the system of countervailing power, to achieve a general balance of interest rested firmly on the conviction that there is sufficient self-interest in individuals and that the selfishness of any one will surely be tempered by the selfishness of the others; thus there is strength in the multiplicity of factions. Patently, his confidence was not entirely misplaced, for there is an element of truth in such a description. It should also be clear that the

[6]Alexander Hamilton, James Madison, and John Jay, *The Federalist Papers* (New York, New American Library, 1961), pp. 77-84.
[7]Hamilton, Madison, and Jay, *Federalist Papers*, pp. 83-84.

element is no more than obvious; there is no total concentration of power in the hands of any single group.

Consequently, politically pluralistic societies with open stratification systems contain a competitive ethos. That is, in nonpluralistic societies with closed stratification systems (closed societies), social rewards are paternistically given to the subordinate group by the dominant group.[8] But the achievement ethos of pluralistic societies demands that social rewards be earned; hence, achievement and competition are prescribed norms; i.e. the competitive factor is a prescribed technique for individual and group advancement in society.

Political pluralism justifies a polity which makes political policy the result of a sort of parallelogram of forces represented by the exertions of self-interested pressure groups. Further, it assumes that all interests have a potentially effective pressure group, and an "intense interest group" — merely numbers multiplied by intensity or feeling engendered by an issue — will put out much more exertion in relation to its numbers than one little affected. In this way intense interest groups, particularly minorities, can exert an influence disproportionate to their numbers.

Technically, political pluralism is a zero-sum game, where winners win, and losers lose, but it is cooperative in the sense that individuals can come together to form an interest group. In so doing they have the freedom to make joint binding agreements to cover their self-interests, since on most matters there is no "common good" in a strict sense, but a clash of interests, and the issue within the group is which interest will prevail. In such situations people take up positions on the basis of where their interests lie, or where they perceive them to lie, rather than on some view of the just society. Individuals are committed to abide by the policy agreed upon, and it is commonly recognized that little or no restraint in the pursuit of "narrow" group-interested ends is necessary for the satisfactory operation of a polity.

Political pluralists, such as R.A. Dahl in *A Preface to Demo-*

---

[8]William M. Newman, *American Pluralism* (New York, Harper & Row, 1973), pp. 25-26.

cratic Theory,[9] have stressed that it is not a failure of pluralism that coalitions of parties are constantly tested and rejected, being superseded by other, newer coalitions. According to the pluralist view, the testing and rejecting is entirely the feature of political pluralism, perhaps its shining accomplishment. Coalitions and group interests have their rise and fall, supplanted by what is taken to be more fruitful and promising ones.

The political theory of pluralism assumes that total concentration of power should not reside for long in any one group and rejoices in balanced power among overlapping economic, religious, ethnic, and geographic groupings. Ideally each group has some voice in shaping politically binding decisions, and each constrains and is constrained through the processes of mutual group adjustment, with all major groups sharing in a plurality of private and public ends. Stability is had, in the long run, because public policy, including, of course, educational policy, outcomes tend to reflect the distribution or balance of power among groups in society. Finally, innovation and change are possible because new groups, created perhaps by population distribution or economic processes can articulate new perspectives and preferences which will eventually seep into the balancing process, affecting the shape of political policy and the direction of policy resolution. Some pluralists, however, see government as the arena where major group conflicts are debated and resolved, while others see voluntary associations, such as labor and management, operating outside of government, and government merely acting as an umpire in setting the rules for conflict resolution.

Now, this simple and truncated description of the theory of political pluralism may seem very much underdrawn, and it is somewhat misleading. The balancing process described commonly experiences difficulty insofar as citizens with new problems encounter institutional and ideological obstructions to the formation of newly organized interest groups which might express their preferences and goals. As Robert Paul Wolff said, "The application of the theory of pluralism always favors the

---

[9]R. A. Dahl, *A Preface to Democratic Theory* (Chicago, University of Chicago Press, 1956).

groups in existence against those in the process of formation."[10]

The previous quote may appear trivial, and indeed in one
sense it is — that is, it fails to give an account of why the
groups in existence first obtained power and how they hold
onto their place. Moreover, we all know the facts of trying to
wrest control from those in power — the problem of "fighting
city hall." But seen in another sense, the way critics of political
pluralism such as Herbert Marcuse, Grant McConnell, Henry
Kariel, John Kenneth Galbraith, and C. Wright Mills stress the
extent to which pluralist politics today is limited, the claim
takes on added significance. They point out that not only are
the issues generated by competing groups constrained by established values and expectations, but groups wishing to bring
about change are encouraged to organize around occupational
categories and expectations, as opposed to other considerations.

My general claim is that CTA is not a basic assumption of
the theory of political pluralism, but rather that it is an accepted part of the rules of the game of the politics of political
pluralism. It is not merely a coincidence that a good deal of
politics is ridden with it, especially on an election eve, and it is
not coincidental that such "hidden hand explanations" are
frequently used to tilt the odds in favor of "groups in the
process of formation" against "those in existence." What I am
claiming, in other words, is that the theory of political pluralism does not necessarily imply CTA, but the application of
the theory of pluralism — politics — potentially does.

Why is CTA potentially part of the politics of political pluralism? For one thing, for groups who perceive a significant
gap between existing social institutions and more desirable
political alternatives, the problem of strategy becomes central.
Someone in the groups must take stock of such questions as,
Which type of pressure is likely to be most effective; which
tactics promise most in the short and long run; how can interest group solidarity be established; and how can inchoate
discontent be generated along the lines of active discontent?

In attempting to answer these questions, interest group pol-

---

[10]Robert Paul Wolff, "Beyond Tolerance," in Wolff, Barrington Moore, Jr., and
Herbert Marcuse, *A Critique of Pure Tolerance* (Boston, Beacon Press, 1965).

itics cannot dismiss out-of-hand the function of CTA. "The groups in existence" and "those in the process of formation" view such a tactic as an acceptable path open to them — a well-trodden path — especially so far as political choices have been circumscribed, the urgent need for practical and quick redress of what is seen as intensely exploitative personal and social situations or when "the groups in existence" have demonstrated frugal responsiveness to other organized pressure, such as boycotts, sit-ins, and the like.

The question arises, however, whether CTA is more likely to be employed in the politics of a pluralist-open society rather than in a nonpluralist-closed society? Most political pluralist theorists would scorn the employment of CTA as ammunition in manipulating the balance of power in society. The important point, at least theoretically, is that the pluralist hopes that by a mechanism similar to the invisible hand of the marketplace, the balancing process will be in the public interest; it needs no CTA to move it along.[11] But even a cursory study of the application of the theory — politics, especially power politics — in recent years shows the naiveté of the benign exercise of political power as well as showing that power is employed by "the groups in existence" to clobber or manipulate the poor and the disadvantaged and keep them in their place.

The important point is that power politics (power, as it were, as the in-and-for-itself of political activity) is a reality against which the new groups wishing to bring about such changes as nuclear control, population control, the prevention of famine,

---

[11]Robert Nozick in his provocative book *Anarchy, State and Utopia* (New York, Basic Books, 1974) argues that some overall pattern of design, which one would have thought had to be produced by a group's successful attempt to realize the pattern, can be, instead, produced and maintained by a process that in no way had the overall pattern or design in mind. He gives the example of the replacement of a barter system by a medium of exchange, showing that "no express agreement and no social contract fixing a medium of exchange is necessary" (p. 18). Following Adam Smith, he calls such explanations *invisible-hand explanations*. These give an account of what looks to be the product of someone's intentional design, as not being brought about by anyone's intentions. Nozick calls the opposite sort of explanation, what I have called conspiracy theory, a *hidden-hand explanation*. He says, "A hidden-hand explanation explains what looks to be merely a disconnected set of facts that (certainly) is not the product of intentional design(s), as the product of an individual's or group's intentional design(s). Some persons find such explanations satisfying, as is evidenced by the popularity of conspiracy theories" (p. 19).

and the rational distribution of natural resources find the judicious exercise of argument and discussion demonstrably impotent. When one finds that the substance of political life — politics — is a grim amalgam of power struggle and material greed, it does seem appropriate to employ CTA as an active force to bring about, or at least call for, a better society. This is viewed as a heresy in many circles, as well it might, but it is an understated truism in American politics. An accepted CTA makes plunder at least legitimate; that is to say it justifies a particular course of action.

The nub here is why CTA is permissible in the application, i.e. politics, of the theory of political pluralism. In an intensely competitive pluralist society, one way to ensure that total concentration of power does not reside for long in any one group is to discredit its aims and tactics. The merit of CTA is as a device to discredit another faction or group in order to maintain or redistribute power in society. But this is more sophisticated and involved. By employing CTA, an individual intends to address the sense of justice of the majority and so serve fair notice that in one's sincere and considered judgment the conditions of a pluralist society are being violated. Someone is not playing fair. This has two consequences for the definition of political pluralism. First, it must be public, and the participants in politics must show that they are willing to accept the consequences of policies, even if not intended. This *fidelity condition* helps to establish to the majority that the CTA is conscientious and sincere, and that it is intended to address the public's sense of justice. Second, while the CTA may warn and admonish, it is calculated to suggest a clear danger, being conjoined with secrecy, plot, and threat.

It is clear, then, that these aspects of CTA issue from a particular type of political society. Recalling again that the force of CTA lies in its appeal to the majority's sense of fair play or justice, the CTA alleges that someone has tampered with the mechanism, and that is unfair. Hence, it may well be that CTA is most frequently (effectively?) applied in American society to the active agents of power — "the groups in existence" or in office — rather than to inactive agents of potential power — "those groups in the process of formation" or seeking office.

In a closed society, on the other hand, the political theory of a self- or group-interest operating in a way similar to the invisible hand of the marketplace producing the public interest is denied. There being no such value, there is no parallel sense of justice to appeal to. But this does not imply that there is no corresponding employment of CTA — quite the contrary. At least in part, it is powerlessness and victimization that lead people to develop CTAs. Thus it would seem that in closed societies CTA is expressed in either of two ways. First, we see those who desire to maintain the status quo against those who wish to change it, as in the case of being applied to "legal" dissidents, "terrorists," "traitors," and similarly labeled groups who, in an illegal way, because no other is open to them, attempt to change the status quo. Second, and more common, although there are no rules about political fair play for groups whose participation is disallowed, there still exists a set of expectations about just distribution of rewards and desirable political outcomes. Since the legitimacy of the regime may depend on the charismatic quality or some such thing of the leader, conspiracy theories spring up to explain why there is injustice despite the acknowledged benevolent intentions of the leader. Thus impoverished Russian peasants blamed the Jews for their plight, not the Czar, claiming "If the Czar only knew." French peasants in the eighteenth century blamed the excessive taxation on a conspiracy of greedy tax collectors and middlemen, and not the king. Indeed, the persuasive characterization of Goldstein in *1984* suggests that there is an important role for CTAs in closed societies, although it is inevitably not the same role as CTAs play in a pluralistic society.

In summary, it is evident that there is a potential in political pluralism for the use of CTA. But this is not to say that it will necessarily be converted over to active CTA. We have to look beyond this point to other factors as well.

A GENERAL MALAISE IN AMERICAN LIFE: THE PARANOID STYLE

The fear of conspiracy as well as the credibility of CTA lies first of all in our prejudices. For example, experiences of the last decade, particularly the Indo-China War and Watergate, have reinforced more or less strong prejudices against those in power, and we easily label those in power with the epithets "politician," "bureaucrat," and "powerbroker," each in its own way conjuring up a person capable of every atrocity, dishonesty, and immorality known to humankind. But the fear of subversion goes far back in American history and has been well documented in the literature.[12] Bernard Bailyn wrote of conspiracy fears and the American Revolution; and David Brion Davis observed that much of the rhetoric of the anti-Masonic crusade, as well as the persecution of the Mormons and the anti-Catholic hysteria during the years following the Civil War, can be explained in terms of a fear of conspiracy.

As Richard O. Curry and Thomas M. Brown in their book *Conspiracy: The Fear of Subversion in American History* explain:

> In attempting to gauge the significance of fears of conspiracy in American politics, some scholars believe that the denunciation of subversion in high places is little more than a sham, a crude tactic designed to discredit political opponents whose domestic policies are the real target. Thus, Federalists who opposed Jefferson's social and economic ideas sought to link him with atheism and the French reign of terror, and Republican opponents of the New Deal hoped to drive Democrats from power by accusing them of advocating socialism and appointing Soviet agents to high government offices. While

---

[12]Hofstadter tells us, "In the history of American political controversy there is a tradition of conspiratorial accusations which seem to have been sincerely believed. For example, Jefferson appears to have believed, at one time, that the Federalists were conspiring to reestablish monarchy. Some Federalists believed that the Jeffersonians were conspiring to subvert Christianity. The movement to annex Texas and the war with Mexico were alleged to many northerners to be a slaveholders' conspiracy. The early Republican leaders, including Lincoln, charged that there was a conspiracy on the part of Stephen A. Douglas to make slavery a nationwide institution. Such pre-Civil War parties as the Know-Nothing and anti-Masonic movements were based almost entirely upon conspiratorial ideology. The Nye Committee, years ago, tried to prove that our entry into the first World War was the work of a conspiracy of bankers and munitions-makers. And now not only our entry into the second World War, but the entire history of the past twenty years or so is being given the color of conspiracy by the cranks and political fakirs of our own age." Hofstadter, *Age of Reform*, p. 72.

this approach to the omnipresence of conspiratorial rhetoric in American political life may be correct, it by no means solves the problem posed by fear of conspiracy. Most writers agree that such tactics cannot be successful unless large numbers of people fervently believe that conspiracies constitute a danger to American security and ideals. In an effort to explain why these fears are widespread, some scholars have used modern sociological and psychological theories of behavior.[13]

The authors include papers by Franz Newmann and Gordon Allport who "emphasize the importance of societal disruption, alienation, and personality disorders in accounting for the success of demagogues."[14] Newmann, for example, considers Caesaristic imputation (the labeling of a situation as dangerous as well as imputing to that situation some sort of man-made machination to win political, economic, or social power) as coming into play when people see themselves as subjectively endangered and are incapable of understanding the historical process itself. Newmann argues that the clue to understanding this phenomenon is to grasp the connection between a positive Caesarism — such that people hope for deliverance from societal distress through the efforts of one person (person on a white horse) — and a negative Caesarism, a situation fraught with anxiety, fear, and dread, in which people ascribe their distress to certain persons who have brought this distress into the world through a conspiracy.[15]

Now, of course, a total view of history predicated on one conspiracy after another is not likely to gain many adherents, but the danger of this view is that there have been, and probably will continue to be, political conspiracies. In other words, this view of history is not entirely false, but always contains an element of possible truth, and indeed must contain some element of possible truth, mixed with propaganda techniques, if it is to have a convincing effect. Hence, the greater the kernel of

[13]Richard O. Curry and Thomas M. Brown, eds. *Conspiracy: The Fear of Subversion in American History* (New York: Holt, Rinehart & Winston, 1972), p. ix.
[14]Curry and Brown, *Conspiracy*, pp. ix-x.
[15]Curry and Brown, *Conspiracy*, pp. 254-255.

truth or possibility of a conspiracy, the greater the possibility of a CTAs acceptance.

In contrast to Newmann, Allport focuses primarily on the manipulative techniques employed by successful demagogues to convince others. Similarly, Eric Hoffer's now classic *The True Believer*[16] provides many clever insights about the techniques of demagogues.

The fear of conspiracy as well as the employment of CTA is more likely to occur when traditional modes of behavior are changed, when a group's identity, security, or core beliefs are challenged, or where there is, most generally, a sense of shared condition as "victims."[17] The person who feels victimized is not necessarily defined by his or her lack of income or status or by exclusion from the mainstream of American economic life, although these usually are elements of "victimization," but by being a member of a dependent class, one that does not own or control the object of its labor or its uses, and is thus subordinate with regard to the distribution of power. Thus, the victimized usually varies from the social norms or archetypes, is economically subordinate, and constitutes a physical, cognitive, or behavioral minority.[18] All of this is accompanied by a high sense of powerlessness that influences profoundly one's angle of vision in terms of charges or fears of conspiracy. Objectively speaking, there must be a person with a set of attitudes, a state of mind, receptive or prepared to accept an emotionally charged allegation about others, particularly those who are superordinate with regard to the distribution of power and who exemplify the most highly valued social norms or archetypes.

The so-called "victimized" are most receptive to those appeals calculated to explain how certain groups in society are responsible for their plight, such as those institutions, organizations, and groups having the power not only to oppress

---

[16]Eric Hoffer, *The True Believer* (New York, Harper, 1951).

[17]The notion of "victims" in American society is not new, and much has been written about it. Recently, however, two books have addressed this condition in terms somewhat different but quite similarly. In Antonia Pantója, *et. al.*, *Badges and Indicia of Slavery* (Lincoln, Neb., University of Nebraska, (1975) the term used is the *unpreferred*: and in Martin Carnoy's *Education as Cultural Imperialism* (New York, David McKay, 1974) the term employed is *colonized*.

[18]Newman, *American Pluralism*, pp. 34-37.

others but to suppress information giving away their efforts.

To fully appreciate the impact of "consciousness raising," that is, of giving the victimized a CTA explanation of their plight, it is necessary to appreciate the use of and multilayered character of "relativistic truth." If others can be convinced of the view of truth that "what is believed to be true is indeed true," then truth is no more than strong belief. Belief alone, that is, is sufficient to account for the truth of a proposition. Hence, "believing makes it so." It is important to note that this view may be coupled to the claim that people's ideas or beliefs differ according to their social position. In other words, the views of the world held by members of society are themselves importantly influenced by the position in society which they fill. Hence, all sectors of society, especially a capitalistic one, are dominated by systems of beliefs which are self-serving, for each different system of ideas necessarily represents the standpoint, interests, aims, and outlook of that segment of society, though often under the guise of speaking for society as a whole. Thus each social sector must be seen as identified with a correlative political tendency and social program, and social programs are merely a passive by-product of thought. They often become an influential cause which stirs people and groups to action, warfare, and genocide. Believed to be false, one-sided, outmoded, oppressive policies and practices are not expected to wither away. They have to be exposed, combated, and uprooted. One way to achieve this is through CTA. Hence, for some, a fear of subversion or the tendency to view the world in conspiratorial terms is not totally misguided.

For example, one form of CTA is that the effective exclusion of women from the production of raw materials and heavy machinery in this country is to be explained neither by technology nor biological necessity as sufficient conditions. Something else must be at work. Exclusion must be the product of a sexist ideology not only of efforts of trade unions, employers, and social reformers to enact legislation to protect their jobs, but of a successful conspiracy.

The very term *sexism* has influenced profoundly our thinking in examining present day society. The word is, of course, an "ism" and refers to a set of attitudes, a state of mind involving prejudice and discrimination, concerning the role women are expected to play in American society. Sexism, qualifying as a prejudice, badly distorts the role of women, threatening their integrity and independence. In the uncovering of "sexism as an ideology," there is a consequent tendency to fix upon a conspiracy as the critical factor in the exclusion problem of women in certain work forces. That is, a calculated male self-interest is not sufficient to explain the exclusion problem; something else is afoot, namely, a conspiracy.

But the fact remains that *conspiracy*, unlike words such as discrimination, prejudice, segregation, and stratification, does not direct attention primarily to actual social processes or conditions. Its meaning lies embedded in a descriptive/evaluative nesting, and its function is to explain with an added moral force. CTA, as an explanation of the exclusion problem of women, obscures the fact that powerful economic and social groups acting in their common self-interest have succeeded through legislation and influence-peddling to further their own ends. What is important here is that it is not a conspiracy of men against women, or the strong against the weak, but it is the wealthy supporting institutions and ways of life which maintain their position of wealth and power. In a politically pluralistic society competitive interest groups pursue distinctive interests chosen largely on the basis of a rough coincidence of interests. In other words, class and status rivalry are along with the ideology of sexism also deeply embedded in American society. These rivalries have arisen, in part, from subjective conditions and are but a part of the process of America functioning as a pluralistic society.

But the matter is not so simple. When a trades union insists that it has nothing against women but it must protect its jobs for its members and their children, do we denounce them by alleging a conspiracy at work? In other words, to ignore the self-interest source, in an exclusive fixation on CTA, will undoubtedly encourage bitterness and acrimony in a community.

To employ CTA as *the* explanation of the exclusion problem of women is not to recognize that historical divergent backgrounds can be causes, not just results, of the problem. Perhaps it is psychologically comforting not to think this way, but to do so may be to miss the crux of the matter. We should realize that American society reflects a political ethos of countervailing power calling for a high degree of competition for goods and services. Everything which differentiates one group from another involves a potential conflict of interest, making common public aims or interests such as human rights and dignity difficult for political pluralists to achieve — outside, of course, of easily perceived threats to national security as in the case of World War II. Under ordinary conditions, the "particularistic ties" of kin, sex, skin color, religious affiliation, and neighborhood, the so-called static or traditional parameters of factions, provide no adequate basis for the shifting to "universalistic" loyalites involved in class political action.

Moreover, the potential for responsible criticism and protest inherent in real and persistent social inequalities of society may be muted at best or, worse still, find no lasting expression if cast only in the form of CTA. Such a knee-jerk response may produce, for example, a predominant pattern of irrational allegation coupled in predictable proportions with resigned political indifference or overreactive hostility. In either case, the arena as well as the means of social criticism is narrowed, and the responsiveness of those in power to the potential for reform is decreased.

In summation, the very conditions that produce an acute sense of injustice among women and other discriminated-against groups also obscure the sources of the injustice. It is important for women and others to grasp the fact that their exploitation results not so much from a conspiracy but from systemic causes within American institutions. The mechanisms of competitive factions have not heretofore included women in significant degree because women are not an oppressed class in any way; they are an oppressed sex.[19] The answer to the problem lies, *only in the short run*, with women developing a positive self-interest designed to strengthen and develop a distinctive group, with a distinctive history, defined interests,

---

[19]Evelyn Reed, "Women, Class or Oppressed Sex?" in Evelyn Reed, ed., *Problems of Women's Liberation* (New York, Pathfinder Press, 1972).

and identifiable styles of social life, culture, and politics. The last point is crucial. Above all else, women and minority groups must develop the political machinery to compete equally in a system of countervailing political power, insofar as the rivalry between interests is believed to be the best regulator of the political process. The public interest, for awhile, must be replaced by group interest.

CTA AND SCHOOLING

Use of the term *conspiracy* to damn schooling policies and practices has become ubiquitous. With respect to the relationship between schooling and society, it is commonly supposed that some schooling policies represent an explicit or implicit conspiracy to reinforce the status quo. Hence, a conspiracy argument, when employed in educational discourse, usually takes the form that a group, controlling school policy, has successfully conspired to maintain a particular socioeconomic order.

What role does CTA play in educational discourse? The following paragraphs present various attacks on schooling consequences, and, thus, the assumptions underlying the employment of CTA surface.

We begin with the disclosure that some educational critics have highlighted the polarity between what schools *say* they do and what they *actually* do. Ostensibly, the purpose of schools and schooling is to educate. Charles E. Silberman indicted school personnel with the charge of "mindlessness."[20] Everett Reimer, a less congenial critic, purported to move beyond the professed aim of school to examine actual functions. In an essay written in 1970, he said, "Schools in all nations, of all kinds, at all levels, combine four distinct functions: custodial care, social-role selection, indoctrination, and education as usually defined in terms of the development of skills and knowledge. . . . It is the conflict among these functions which makes schools inefficient. It is the combination of these functions which tend to make the school a total institution . . . and which

---

[20]Charles E. Silberman, *Crisis in the Classroom: The Remaking of American Education* (New York, Random House Vintage Books, 1970), pp. 11, 16.

makes it such an effective instrument of social control."[21]

Paulo Freire asserted that there is no such thing as neutral education; education is either for domination or for freedom. Schools and schooling, he contended, effectively domesticate and pacify the masses.[22] Ivan Illich declared that obligatory education, schools, and teachers must be abolished.[23] There is no doubt in his mind about the possibility of reforming the present system; it is beyond reform. With respect to the relation between schooling and society, Illich suggested that schooling is a reflection of society and serves as a reinforcement of the status quo, and that schooling is not, and cannot be, an instrument of social change.[24]

In a similar vein, Edgar Z. Friedenberg claimed, "In school . . . [it] is indeed true that the medium is the message . . . what is taught isn't as important as learning how you have to act in society, how other people will treat you, how they will respond to you, what the limits of respect that will be accorded to you really are."[25]

Common in writing of these and other current educational critics is the claim that schooling functions as an agency of socialization. That proposition is well-documented in the literature, particularly in Robert Dreeban's *On What is Learned in School.*[26] What the critics take umbrage with is the claim that

[21]Everett Reimer, *An Essay on Alternatives in Education* (Cuernavaca, Mexico, CIDOC Guaderno No. 1005, 1970); *See* also *School Is Dead: Alternatives in Education* (Garden City, N.Y., Doubleday & Co., 1971).

[22]Paulo Freire, "Cultural Action for Freedom," *Harvard Educational Review*, Monograph Series No. 1, Cambridge, Mass., 1970, p. 1.

[23]Ivan Illich, *Deschooling Society* (New York, Harper & Row, 1970); and *Celebration of Awareness: A Call for Institutional Revolution* (Garden City, N.Y., Doubleday & Co., 1970).

[24]Ivan Illich, "The Alternative to Schooling," *Saturday Review*, June 19, 1971, p. 44.

[25]Edgar Z. Friedenberg, "What Do Schools Do?" *This Magazine Is About Schools* 3(1):33, 1969.

[26]Robert Dreeban, *On What is Learned in School* (Reading, Mass., Addison-Wesley, 1968). The author's main argument concerns the relationship between school structure and learning outcomes, and the relevance of those outcomes to surrounding institutions. His point is not that schooling is a reflection of society and serves as a reinforcement of the status quo, but that schooling is not necessarily an instrument of social change. Although schooling contributes to the acquisition of knowledge and skills through instruction, these developmental changes constitute only components of the total outcome of schooling, and particularly important are the normative outcomes that emerge through students coping with the structural aspects of schools.

schools and schooling are meant to be educative. Some critics claim that schools pay lip-service to an ideology of equality, but in reality perpetuate traditional sex roles; others charge that the schools foster colonialism, using the language of cultural deprivation; still others claim that schools process youth for life in a consumer society.

While sociologists of education have sensitized us to the hidden curriculum and unintended consequences of schooling, some education critics seem to disregard altogether the sociological data and claim that hidden curricula and unintended consequences are not mere accidents but are purposeful or intentional. Thomas F. Green said, "It is sometimes argued, for example, that it is the intent of educational policy in contemporary America to lead the 'underclass' or the 'disadvantaged' to be content in their position of 'disadvantaged.' The evidence often cited for such a position is the outcome of policy."[27]

The point is simply that it is sometimes claimed that schools are by their very nature, their structure and purpose, designed or intended to have "so-called" unintended consequences.[28]

If this description of the state of the critic's literature is correct, it is my conclusion that the critic's dismissal of unintended consequences and hidden curricula has arisen out of a rejection of sociological accounts of schooling in favor of a causal theory that posits free, deliberate, opportunistic, and secretive human courses of action imputed to bring about "intended consequences." Hence, conspiracy theory rests on the belief that there is no such thing as a hidden curriculum or unintended consequences; rather, some group has conspired to bring about the "so-called" unintended consequences of schooling. Once this point is understood, it is easier to assess the role of conspiracy theory.

To show that the above is plausible, I shall turn to three educational critics and their assessment of selected schooling processes and effects.

Reimer, for example, talks of "secrecy":

> The quality of . . . education will depend only upon the
> quality and completeness of their records that are available to

---

[27]Green, "What Is Educational Policy?" p. 14.
[28]Nozick, *Anarchy, State and Utopia.*

the public. Information upon which corporate and national advantage presumably depends will not be available . . . neither will other information deemed vital by some groups for the maintenance of their advantage over others. These are problems that organization alone cannot solve.

The multiplication of product shells and factory walls, behind which tools, instruments, and machines are hidden, has the same effect educationally as the hiding of records behind the veils of national security and corporate privilege. The result is to deny people the information they need to act intelligently in their own interests. The reasons behind all this secrecy are also the same, even though the conscious motives may be different. Manufacturers guarded their equipment and their products from the eyes of their customers, perhaps not consciously to keep them ignorant, but certainly in order to maintain an advantage in which ignorance is a critical factor.

Secrecy is by no means confined to capitalist countries. Professionals, managers, and specialized workers guard their privileges as jealously as owners.

So long as large-scale production continues to monopolize tools, instruments, machines, and other products that have special educational value, it will be necessary to include such products in educational directories and to arrange for general access to them.

Secrets seem natural and inevitable in the world to which we are accustomed, but the cost of keeping them is very great. . . . In a world controlled and owned by nations and corporations, only limited access to educational objects will ever be possible. Increased access to those objects then can be shared, however, may increase men's insight enough to enable them to break through these ultimate educational barriers.[29]

Here Reimer asserts that access to tools, records, machines, games, natural preserves, and other not commonly considered to be but extraordinarily useful "educational objects" have been locked into national and corporation businesses denying citizens cheap and powerful educational tools. Educational ac-

---

[29]Reimer, *School Is Dead*, pp. 116, 119, 120, 123.

cess, along with demonstrations and first-hand opportunities to experiment with tools, gadgets, etc., are somehow denied people, making them unable to act intelligently in their own interests. They are being manipulated by others. Educational access to scientific, military, economic, and political objects are denied by carefully guarded mechanisms — but who is responsible for this is not revealed.

Ivan Illich employed conspiracy theory in another, somewhat parallel, way. He claimed:

> If a person is to grow up he needs, first of all, access to things, to places and to processes, to events and to records. He needs to see, to touch, to tinker with, to grasp whatever there is in a meaningful setting. This access is now largely denied. When knowledge became a commodity, it acquired the protection of private property, and thus a principle designed to guard personal intimacy became a rationale for declaring facts off limits for people without the proper credentials. In schools teachers keep knowledge to themselves unless it fits into the day's program. The media inform, but exclude those things they regard as unfit to print. Information is locked into special languages, and specialized teachers live off its retranslation. Patents are protected by corporations, secrets are guarded by bureaucracies, and the power to keep others out of private preserves — be they cockpits, law offices, junkyards, or clinics — is jealously guarded by professions, institutions, and nations.
>
> The reason usually given for the impotence of the majority is stated in terms of political or economic class. What is not usually understood is that the new class structure of a schooled society is even more powerfully controlled by vested interests. Deschooling the culture and social structure requires the use of technology to make participatory politics possible. Only on the basis of a majority coalition can limits to secrecy and growing power be determined without dictatorship. We need a new environment in which growing up can be classless, or we will get a brave new world in which Big Brother educates us all.[30]

---

[30]Ivan Illich, "The Alternative to Schooling," pp. 48, 60.

Finally, according to John Holt:

> I think that schools and schooling, by their very nature, pur-
> poses, structure, and ways of working are, and are meant to
> be, an obstacle to poor kids, designed and built not to move
> them up in the world but to keep them at the bottom of it and
> *to make them think it is their own fault.* The odds against
> not just all poor kids but any poor kid being helped rather
> than hurt by schools are enormous. For the parents of poor
> kids to put all their hopes into getting good schooling for
> their kids seem to me to have about as much chance of
> paying off as putting all their money into sweepstakes.[31]

It seems that Holt asserts that schooling has had not only
certain consequences, but also the intent ("meant to be," "designed and built") was to produce these consequences. If
schools and schooling have had this content or design, who are
the perpetrators of this unconscionable, dastardly plot or
scheme? Who is responsible, for surely, irresponsibility bespeaks
responsibility? But Holt does not tell us who was involved, or
when and how the power was mustered to do so.

In the foregoing we see a rather common discourse centering
on the view that schooling consequences are generally un-
wholesome and destructive of "educational" processes and
ends. It is alleged that they often cannot do what they ought to
do and they often do what they ought not. In short, the consequences of schooling policies are deemed inappropriate in one
way or another. We are quite familiar with this discourse and
only a little less familiar with how conspiracy theory deals with
it.

CONCLUSION

One obvious answer to the problem we have considered is to
modify certain of the norms of political pluralism such as
achievement and competition, but this may not be possible in
the long run because the very process of change entails achievement and competition. Perhaps the most plausible modifica-

---

[31]John Holt, *Freedom and Beyond* (New York, E.P. Dutton & Co., 1972), p. 186.

tion would involve dropping the "particularistic ties" of group affiliation so that groupings or affiliation with groups simply would not count in determining, at least on the level of polity, who gets what. The proposition here is that in the new society group affiliation based on a narrow self-interest — kin, sex, ethnicity, religion, national orgin, race — would be irrelevant. Liberty and free association would, of course, be encouraged, but association for the purpose of keeping afloat the narrow system of countervailing forces would be discouraged, at least on the level of polity. Grouping would be irrelevant or unimportant in having any practical consequences as criteria for admission into or participation in the structural institutions of society. This becomes, in reality, an open society, where individuals find themselves not in some atavistic group interest but in the polity of civic society itself, and this is precisely what is meant by an open, secular society.

The decisive significance of a change from a pluralistic to an open society may be had from the lessening of the use of "particularistic ties" but may also be gauged from the weakening of the tendency of political leaders and their followers to view the functioning of society in conspiratorial terms. If politics can be made a more open process, there is a smaller chance that citizens alarmed over disruptions produced by war, protest, and economic recessions and depressions will see behind these secret, sinister conspiratorial plots. We may never be able to rule out the fear of subversion altogether, but conspiratorial interpretations or allegations can be somewhat muted by openness in politics. In short, a change in political pluralism may effect a change in the way people perceive the policy-making process and its results.

Chapter Five

CULTURAL PLURALISM AND THE
PUBLIC SCHOOL MOVEMENT*

IT may be argued that the principal charge
against the Public School Movement (PSM) today has yet to be
raised, namely, that it has failed to provide a genuine commitment to the toleration of the life-styles of the various ethnic,
religious, and racial subgroups that make up the American
social order. Just as critics of postindustrial society have be-
moaned the depersonalization of man which they see accom-
panying technological expansion, so other critics bemoan the
degree to which the PSM depersonalizes and demeans its
charges by adhering to a theory of assimilation which posits an
"invisible" label for all but a few — those who can make the
most of it — while the less fortunate are relegated to the position of second-class citizens. Considerable pessimism exists
today, especially among the threatened minorities, about the
possibility of seriously improving the PSM by any of the reforms mentioned previously. Many have come to believe that
the PSM has failed and will continue to fail as long as it
promotes a one-dimensional view of what it is to be an "American."

Basic to an understanding of this problem is the recognition
that this criticism of the PSM is symptomatic of a rejection of
the dominant goal-system ideology of assimilation that has
dominated American schooling since the second half of the
nineteenth century. Earlier we saw that a major function as-
signed the PSM in the previous century was that of solving the
social problems of a growing nation, particularly the problems
created by millions of immigrants to the United States from
Southern and Eastern Europe. Part of the criticism of the PSM
today is that it succeeded too well in this regard. In effect, many
critics are saying that the reality of America today is cultur-

---

*Adapted from *The Public School Movement: A Critical Study* by Richard Pratte.
Copyright© 1973 by Longman Inc. Reprinted by permission of Longman.

121

al diversity and cultural pluralism, both of which are virtually ignored by the PSM. Legendarily the vehicle for Anglo-conformism, the PSM now finds itself faced, at best, with irrelevance or, at worst, with extinction.

Controversy over this matter has come to a head only in recent years. The minorities are now aware that the PSM is organized and functions along social and economic lines. One of the most obvious manifestations of this is the fact that the PSM is a biracial system wherein approximately 90 percent of American children attend segregated schools. Moreover, there have been flagrant sources of opposition to any effective desegregation of the PSM.

Strangely enough, until the comparatively recent influx of blacks and Puerto Ricans into urban public schools, the PSM was justifiably credited with being the chief instrument for making the American dream of upward social, economic, and political mobility a reality. The depressed immigrants from Europe used the PSM as the ladder toward the goals of assimilation and success. But the fact that the PSM was an effective vehicle for white American immigrants makes its inefficiency and malfunctioning in the mobility of blacks, Chicanos, Puerto Ricans, Cubans, and Native Americans even more intolerable. American minorities are challenging the PSM to provide social justice and deliver positive results, particularly in the area of full civil rights for all Americans.

An oft-heard position in this regard is that it is the responsibility of the PSM to nurture what has been described as "cultural democracy" — the values of cultural diversity and toleration — since it posits the right of all groups in a democratic society to maintain their communal identity and their own subcultural values. This position is frequently called "cultural pluralism" (hereinafter abbreviated CP). It seems to involve the mutual exchange and respect for the diverse cultures that comprise the nation and requires that different groups respect or at least tolerate different views of the Good Life. To the extent that people believe, and the schools reinforce — as it is charged they so often do — a particular life-style as the only right one, a culturally diverse society will continue to have many unresolved inherent tensions which spill over into the economic, political, and social arenas of life.

Thus the question, Ought the PSM educate for a culturally pluralistic society? is an ideological one and crucial for anyone even remotely concerned with the problems and tensions of American society today. But we must not be too hasty to answer this question, because it is an extremely complicated one, requiring all the care and attention we can possibly bring to bear in answering it. For example, the question seems to be of a type to which we would respond yes or no. But we should recognize that an assumption underlies the question: Can the PSM educate for a culturally pluralistic society? That is, if the PSM cannot educate for such a society, then the question, Ought it educate . . . ? simply does not arise, for it can be rebutted as a complex question.

Therefore, in order to deal adequately with the question, it would be prudent to examine some problems involved in achieving a culturally pluralistic society. John A. Ether has outlined three basic problems.[1] He begins by saying that before an investigation of these problems can be undertaken, we must face the basic fact that " . . . cultural diversity has always existed in the United States, but as a nation we have ignored it or denigrated it."[2] He cites as examples the reluctance of textbook authors to recognize the existence of blacks in American history. Also, he offers the case of the teacher who helps to eliminate the foreign accents of students. Ether charges that this is done in the name of "Americanizing" the students, when in fact teachers are destroying a cultural diversity basic to American political philosophy. In general, Ether cites three fundamental problems associated with CP: cultural diversity as a threat; the viability of CP as a model; and cultural supremacy. These are the pitfalls that must be overcome in order to begin promoting the culturally pluralistic society Ether so clearly desires.

Ether claims that many Americans view cultural diversity as an intense threat. Too many members of subcultures want to be

---

[1] John A. Ether, "Cultural Pluralism and Self-Identity," *Educational Leadership* 27:232-234, 1969.
[2] Ether, "Cultural Pluralism and Self-Identity," p. 234.

totally Americanized, and this means leaving their ethnic identity behind them. Second, Ether claims that the concept of CP itself may or may not be viable. There is little proof that such a model has been tried and could be successful. Finally, Ether suggests that the ethnocentrism of American society makes it difficult for Americans to accept all cultures as being equal. This tendency he calls "cultural supremacy" and considers it deeply ingrained in American thought.

Ether thus raises the question of whether CP not only does exist but whether it can exist in the United States. He says, "I know of no evidence that indicates that a pluralistic society has ever existed or can exist. . . An examination of supposed examples reveals that each has a dominant culture with subservient cultures. . . . This is not to say that a culturally diverse nation cannot exist. The notion that it can is, however, at the present time based upon faith and not upon evidence."[3]

Ether seems to be making two very important points. On the one hand, he said that every example of a so-called culturally pluralistic society is in fact dominated by a core or dominant group to which all other groups are subservient. This point is seemingly in accord with the theory of Anglo-conformism dealt with previously.[4] On the other hand, Ether's claim also supports a very loose interpretation of the melting-pot theory of amalgamation which calls for the cultures of the subservient groups "melting" into the culture of the host society. In either case, however, he is not talking, strictly speaking, of what was delineated earlier as the theory of cultural pluralism.[5] Moreover, it is clear that Ether employs "pluralistic" and "diverse" without a distinction. This is not an unusual move, but one that obliterates a fruitful way of gaining an understanding of the concept of CP. We shall not attack this problem here, but will turn to it later.

Another problem needs to be explored briefly before pushing on with our original question. Thomas F. Green asserted that " . . . what we have seen happening in the United States is not in fact the growth of a pluralistic society, but the growth of an

---

[3]Ether, "Cultural Pluralism and Self-Identity," p. 234.
[4]Ether, "Cultural Pluralism and Self-Identity," *see* Chapter 2, pp. 63-65.
[5]Ether, "Cultural Pluralism and Self-Identity," pp. 67-68.

open society. . . . "[6] The clear-cut judgment of Green is that we are moving toward the reality of an open society in the United States and away from the ideal of CP. He further believes that our educational goals and practices should more and more reflect the reality of an open society rather than a pluralistic one. In other words, Green challenges us to question the value of "educating for a culturally pluralistic society" at the expense of achieving the reality of an open society. Green's assertion appears to make over our original question, Ought the PSM educate for a culturally pluralistic society? to Ought the PSM educate for an open society?

But where does this leave us? Our rather long detour by way of exposure to Ether's views and Green's position on CP has not made easier the framing of an answer. If anything, we may perhaps be more confused because of the ideas put squarely before us. Both men have seriously questioned the feasibility of answering the original question in the affirmative, but for quite different reasons. Ether favors the model of CP for American society but raises the distinct possibility that the model may not be a viable one. He sees, in other words, the theory as based more on faith than on evidence. Green, on the other hand, regards CP as a limiting theory for American society. He prizes the values of an open society over those of a culturally pluralistic one, for the latter promotes differences between people, whereas the former regards differences between people and groups as no longer relevant or important in evaluating the position or merit of individuals. But despite their differences, Green's position supports Ether's claim that "No evidence indicates that a pluralistic society has ever existed or can exist." Indeed, Green questions whether CP could exist at all for any length of time.

It seems necessary to say here that although we appear to use and understand the concept of CP with ease depending upon the context to specify the meaning, even so, there are problems in its use. For one, CP has become very closely linked with the American democratic concept. It has almost become syn-

---

[6]Thomas F. Green, "Education and Pluralism: Ideal and Reality" (Twenty-Sixth Annual J. Richard Street Lecture, Syracuse University School of Education, 1966), p. 25.

onymous with the democratic concept which offers a "piece of pie for everyone." Educational curricula are being developed to demonstrate a high regard for CP, and the model is considered by many as a new social force which could truly make American society a more democratic, tolerant, and peaceful one.

The questions arises, then, What is CP? Also, why would such thoughtful men as Ether and Green question, albeit for different reasons, its validity? These are difficult questions, and until they are dealt with, we will merely talk past one another and be at a loss to understand how to go about answering our original question as well as failing to understand much of the controversy surrounding the PSM today. Moreover, one should reflect on the distinctions made so far and consider these fundamental questions: How viable is the model of CP? What aims and methods of schooling are most appropriate for its realization? How viable is the model of an open society? What aims and methods of schooling are most appropriate for its realization? These are critical questions because the claims made in each will go far in giving us direction not only for the future of the PSM but for our society as well.

Therefore, let us begin with an examination of Green's view, that the United States ought to discard the model of CP in favor of an open society. The latter tolerates all points of view; factors of ethnic, racial, or religious backgrounds are not relevant due to the rejection of traditional cultural biases and prejudices and the increasing secularization of the American social order. This view, it is suggested, is a significant issue worthy of the consideration of all Americans, but particularly of those interested in the PSM.

CULTURAL PLURALISM: IDEAL VERSUS REALITY

Green, in his discussion of CP, suggests two traditions that have helped shape societies in the Western world.[7] The first is the "Anglo-American tradition," and the second is the "French democratic tradition." The former is that type of social struc-

---

[7] Green, "Education and Pluralism," pp. 8-9.

ture which encourages many voluntary subgroups and associations to combine in order to represent their interests collectively. The latter type of social structure puts its emphasis on individual equality and national unity more than diversity; citizens, in this view, achieve their identity in their common status as "citizens" rather than as members of subcultures.

The distinction is important because it establishes, on the one hand, a relationship between the Anglo-American tradition and CP, and, on the other, between the French democratic tradition and Green's conception of the secularized open society in which traditional cultural, ethnic, racial, or religious differences are no longer considered relevant. Green argues that we are moving toward the reality of the open society in the United States and away from the ideal of pluralism. He further argues that our educational ideal as embodied in schooling should reflect the reality of a more open society than a culturally pluralistic one.

It is not very difficult to see here that in promoting the model of an open society as opposed to a pluralistic one, we should discourage the cultural separation of those who wish to live separately from other groups. This is a very serious matter. We must examine Green's arguments very closely, because his position leads to a policy proposal for the PSM and encourages certain policies and practices at variance with the policies and practices of those who wish CP promoted by the PSM.

Briefly, what follows is a rather close rendering of Green's analysis of pluralistic social structures as appearing on a scale. He discusses three stages of social relationships often referred to in debates concerning CP in American society: (1) "insular pluralism," (2) "halfway pluralism," and (3) "structural assimilation" or what Green calls "make-believe pluralism."[8]

Insular pluralism, the first type, is a stage of social development in which the differing subgroups comprising the social order decide that they will live, as much as possible, in separation from one another. Within each group both primary and secondary levels of association are restricted to members of the

---

[8]Green, "Education and Pluralism," pp. 13-28.

group. The subgroups develop their primary or close filial and secondary or extended relationships among members of their own groups, while intergroup contact occurs only at the level of polity.

Moreover, it is a type of pluralism which, although successfully expressing the value of cultural diversity in society and the desire to preserve it, is restrictive of each individual who must remain within the cultural confines of his subgroup or "birthright" regardless of his wishes in the matter. In other words, although insular pluralism lays claim to being truly democratic because it allows each group to maintain its communality and culture, how democratic is it when it places such a severe limitation on the freedom of association for the individual? In Green's words, " . . . although insular pluralism expresses the social value of freedom of association, it does so for groups and not for individuals."[9] Milton M. Gordon agrees with Green: "To put the issue more succinctly, while cultural pluralism may be democratic for groups, how democratic is it for individuals?"[10]

If this is the case, then it seems to follow that insular pluralism, to the extent that it is effective, excludes any kind of functional contact between and among groups on both the primary and secondary levels of association. It can thus be argued that this type is not representative of an interactive society at all; rather it applies to a type of social structure where diversity is valued but at the cost of canceling out any functional contact between groups.

"Halfway pluralism" is a second type discussed by Green. In this model there is a partial integration of social relationships among differing cultural, ethnic, racial, or religious subgroups on the level of secondary relations, in schools, hospitals, churches, stores, housing, restaurants, occupations, etc. But on the primary level of relations — social filial, and avocational or leisure activities — insularity is rigidly maintained. There is no dating, no intermarriage, and no heterogeneous children's play

[9]Green, "Education and Pluralism," p. 15.
[10]Milton M. Gordon, *Assimilation in American Life: The Role of Race, Religion, and National Origins* (New York, Oxford University Press, 1964), p. 152.

groups in this model.

The principal difference between insular pluralism and halfway pluralism is that the former involves a thorough structural separation between the many subgroups within the social order at the level of primary and secondary associations. Halfway pluralism, on the other hand, demands thorough structural insularity only at the level of primary relations and encourages a high degree of functional contact between members of subgroups at the level of secondary associations.

The fundamental difficulty inherent in the dynamics of the model of halfway pluralism is that the increased contact among groups on the secondary level of association may and often does promote cultural assimilation. To the extent that it succeeds in this, the distinctive inheritance or cultural identification of a person is often challenged when it inconveniences assimilation at the secondary level. Engaging in considerable functional contact with members of other subgroups encourages a willingness for one to sacrifice ancestral values in the face of gaining economic or political success. Willingness to sacrifice one's cultural identity may be indispensable if one is to function effectively in the complex secondary associations of society.

It is not difficult to see that the model of halfway pluralism represents a position that requires integration of groups at the secondary level of association, but in the process it often sacrifices whatever in the ancestral heritage is dysfunctional in the vast and complex arena of secondary relations. It is thus assumed that minority group members can and do achieve positions of influence and high status in the larger society but only to the extent that they submerge or, in some cases, totally repudiate their ancestral origins. This means for many subgroup members the progressive displacement of particular ethnic, religious, or cultural values insofar as these limit one's acceptance into areas of secondary association. If this process makes considerable headway, then diversity is not being promoted; rather, the locus of importance shifts from personal identity in an ethnic subgroup or a religious subgroup to the vocations — the offices and professions of a secular community that is increasingly corporate and monolithic.

"Structural assimilation," Green's third stage, is regarded by many as the fulfillment of a pluralistic society. In this stage, in Green's words, " . . . integration occurs at both the primary and secondary levels of association."[11] But, according to Green, it is not a case of cultural pluralism at all, for upon closer analysis of the model it is the ultimate culmination of a situation in which differences between groups or individuals are simply irrelevant "as long as they do not inconvenience the conduct of affairs either in the polity, in the economy or in the family."[12] It is remarkable how closely John Cuber is to Green in his definition of assimilation. Cuber defines assimilation as *"the gradual process whereby cultural differences (and rivalries) tend to disappear."*[13] Green displayed similar ideas when he argued that structural assimilation is not a form of pluralism where diversity is promoted, but rather a form of "make-believe" pluralism, i.e. when there are no relevant differences in a society, as in structural assimilation, then there is little diversity that counts. Such a position, Green asserts, represents "not in fact the growth of a pluralistic society, but the growth of an open society, in which the criteria for determining status are less and less connected with ethnic and religious origins and more and more connected with achievement and this development may mitigate against pluralism."[14] In other words, when people of different groups live side by side and do not find anything seriously at stake in their ethnic, racial, or cultural backgrounds, then we cannot call this pluralism. It is, Green said, the way we commonly refer to an open society.

The model of structural assimilation may be, as Green contends, not a case of CP at all; his labeling of it as make-believe pluralism appears fitting. One way to view this stage is to see it as the ultimate end of single melting-pot formula, as the ultimate end of a universal amalgamation. It is an effort out of which a vast intercultural mixture emerges — a new cultural amalgam representing a new form of national character. This

---

[11]Green, "Education and Pluralism," p. 22.
[12]Green, "Education and Pluralism," p. 23.
[13]John Cuber, *Sociology: A Synopsis of Principles*, 3rd ed. (New York, Appleton-Century-Crofts, 1955), p. 609 (italics in original).
[14]Green, "Education and Pluralism," p. 25.

is precisely the position the stalwarts of CP and the advocates of ethnic communality find most dangerous. To assume the correctness of the structural assimilationist stage is to reject the strong possibility that "Probably the vast majority of Americans, as revealed in their choices of primary group relations and organizational affiliations, desire ethnic communality, at least in essential outline."[15] According to Gordon, the goal of a truly open society has yet to be fully realized. Ethnic, racial, and religious origins may not be as important as they once were, but they still exist, and one may question any system of social structure that rules them out.

Green's syndrome of healthy-minded confidence in structural assimilation is not shared by Gordon. The latter, investigating the actual experience of minority groups in the United States, reached a conclusion that runs counter to a crucial assumption made by Green and suggests that there is yet a further stumbling block in the path of achieving CP. Implicit in Green's model of halfway pluralism and the model of structural assimilation is the notion that some degree of structural integration, i.e. participation in the social network of the broader or larger society, is necessarily prior to structural assimilation. Gordon's findings contradict such an assumption by demonstrating that many American minority groups have typically given up much of their cultural distinctiveness while yet participating only minimally in relationships across group lines. Gordon, having analyzed the process of assimilation into seven component processes, including cultural and structural assimilation, and having observed the relations which have been obtained between the subprocesses, concluded that "(1) cultural assimilation, or acculturation, is likely to be the first of the types of assimilation to occur when a minority group arrives on the scene; and (2) cultural assimilation, or acculturation, of the minority group may take place even when none of the other types of assimilation occurs simultaneously or later, and this condition of 'acculturation only' may occur indefinitely."[16]

In support of propositions 1 and 2, Gordon cites the histor-

[15]Gordon, *Assimilation in American Life*, p. 263.
[16]Gordon, *Assimilation in American Life*, p. 77 (italics deleted).

ical evidence of immigration into the United States, as each succeeding wave of immigration spread over America:

> ... the first process that has occurred has been the taking on of the English language and American behavior patterns, even while the creation of the immigrant colonies sealed off their members from extensive primary contracts with "core society" Americans and even when prejudice and discrimination against the minority have been at a high point. While this process is only partially completed in the immigrant generation itself, with the second and succeeding generations, exposed to the American public school system and speaking English as their native tongue, the impact of the American acculturation process has been overwhelming. . . . [17]

Consistent with this analysis is Gordon's only mildly surprising statement that the pluralism evident in American society today — ethnic groups and neighborhoods, fairly low rates of intermarriage among religious and racial groups, etc. — is principally structural pluralism rather than cultural pluralism.[18]

Gordon's distinction between structural pluralism and cultural pluralism is a crucial one. The former, he said, "is the major key to the understanding of the ethnic makeup of American society, while cultural pluralism is the minor one."[19] Gordon characterized structural pluralism in a clear language. "Structural (pluralism) denotes a situation in which primary group contacts between members of various ethnic groups are held to a minimum, even though secondary contacts on the job, on the civic scene, and in other areas of impersonal contact may abound."[20] Although the words are different, this could be Green explicating his concept of halfway pluralism. As for the distinction between cultural pluralism and structural pluralism, Gordon "saves" cultural pluralism for a point of view which offers legitimization of the preservation of cultural differences in the nation's various ethnic groups.[21]

---

[17]Gordon, *Assimilation in American Life*, pp. 77-78.
[18]Gordon, *Assimilation in American Life*, p. 159.
[19]Gordon, *Assimilation in American Life*, p. 159.
[20]Gordon, *Assimilation in American Life*, p. 235.
[21]Gordon, *Assimilation in American Life*, p. 13.

Now, if the PSM did in fact take upon itself the goal of schooling the young for a culturally pluralistic society, what would the model be? Clearly CP seeks the preservation of communal life and significant portions of the culture of all groups within the context of American citizenship. To borrow a justly maligned phrase, CP seems to involve a relationship in which freedom of association is enhanced and groups are "separate but equal." Seymour W. Itzkoff expressed this idea more palatably as "equality in difference."[22] But a problem still exists. Any model of CP implies contradictory practices with respect to social interaction. For example, to maintain its cultural distinctiveness the minority subgroup must confine its most primary and meaningful relationships to its own membership; while to achieve and maintain political, economic, and social equality vis-à-vis the dominant culture, the minority group must participate in certain relationships with the broader society. According to Gordon:

> The presumed goal of the cultural pluralists is to maintain enough sub-societal separation to guarantee the continuance of the ethnic cultural tradition and the existence of the group, without at the same time interfering with the carrying out of standard responsibilities to the general American civic life. In effect, this demands keeping primary group relations across ethnic lines sufficiently minimal to prevent a significant amount of intermarriage, while cooperating with other groups and individuals in the secondary relations areas of political action, economic life and civic responsibility.[23]

Gordon concluded that CP in the American experience was a less than ideal type of model.

Now to return to the question raised earlier, Ought the PSM educate for a culturally pluralistic society? Anyone sensitive to the nuances of ordinary discourse or alert to the problems of undisciplined argument will detect a certain ambiguity in this question. This was in part recognized earlier when it was pointed out that the term "ought" presupposed the condition of "can." We shall say that a term is ambiguous if it can receive

---

[22]Seymour W. Itzkoff, *Cultural Pluralism and American Education* (Scranton, Penn., International Textbook, 1969), p. 148.
[23]Gordon, *Assimilation in American Life*, p. 158.

more than one meaning. Thus to "educate for" might mean "educating for an existing culturally pluralistic society." Or, on the other hand, to "educate for" might mean "educating for the creating of a culturally pluralistic society." Moreover, we have not yet specified what is meant by cultural pluralism. Thus it might not be inappropriate to inquire whether the ambiguity and vagueness which have come to enshroud the term CP have not now led to a state of confusion in which it might be more profitable to center our attention upon certain facets of the concept, namely, those associated with an ordinary language use; then we may return to the original question.

CONCEPT OF CP

If someone said, "I know of no culturally pluralistic society that has ever existed," how do we determine the truth or falsity of the claim? What kind of evidence confirms or disconfirms it?[24] One may say that if those concerned are able to agree as to what would count as evidence, then the data may be collected and the claim may be verified. Suppose they agree that an examination of societies based on patterns of social organization and their effect on promoting cultural diversity and the data collected will count as evidence. Suppose they collect such data, can they then conclude from this that a culturally pluralistic society has ever existed? Of course not. Although agreeing as to what would count as evidence is no mean achievement, a second-order question of what counts as CP needs to be raised. This is obvious. The claim is not empirically answerable until the conceptual question of what counts as a culturally pluralistic society is answered.

Broadly speaking, there are two basic ways in which the term CP is literally used. First, the term is used in a purely descriptive sense to characterize the coexistence of many political,

---

[24]The analysis that follows is based on my paper, "The Concept of Cultural Pluralism," delivered at the annual meeting of the Philosophy of Education Society in 1972 and subsequently published in *The Proceedings of the Philosophy of Education Society* (Edwardsville, Ill., Philosophy of Education Society, 1975).

racial, religious, ethnic, geographical, and age groups living together in a way that allows the social system to function and maintain itself. The term is descriptive of a situation in which any number of subgroups in the total society retain their identity and culture while functioning with each other. Thus in this usage, CP is equivalent to "cultural diversity," and writers on the topic commonly employ metaphorical melting pots to characterize such a society. Second, we use the term CP not only to convey descriptive data but to evaluate as well; the term is thus "mixed," serving both to describe and evaluate. Hence, for some, the term carries a positive connotation. This is implicit in the claim that CP "develops the skills of democratic politics," the assumption being, of course, that participation in a pluralistic society encourages the use of bargaining and negotiation. We also hear this implicit sense when someone says that CP implies a kind of "equality without conformity," or it "reflects a spirit of universal brotherhood." The evaluative sense is explicit when someone says that "CP and democracy are equivalent."

This last point is an important one. It seems to me that the mixed use of CP connotes at one and the same time a theoretical construct and a programmatic value position. Green argued that CP, as a social ideal,

> ... involves a belief in freedom of association. Secondly, it contains the belief that there is no single way of life which can without question claim to be best; thirdly, it implies the belief that a humane society must afford room for many competing ways of life. And, finally, the ideal of pluralism implies that it is good to have such ways of life in competition and in contact and that the differences between them will not be endangered but enhanced by the contact between them.[25]

The value commitments of this use suggest a reason why it is uncommon or peculiar to employ the term CP when one disapproves of the values. If one rejects that values or program implicit in the mixed use, then the tendency is to rely upon a

---

[25]Green, "Education and Pluralism," p. 11.

purely descriptive use. The term "subsocieties" or "subgroups" may serve, or one may speak of "social structures," "intergroups," "various groupings," and "communities." In effect, the use of such terms takes note of the many or diverse groups in a society, but does not accord this situation a "halo" effect. What I wish to suggest is, of course, that the mixed use of CP is commonly a positive or yea sort of connotation rather than a negative or nay sort.

Are there other situations where the term CP is not commonly applied? In short, the question becomes, Is it possible to have CP without a particular condition? Or to put it another way, Is it possible to have A without B?[26] This line of conceptualizing should allow us to determine some characteristics of the concepts CP by establishing the nature of its relations to some other concept.

Let us take the descriptive sense of CP and begin with an ordinary example. Suppose we were to hear of state X, wherein many racial, ethnic, religious, and geographical groups coexist side by side, each retaining its historic identity. For instance, all ethnic groups can be identified by certain cultural life-styles which are expressed in special eating habits, attitudes toward time and property, unusual emphasis on primary relationships such as the value of familial ties, and distinctive speech patterns and dress. No explicit sanctions are needed to enforce this condition beyond the satisfying participational roles of the group members in the larger society.

Let us acknowledge that this description characterizes a situation in which any number of subgroups in the total society retain their identity and culture while functioning with each other. These diverse groups exist side by side, preserving their ancestral heritage, contributing not only to their own welfare and development but also to that of the society as a whole. In this case, one might be quite sure that this is an instance of the concept of CP, something of which we might say, "Well, if that isn't an example of CP, then nothing is."

---

[26]Thomas F. Green, *The Activities of Teaching* (New York, McGraw-Hill, 1971), pp. 17-18, 116-117, 209-210.

The case described does point out an essential feature for applying the term CP to a society, namely, that a society in fact exhibits cultural diversity. But the problem with the case is its failure to discriminate — that is, to make a significant distinction between CP and cultural diversity. The example illustrates that the two concepts are closely related in the sense that cultural diversity is a necessary condition for applying CP to a society.[27] And we may note that there are many contexts within which it is a matter of indifference whether the term CP or the term cultural diversity is used. Nevertheless, it would be a mistake to conclude that they are the same thing. They are not, for there are some contexts in which it would be an obvious distortion to substitute one idea for the other.

For example, imagine a fifth-grade classroom. The students include children from many religious, ethnic, and cultural origins. Moreover, their abilities vary considerably. A visitor, after spending an hour or so with the students and their teacher, comments, "I note that your students come from many different backgrounds." But he would not likely say, "I note that your class is decidedly pluralistic." We recognize, of course, that every human group is diverse, heterogeneous, different, distinguishable, or varied from some point of view. The important question is, When are we likely to use the term culturally pluralistic rather than the terms culturally diverse, culturally heterogeneous, or culturally different? Perhaps employing the A-without-B procedure may clarify this situation.

We can begin with the concept of CP and the concept of political status. The question might be raised whether CP can be considered to apply to a social order in the absence of equal or approximately equal political status in the polity. Such a question could be answered by attempting to describe a case that would meet the conditions set by the question. For example, let us imagine the case of state Y, wherein although there coexist different racial, religious, ethnic, and cultural groups, only the members of cultural subgroup$_1$ enjoy legal

---

[27]The example makes it clear that in attempting to elucidate the requirements for the application of the term CP, diversity of groups is a necessary condition for CP, but other things are needed, too, and so cultural diversity is not a sufficient condition.

and political privileges. All other groups (subgroup$_2$, subgroup$_3$, subgroup$_4$, subgroup$_n$) are disenfranchised and do not enjoy even the minimum equality of educational and economic opportunity.

What does this line of investigation reveal about the ordinary language concept of CP? With this relation existing between CP and political status, it can be seen that, although we do have subgroups making up the total society, although cultural diversity abounds, the value aspect of CP is not met; we have caste (a nay word) instead of CP. The example shows that for a society to be called culturally pluralistic as well as culturally diverse, members of the constituent groups must possess the status of roughly equal legal status and enjoy some minimum of equality of educational and economic opportunity. Hence we do not ordinarily apply the term CP to a rigidly defined caste society. This is the second condition that permits the term CP to be applied in some contexts and not in others. We can speak of this as a necessary condition.

Two important points need to be made at this juncture. Obviously, I do not wish to suggest that everyone must achieve equal political, economic, and educational opportunity in order for the condition to be met. This constraint means only that the range of opportunity and the distribution within that range should be about the same for each group. The restrictions on individuals achieving equally would be those normally attached to job performance, such as mental and physical health, intelligence, initiative, and motivation. But no group would be discriminated against as a group. Second, to argue that approximate equal political, economic, and educational opportunity must exist before the term CP can be applied to a society may seem too much to claim, but it is not too much to claim from a normative point of view, for under this condition, the various subgroups in society would no longer be politically, economically, or educationally disadvantaged. Yet, while it would be correct in one sense to describe a culturally pluralistic society as a "cultural democracy," since it implies the right of all groups in society to equal political, economic, and educational opportunity, it would not be correct in another sense to describe a system of CP as a cultural democracy insofar as CP does not demand this value for all individuals or, for that matter, for any one individual.

Does another constraint on the ordinary language use of CP suggest itself by application of the A-without-B procedure? Consider the following searing query, especially important to militant black Americans and militant French Canadians in North America today. To some black Americans the question, Is the United States to be two separate nations or one? and to some Quebecois of the Quebec Liberation Front (FLQ) the question, Is Canada to be two separate nations or one? has but one possible answer. Each revolutionary type responds, "Let there be two nations." To both types, a behavioral commitment to the values of CP is unreal. Nor is diversity valued, at least in respect to the level of polity. Two cases may make this position clearer.

First, let us consider the case where the white dominant or host group refuses to allow a black minority to achieve anything but second-class citizenship status, even though the vote is had by both whites and blacks. In effect, despite the achieving of most legal and political rights, the black minority continues to be discriminated against and denied equal economic and educational opportunities. Recognizing the hardened bias and prejudice of the white dominant group, some members of the black minority claim that the major problem of the black minority is to create a contraculture based on a theme of conflict with the values of the dominant host white culture. One major theme of the white culture is its ideological commitment to liberalism. The white liberal ideology emphasizes egalitarianism and has the goal of eliminating differences among peoples in order to create a democratic society. Racial integration in education is regarded as an important means for eliminating societal inequities. White liberals thus claim that race is irrelevant and ought to make no difference in determining one's societal roles, that it is merely a difference of skin color, an accident of birth.

But these ideals, some black Americans aver, have little basis in reality, and, in fact, the PSM has consistently failed to prepare black children to achieve in society. The liberal conception of integration is conceived of as training black children to be white and at the same time making clear to them that it is impossible to be white. In being taught the values of the host dominant white culture, black children are often taught to despise themselves for their "blackness." Hence, compensatory education programs for the "disadvantaged" are regarded by some blacks as attempts to uphold or save the liberal ideology by placing the blame for the school's failures on black children and their disadvantaged families and "deprived" environments.

A second theme of the dominant white culture is that of ideology which regards highly the social ideal or mixed sense of CP: the belief in freedom of association, for groups and for individuals; that there is no single way of life which can without question claim to be the best; the belief that a humane society must afford room for many competing ways of life; and that it is a value to have such ways of life in competition and in contact, and that the differences between them will not be endangered but enhanced by the contact between them.[28] But the black revolutionaries argue that the majority of the dominant culture do not act upon this ideology and thus promote the theme of black conflict with the dominant culture. Hence, at least one black ideology is a specific contradiction of the social ideal of the dominant culture. It argues that there is value in freedom of association with blacks only; that a black way of life can without question claim to be best; that there is no room for competing ways of life; and that there is no value in having contact with the white culture; indeed, differences between blacks and whites will be endangered by the contact between them. In short, one black ideology is the goal of separatism, which may or may not threaten the unity of the larger social system, but, above all else, rejects the values of CP itself.

The second case is seen in Canada today. Some French Canadians reject the values of CP in favor of a monolithic French Quebec. Here too is seen the goal of separatism, which threatens the unity of the larger social system, even though the

---

[28]Green, "Education and Pluralism," p. 11.

separatist group possesses legal equality and roughly comparable educational opportunities.

But what is the importance of these cases? Do they point to any conclusions? They suggest that when a group in society develops separatist goals and becomes powerful enough to endanger the freedom of individuals and of other groups in the society as well as threatening the polity itself, then we may question whether such a goal is compatible with the ordinary language use of CP. That is, in respect to an exclusivist group which threatens the unity of the larger social system, it seems clear that we have not examined a case of CP at all. Rather, it is a contrary case. CP, as an ordinary language term, appears to involve the mutual exchange of and respect for the diverse subgroups that comprise the social order. Its application requires that groups respect or at least tolerate different views of the Good Life and conceptions of the good state. To the extent that a group believes that its life-style is the only "right" one and does not tolerate other life-styles, then we have a culturally diverse society with inherent tensions. Hence the concept of CP (A) without a behavioral commitment to the values of CP (B) turns out to be "unhappy." We find it quite odd to apply the term CP to a culturally diverse society wherein a group rejects the values and the validity of CP as a viable system for regulating group competition, assuaging rivalries, and reducing monopolies of power and vested interests through interest representation. Thus the third constraint on the use of the term CP — the third necessary condition which permits the term to be applied in one context and not in others — is a behavioral commitment to the values of CP as a basis for a viable system of social organization.

One might now argue that the ordinary language use of CP applies only when (1) cultural diversity, in the form of a number of groups — be they political, racial, ethnic, religious, economic, or age — is exhibited in the society; (2) the coexisting groups approximate equal political, economic, and educational opportunity; and (3) there is a behavioral commitment to the values of CP as a basis for a viable system of social organization.

What is involved here cannot be described easily in one or two paragraphs. The three conditions represent, among other things, inherent tensions not easily perceived or dealt with by any existing or possibly foreseen society, and these conditions are illustrated on the following pages.

Condition 1 is the most obvious. The tension here is between ensuring the viability of subcommunity organizational life while maintaining free choice for the individual. That is, the individual should be allowed to choose freely whether to remain within the confines of his birthright community enclave or to branch out or change affiliation to another group should he wish to do so. If the birthright community places very heavy pressures on its members to stay confined to the subgroup community, so much that the members remain confined to the subgroup, then we have, in effect, CP for subgroups but not for individuals.

Condition 2 is the most challenging. The tension here is between ensuring the equality of minority groups by state intervention and justifying the practice of specific discrimination in favor of or against certain individuals or groups. This tension may be illustrated as follows. It is generally accepted that the proper role of government is to effect desegregation — that is, to eliminate racial, sex, religious, and ethnic criteria — in the operation of all its facilities and services at all levels, local, state, and national. But it is also generally accepted that the proper role of government is not to interfere in any way with those personal choices in primary group relationships and organizational affiliations which make for the ordinary processes of communality, whether intra- or interethnic, religious, racial, or otherwise. An obvious solution is to grant to each group a substantial amount of power over its own affairs, but as the outcry over recent campaigns for community control of schools attests, this is more easily proposed than enacted.

Condition 3 is the most problematic. The tension here is between the virtue of tolerance and efficiency, between the "ideal" of CP and the pluralistic reality of the hyphenated-American. One of the major virtues of a flourishing pluralistic society would be its tolerance, particularly tolerance of various ethnic, religious, or cultural subgroups as the locus of the individual's participational effort in the functions of the polity, in his economic life, and in the functioning of social interests. But such a pattern may be, and is, grossly inefficient: for example, the dual languages French Canada, or the "problem" of bilingualism in the teaching of Puerto Ricans, Cubans, Chicanos, and Native Americans. How much more efficient it is to demand that all children speak the one approved language of English, but how intolerant.

There are, I believe, no clearly marked courses of action which neatly resolve the tensions mentioned. The point, in this discourse, simply has been to make the conflicting views apparent. They are dilemmas close to many of today's social problems, and they point to the need to go beyond the assumptions of CP to the underlying conflicts.

Now we can recall the claim, "I know of no culturally pluralistic society that has ever existed." Are we in a position to deal with this claim? For instance, if we take the case of Northern Ireland today, employing the conditions governing the use of CP, we determine that cultural diversity does exist, but in its fifty or so years of political life, Ulster has been governed only by Protestant Unionists. The Roman Catholic minority, although one-third of the total population, has not actually participated in Ulster's governance. Hence, the state of Ulster fails to meet condition 2. And with regard to condition 3, Ulster appears to fail. Patently, little or no behavioral commitment to the values of CP, either by the Roman Catholics or by the Protestants, exist as the bloody battle rages on.

What of the case of Canada? Condition 1 is clearly met, and as previously mentioned, condition 2 is also met. French Canadians have never been without the vote, and they enjoy approximate educational and economic opportunities. But it is condition 3 that is not met as long as the FLQ terrorists threaten the unity of the social order and continue the tactics that led to the brutal murder of Pierre Laporte in their effort to achieve an independent/monolithic French Canada.

What of the United States? Does the United States meet the

conditions of a culturally pluralistic society? The United States appears to be eligible for the following reasons: It has undergone an agonizing period of change in behavioral standards and in the affirmation of freedom of groups and the individual; it rejects a monolithic system of social organization in favor of pluralistic styles — especially in art forms, life-style, and value judgments — and promotes the coexistence of a diversity of mutually complementary alternative subcultures. At the present time the following are being promoted on a large scale: radically new approaches to moral values; a black consciousness and pride; a feminist attack on masculine domination; rejection by many young people of exclusively political, economic, and technical social goals; an insistence on economic and educational equality; many views which suggest that the natural environment is more important than commercial profit; and demands for absolute individual and cultural freedom.

To sharpen our analysis, I suggest we scrutinize condition 2 vis-à-vis American society. Surely the many diverse groups — religious and nonreligious, ethnic, racial, and geographical — in the United States enjoy approximate political equality. The recent lowering of the voting age to eighteen has extended political equality to millions more. And the Hispanic, Native American, and black American civil rights movements as well as the Bilingual Education Act are providing excellent economic and educational opportunities not heretofore had by these minority groups.[29]

But what of condition 3? Is it met? Despite the public utterances of a black separatist element in the United States, formulated in such demands as "a land of our own" and "three, four, or more black states forming a black nation," actually little has been done in this regard. The action taken by secessionist groups such as Marcus Garvey's Universal Negro Improvement Association (UNIA) or the Peace Movement of Ethiopia are

[29]The Bilingual Education Act grew out of a 584-page report entitled "Bilingual Education Programs" which was the result of hearings held by the House of Representatives, 28-29 June 1967. The purpose is to offset the economic desperation of ethnic groups who are failing to acquire labor potential because of major deficiencies in English. Also significant is HEW's Office of Civil Rights Memorandum, 25 May 1970, guaranteeing equal educational opportunity for the culturally different.

exceptions to the recent investments in land by a number of Black Muslim groups. In effect, to some blacks the idea of black nationalism is appealing and real, but within the concept of "black nationalism" (it is recognized that there are several programs of black nationalism) the goal of separatism is not supported in any real sense. Although the idea of political separatism is very special and often appears in discourse, it is not widely supported; there appears to be symbolic rather than actual support for it. In effect, there is no Black Israel for Afro-Americans.

However, we also have reason to believe that the values of CP are not subscribed to in a behavioral sense by a majority of Americans. Specifically, I refer to the values of (1) a belief in freedom of association; (2) the belief that there is no single way of life which can without question claim to be best; (3) the belief that a humane society must therefore afford room for many competing ways of life; and (4) it is good to have such ways of life in competition and in contact and that the differences between them will not be endangered by the contact between them.[30]

The reasons for this judgment are grounded in the empirical evidence of recent years issuing from broad voter dissatisfaction with busing ordinances, fair-housing ordinances, and other attempts to achieve racial balance and equality. That is to say, although the values exist as a social ideal, reality suggests that the values are merely guides, not behavioral commitments. As a social ideology, CP has the potential to encourage the meaning of democracy, but as a social reality it remains pregnant with possibilities for what might be.

With this last consideration it is conceivable to argue that the United States today represents neither a model case nor a contrary case of CP. Rather it appears to be a case in which we are not sure, a borderline example of the concept. Some will argue that it is a matter of commonplace observation that the United States has become a society of the many, of diversity. The popular prefixes of today are "hetero," "multi," and "poly"; we are somewhat ill at ease with "mono." For some, it is sufficient

[30]Green, "Education and Pluralism," p. 11.

that American society has undergone the profound and agonizing period of change mentioned previously. They view
American society as having made great gains toward achieving
the goal of a truly culturally pluralistic society actively committed to the normative aspects of CP. Others argue that the
major changes wrought in American society in the past few
decades still fail to give evidence of an American society actively committed to the normative elements of CP. They can
and do contend that American society has become even more
polarized in recent years.

What, then, is the answer to our question? Is the United
States a culturally pluralistic society? Clearly, a response to the
question is *No* if American society is seen as failing to meet
condition 3. Whether the former or the latter claim is true
should be approached as a value question. The point is that the
answer is doubtful because we are asked to assign some kind of
value to CP: We are asked whether CP is desirable or undesirable, wise or unwise, good or bad. But when we are asked to
make such a decision, before the question can be answered, it is
important to recognize that we are not dealing with a question
of fact, but with a question of concept. Until the "unpacking"
of what is meant by cultural pluralism is engaged in, until we
know the sense in which the term is being employed, we will be
in no position to deal with the question as a question of value.
Succeeding in that, when we are asked to make such a decision,
it might better be viewed as a value judgment involving standards, criteria, and principles rather than mere preferences, feelings, attitudes, or favorings. The question, then, is a matter of
judgment, a value judgment, and should be treated as such.

We thus have reached the end of a long and difficult examination of the concept of CP. We began initially with a question, Ought the PSM educate for a culturally pluralistic
society? We found that this question raised certain prior questions: Can the PSM educate for a culturally pluralistic society?
What is cultural pluralism? On the whole, this analysis of the
concept of CP is a difficult and tentative affair. Very little in
the way of a really thorough, logical investigation of the concept has been done. Nonetheless, it suggests some theoretical
and basic questions that must be asked. In the first place, it is

important to ask whether the PSM, as an instrument of the
social order, could be realistically charged with the task of
"educating for a culturally pluralistic society" when such confusion and value conflict exist relative to the concept of CP
itself in the broader society. That is, it is a value question and
value judgments are involved. It might be argued that the PSM
ought to take a neutral position in this regard, or the PSM
cannot remain neutral, and so on. Whatever the case, it is
essential for us to realize that a question of value is involved,
and as such, disagreements, uncertainties, and confusions will
plague the PSM in this regard. All this being so, it would
appear evident that anyone who seeks to understand what we
might reasonably decide to make happen in education will
perforce be obliged to think hard on the matters raised in this
chapter. And if, as most of us profess to believe, a grasp of the
communal way of life is essential to intelligent participation in
the guidance and control of human affairs, then the study of
these matters must not end with the reading of a particular
book or the completion of a course.

A PROPOSAL FOR AN ALTERNATIVE TO CP

Since I believe that the model of CP is in itself an ambiguous
one and that the belief in freedom of association of individuals
is not necessarily bound up to a culturally pluralistic society
but may be basic to another type of model, we begin in this
section by conceptualizing an alternative model to CP, one that
assumes the necessity of cultural diversity but moves beyond
cultural subgroup association to continuously emergent groups
which form over matters of shared concerns in the context of
ever-changing social, economic, and political conditions. The
major issue from this point of view is whether or not we can
find a viable model for people willing to begin serious discussion on problems and consequences rather than only on subgroup identification and goals.

To answer this we commence with the fact that the individuals who form a society at any point in time are held together
by their formal patterns of cultural participation and by the
mutual interdependence arising from their divergent social her-

itages which commonly derive from the subcultural pattern of habitual association and emotional attachments. But it is an equally important fact that the people who form a society at any point in time may be held together by a "community of interest." John Dewey claimed that "conjoint, combined, associated action is a universal trait of the behavior of things."[31] Now such a claim may strike even the casual reader as a vague, metaphysical statement. I would agree; the less said about it the better. But perhaps Dewey is less metaphysical when he argued that one such associated action is seen when " . . . interest and control are limited to those directly engaged: in the second, they extend to those who do not directly share in the performance of acts."[32] He further contended that those indirectly and seriously affected for good or evil form a group distinctive enough to require recognition and a name. The name he selected is The Public.[33]

Although Dewey was not consistent in his use of the terms *public* and *The Public,* enough consistency is evidenced to make the distinction here. The term *public* is used to refer to the community of interests of those directly engaged in an act of conjoint behavior or association. The term *The Public* refers to those who do not directly share in the performance of the acts of conjoint behavior but whose interests are involved insofar as they are affected by the actions in question. Thus, those indirectly and seriously affected by the performance of an act may form a group distinctive enough to be called The Public. When such an association endures and adds to itself political organization, The Public becomes a political state.

The terms *public* and *The Public* represent an attempt on Dewey's part to develop mediating terms to delineate the various communities of interest in the United States. Dewey sought to develop the concept of a public in such a way as to provide the basis for accounting for the pluralistic nature of American society. He realized that there are human associations too isolated or restricted in scope of operation to give rise to the formation of a public, "just as there are associations too iso-

---

[31]John Dewey, *The Public and Its Problems* (Chicago, Swallow Press, 1927), p. 34.
[32]Dewey, *Public and its Problems*, p. 35.
[33]Dewey, *Public and Its Problems*, p. 35.

lated from one another to fall within the same public."[34] But when conjoint activity is transformed into a community of interest, a public may be born. When such a community of interest involves a number of people, directly or indirectly, and consequences are foreseen, then The Public may be born. The latter, according to Dewey, is the symbol by which he represents the struggle within the United States to achieve national unity while protecting ethnic, religious, and racial diversity within a democratic framework.

This brief foray into the thought of Dewey is aimed at offering an alternative and viable model to the models of CP and the open society. When Dewey used the term *community*, one sense signified geographical or spatial marks of special places, as in "local community" and "neighborhood community." His second sense is the broader one in which he characterizes a system of human relations in a societal matrix. Thus in his discussion of the method for achievement of the "Great Community," Dewey envisaged a great emerging nation-community of shared interests, achieved through maximum development of local community institutions working in coordination with the state and national governments. He said, "The Great Community, in the sense of free and full inter-communication, is conceivable. But it can never possess all the qualities which mark a local community. It will do its final work in ordering the relations and enriching the experience of local associations."[35]

Taken literally, Dewey seems to suggest that a community of interest is necessarily a local community or, at least, found in face-to-face relations characteristic of a kind of localism. There is, however, a second plausible interpretation of this concept in his thought. This second use is a "problems" approach which takes shape in the form of various interested persons coming together to discover their commonly shared interests and values and organizing for effective pursuit of these. Dewey assumed that members of human groups share "common problems." He also contended that each or different members of any human

[34]Dewey, *Public and Its Problems*, p. 39.
[35]Dewey, *Public and Its Problems*, p. 211.

group may deny or be unable to perceive such common problems. He realized that America was only a "Great Society" because the various human groupings — the economic, religious, geographic, age, sex, occupational, political, etc. — in the culturally pluralistic American social order had been unable or unwilling to develop the methods of communication and intelligent interaction required to approximate the standard of a Great Community. That standard is, namely, the "method of intelligence" operating in the associational life patterns of the urban-industrial, technologically advancing American social order. Dewey's concept of community is, then, fundamentally the voluntary implementation of the method of intelligence.

In effect, Dewey argued that men may associate and interact for many reasons, not the least of which is cultural subgrouping. But cultural subgrouping is not always conscious, reflective action. Nor is cultural subgroup recognition of a common problem the same as mutual concern for common problems. Cultural subgroups, like any human group, may deny a common problem, or they may perceive their own special interest at the basis for dealing with the problem. Dewey was aware that what should be desirable in a social democracy may in fact not be admitted as a mutual concern by groups out to protect their interests regardless of the public consequences of their acts and without regard for the public interest. His plea was a call for an individual becoming socially mature in terms of his social interaction by exhibiting a concern for the problems of others and concern for the public consequences of his acts.

We have but touched lightly and in passing upon the ideas of Dewey, but a sense of what he dealt with comes through. "If the Great Society is to become a Great Community; a society in which the ever-expanding and intricately ramifying consequences of associated activities shall be known in the full sense of the word, so that an organized, articulate Public comes into being."[36] then a kind of social structure within which family

---

[36]Dewey, *Public and Its Problems*, p. 184.

and other primary group loyalties dominate can serve as only
the starting point. To go beyond the special interests of cultural subgroups to the forming of a public as the result of a
mutual concern for a problematic situation is the alternative
proposed here. This position may be called "dynamic pluralism." It begins with the existence of cultural subgroups with
a ready agenda of politics and values to buttress the individual
in a problematic situation, but moves beyond this situation to
the forming of publics or factions through which people give
concrete expression to a multiplicity of different, even incompatible values.

Dynamic pluralism is characterized by a commitment to the
worth of cultural diversity and factions promoting an agenda
of politics, but it goes beyond the promotion of the values of
cultural subgroups to the forming of a public as the result of a
recognition of a problematic situation having direct and indi-
rect consequences. Dynamic pluralism is thus continuously
emergent insofar as each of the society's members must reinter-
pret shared concerns and goals in the context of ever-changing
social, economic, and political conditions. To achieve an understanding of such a state of affairs requires of each citizen the
development of intellectual capacity whereby he can thought-
fully assess the relative pros and cons of the problematic situation.

Such a pluralism demands opportunity for the different factions to come together as well as a free circulation of evidence,
experience, and ideas. Recent developments such as the movements for police review boards in many cities, the sit-ins and
marches, strikes and protests by people from many different
subgroups and from many walks of life — all these and many
others are evidence of increasing dissatisfaction with the established ways of dealing with social problems and conflicts. Far
from insignificant as evidence of the viability of this position is
the recent emergence and growth of national communities of
interest in opposition to the wanton waste and abuse of natural
resources.

The working model of dynamic pluralism is the "concerned
community of interest" of Dewey. It views as both necessary

and good that the policy agenda and the public interest be
defined in terms of communities of interest, are necessarily
homogeneously organized groups, rather easy to define, quite
often monolithic, and that any duly elected spokesperson for
any interest can speak in close approximation for each and
every member.

Out of this discussion emerges the recognition that dynamic
pluralism offers the advantage of preserving the value of
freedom of association and diversity in society. The very existence of many communities of interest is ample testimony to
that claim. Also, it expresses other values of pluralism. For
example, it is a form of free association not only for groups but
for the individual as well. The fact that this is a consequence of
this concept is not an empirical fact; it is simply a logical
consequence of this type. That is, it contains the belief that a
democratic society must afford room for many competing "interests." The least evident, yet perhaps the most important,
aspect of this type is its valuing of consensus problem solving,
with a strong reliance on the logical, rational evidential
avenues of decision making.

But how does dynamic pluralism differ from structural assimilation (Green's "make-believe" pluralism)? I would like to
suggest in the strongest possible way that, though the two
concepts are similar in one important aspect, they differ in at
least two crucial respects.

The two concepts are alike insofar as both suggest the insig-
nificance or relative unimportance of cultural, racial, ethnic,
and religious subgroup affiliation as the sole determinant of
the individual's participation in the civic arena. They suggest,
in other words, explicitly and implicitly, that cultural differences are unimportant, at least to any matter of practical concern in the polity. But structural assimilation posits a negation
or denigration of matters of, say, religious distinction. As structural assimilation occurs in a society, the inevitable happens.
"The Jew has less identity as a Jew, the Catholic less as a
Catholic, and even the Episcopalian."[37] Consequently, the

---

[37]Green, "Education and Pluralism," p. 21.

sense a person has of historical cultural identity becomes less and less viable, less and less valid. In a word, religious backgrounds and affiliations are regarded as divisive, and the hyphenation, for example, of the Jewish-American is seen not only as reflecting the fact that the individual is a hyphenated type — that he is part Jewish and part American — but that the hyphen is seen as separating rather than connecting.

Dynamic pluralism, on the other hand, recognizes the existence and role of subgroup pluralisms in American society, and it assumes pluralistic interests and values as the starting points for establishing "communities of interest." This point can be seen in the following. Whenever a problematic situation arises, it is in doubt because of conflicting, often mutually exclusive, interests. If there exists no commitment on the part of the individual to a particular value, then it is unlikely that the individual's participation in resolving a problematic situation will likely occur. A community of interest cannot emerge when there is no commitment on anyone's part to anything. Surely, a problematic situation, if it is to be resolved by those who are and should be most interested, cannot exist unless persons are committed to some point of view. That individuals first identify themselves with regard to primary group relations and, quite often, with a subgroup or subgroups, is well documented. This initial commitment is the essential starting point for developing a community of interest. Subgroup-associated behavior may be converted into a community of interest by a desire to find and sustain a shared meaning, common values, and commitment to common purpose.

Dynamic pluralism differs from structural assimilation in another important aspect. Structural assimilation, in denying or denigrating the heritage of cultural subgroups, would assign to the PSM the task of mitigating or softening the individual's cultural heritage. In the case of religion, for example, the PSM would not take into account the development of religious thought and institutions in the colonial and national state experience. In the case of ethnicity, the PSM would not take into account the contributions of immigrants following the great waves of migration by which America was built up over

three centuries. Viewing religion and ethnic group backgrounds and affiliations as divisive, these would be, at worst,
played down, and at best eradicated.

Dynamic pluralism, on the other hand, although not hon-
oring cultural values as good in themselves — as ends in themselves — demands the taking into account of these as the PSM
attempts to teach each faction to respect each other, but emphasizing these values as the mere starting points, the ini-
tiating elements, of a problematic situation which will
inevitably arise. Teachers should know how to recognize, discuss, appraise, and resolve value conflicts in the classroom.
They will thus teach an appreciation of diverse values and will
broaden the students' cultural perspectives, but, in a larger
sense, the PSM will have the special responsibility of guiding
the decision-making process of students with respect to
pointing out hidden assumptions of racial inferiority, the inherent tensions between subgroup enclaves and the larger society, and will oppose prejudice and discrimination. In the last
analysis, the struggle to eliminate racial, ethnic, religious, and
cultural prejudice and discrimination from American life must
go on against the underlying social reality of diverse cultural
subgroups tenaciously maintaining their identities and values
in today's society.

It seems, in short, that dynamic pluralism can occur only
under certain rather specific conditions. In the first place, the
society must contain many cultural subgroups designed to
permit, even encourage, the expression of different value commitments in individual behavior. This means that the PSM, a
society that takes pluralism seriously, would have to provide
not only different curricula and different career choices for
students, but varied and in-depth opportunities for students to
discuss the importance of learning, work, and leisure: how
we become members of a community in terms of perceived consequences of conjoint activity; what effect signs and symbols
have in human associational activity; the nature of communication and its shaping power; and above all, the need for
each student to understand the various viewpoints of other

ethnic, cultural, and religious associations.

Not even this, however, is sufficient. The second condition that must be met in dynamic pluralism is that the alternative value and interest choices involved must be fundamental enough to reflect different points of view vis-à-vis a problematic situation, but those differences must not be so fundamental as to be nontransformable or nonnegotiable. When interest and values, behaviorally expressed, are not regarded as significant, then we do not have a condition for pluralism, but a likeness or sameness in values. And when interests and values are held so strongly that they are not considered transformable, then we do not have a condition for establishing a community of interest.

We thus reach our conclusion. Now that the immigrant tide has subsided, now that we recognize and understand the plight and goals of minority groups in the United States today, now that we comprehend the inherent tensions and difficulties involved in a pluralist model, it is time to commit ourselves to more than a bland tolerance of interest and value differences which denies that diversity represents anything serious. Ethnic and religious origins may not be as important as they once were, but they exist, and in some aspects they may and do contribute to the scope of those areas of free choice guaranteed by democratic values. As has been suggested here, some individuals have their identity rooted in subgroup organizational life, and some minority-group members fear the loss of their respective groups' unique contributions to American life and culture if a single melting-pot model or an open-society model is adopted. Dynamic pluralism takes these aspects into account and offers to all individuals and groups the opportunity to branch out or move away from the strictures of subgroup factions to communities of interest which have as the main justifying function the employment of man's essential powers — including human dignity and respect, and making men responsible by developing their powers of deliberate action. These gains, it would seem, are a small price to pay for the impact of unsettling the relations of school and community that may be visited upon the PSM in particular and society in general.

CONCLUSION

Looking back in American social history, especially with the aid of ex post facto experience, it would be hard to deny that Americans have not adopted ideologies of cultural diversity simply because they have been available. They have embraced them only when it has become socially advantageous, economically feasible, or politically necessary. For example, Anglo-conformism served a nation fearful of being engulfed by waves of immigrants; the melting-pot ideology mitigated the concern of immigrant children who feared for the loss of their ancestral heritage; and cultural pluralism offered to subgroups, be they ethnic, religious, or racial, a world of self-respect and inherent tensions.

It is due time, or well past it, to devise a way out of traditional demeaning and subservience to racial, religious, and ethnic labeling and to look toward a new model that is both "conserving" and "liberal" in the everyday use of those terms. Dynamic pluralism is conservative in that it guarantees the right of any individual in the social order to ethnic, religious, or racial communality. But it is liberal insofar as it goes beyond the strictures of subcultural values to broader group relations where criteria of objective judgment and assignment are primary and where the subgroups are given passing consideration. The attainment of this objective calls for good sense and reasonableness on the part of all Americans as well as making it a primary concern of the PSM. Thus, the original question has become, Ought the PSM educate for a dynamic pluralism in American society?

Chapter Six

CULTURAL PLURALISM AND ITS RELATIVISTIC COMPONENT*

INTRODUCTION

CULTURAL pluralism is important to social thought in at least two ways. First, it may be used in justifying the overriding concern for cultural and self-interest groups who wish to share more fully in the goods and services of American society. Second, institutional authorities are pressured on many fronts either to take greater account of cultural pluralism or to suppress it altogether. Hence, the following comments regarding cultural pluralism will be shown to have significant consequences for the way in which policy making may be affected and the way society's commitment to the provision of cultural pluralism might be formulated. The comments about cultural pluralism will revolve around an explication of how cultural pluralism is intimately connected to ethnicity, and how both cultural pluralism and ethnicity have a relativistic component.

CULTURAL PLURALISM: A NEED FOR PERSPECTIVE

There is growing interest in cultural pluralism (hereinafter CP) among American politicians and political scientists as well as among those who are not specifically and practically concerned with social problems and policies. CP is not, of course, a new term, but varying degrees of confusion have surrounded the concept since its first realization by Horace M. Kallen. In 1915, it will be recalled, Kallen hopefully prognosticated the realization of CP in the United States as the following:

. . . the outlines of a possible great and truly democratic com-

---

*Adapted from *Review Journal of Philosophy and Social Science*, 1(1, 2), 1976.

monwealth becomes discernible. Its form would be that of the federal republic; its substance a democracy of nationalities, cooperating voluntarily and autonomously through common institutions in the enterprise of self-realization through the perfection of men according to their kind. The common language of the commonwealth, the language of its great tradition, would be English, but each nationality would have for its emotional and voluntary life its own peculiar dialect or speech, its own individual and inevitable ethical and intellectual forms. The political and economic life of the commonwealth is a single unit and serves as the foundation and the background for the realization of the distinctive individuality of each *natio* [sic] that composes it and of the pooling of these in a harmony above them all. Thus, "American civilization" may come to mean the perfection of the cooperative harmonies of "European civilization" — the waste, the squalor and the distress of Europe being eliminated — a multiplicity in a unity, an orchestration of mankind.[1]

Kallen's overly optimistic characterization of CP as America stood at a kind of cultural crossroad early in this century rested squarely on the *fact* that the form of government of the United States is that of a federal republic and on the *ideal* of various ethnic cultures working harmoniously within the framework of a democratic society. A corollary of this view is that each of the ethnic cultures has something positive, something of value, to contribute to American democractic life. Finally, Kallen maintained that the idea of democracy, in the words of the *Constitution*, of "all men being created equal," carries an implicit assumption that there are ostensible differences between persons and groups that can be viewed as "equal." In the face of WASP domination, Kallen attempted to prove that CP — freedom for groups and unity through diversity — was the real meaning of American democracy.

The social·theory of CP has been one of the central themes in the literature on minority groups in the United States.[2] Funda-

---

[1]Horace M. Kallen, *Culture and Democracy in the United States* (New York, Boni and Liveright, 1924), p. 124.

[2]Nathan Glazer, "Ethnic Groups in America: From National Culture to Ideology," in Monroe Berger, Theodore Abel, and Charles H. Page, eds., *Freedom and Control in Modern Society* (New York: Van Nostrand Reinhold, 1954); Nathan Glazer and Daniel Patrick Moynihan, *Beyond the Melting Pot*, 2nd ed., (Cambridge, Mass., MIT Press,

mentally, cultural pluralists contend that, over time, ethnic groups should maintain their differences and American life will be enriched by their effort. But it has become apparent that the United States has not become over the passage of sixty years or so "a democracy of nationalities, cooperating voluntarily and autonomously through common institutions." Nor are the relationships which exist among the various cultural, racial, and national groups conducive to "self-realization through perfection of men according to their own kind." Cultural assimilation for many white ethnic groups has occurred; thus we have, for example, Italian-Americans, Polish-Americans, and Irish-Americans. But many minority groups, particularly blacks, Hispanics, and Native Americans, have remained outsiders, omitted from participating in the "orchestration of mankind," at least in American society.

In the case of the nonwhite groups in American society the reasons are analyzed by sociologist Robert Blauner as follows:

> The fundamental issue is historical. People of color have never been an integral part of the Anglo-Saxon political community and culture because they did not enter the dominant society in the same way as did the European ethnics. The third world notion points *to a basic distinction between immigration and colonization as the two major processes through which new population groups are incorporated into a nation.* Immigrant groups enter a new territory or society voluntarily, they may be pushed out of their old-country by dire economic or political oppression. Colonized groups become part of a new society through force or violence. They are conquered, enslaved, or pressured into movement. Thus, the third world formulation is a bold attack on the myth that America is the land of the free or, more specifically, a nation

1970); Milton Gordon, *Assimilation in American Life* (New York, Oxford University Press, 1964); Thomas F. Gossett, *Race: The History of an Idea in America* (Dallas, Tex., Southern Methodist University Press, 1963); Oscar Handlin, *The Uprooted* (New York, Grosset & Dunlap, 1951); Maldwyn Allen Jones, *American Immigration* (Chicago, University of Chicago Press, 1960); Harold Abramson, *Ethnic Pluralism in the Central City* (Storrs, Conn., Institute for Urban Research of the University of Connecticut, 1970); Christopher Jencks et al., *Inequality: A Reassessment of the Effect of Family and Schooling in America* (New York, Basic Books, 1972); Peter Rose, ed., *Nation of Nations: The Ethnic Experience and the Racial Crisis* (New York, Random House, 1972); Peter Schrag, *The Decline of the WASP* (New York, Simon and Schuster, 1971); Melvin Steinfield, *Cracks in the Melting Pot* (Beverly Hills, Glencoe Press, 1970).

whose population has been built up through successive waves of immigration. The third world perspective returns to the origins of the American experience, reminding us that this nation owes its very existence to colonialism, and that along with settlers and immigrants there have always been conquered Indians and Black slaves, and later defeated Mexicans — that is colonial subjects — on the national soil.[3]

It is precisely this point that bears so mightily on today's rediscovered CP. During the 1960s to the present there has been a considerable amount of attention and debate given to the fact that a pluralistic pattern remains significant in American life. In simple terms, the ethnic, racial, and religious enclaves of American society have not totally disappeared. First- and third-generation groups reveal a pattern of CP.[4] Ethnicity, not a new term to be sure, is currently prevalent. Where cultural, racial, and national groups were formerly viewed as regrettable survivals from an earlier period, to be treated with disdain or sympathy, there is now a growing sense that not only are such groups necessary but they may be the forms of social life most capable and worthy of saving the American form of government and its espoused values.[5]

One may wonder, What about this ethnic resurgence? Does it capture a new reality, or is it simply a revived way of expressing something old, perhaps primordial? One way of getting at the problem is to recognize that to many Americans today CP seems to express accurately the current wave of ethnic feeling which is sweeping over the United States. CP appears to those in search of a new ideology as the proper substitution for class ties that have been weakened, a lost faith and pride in our national destiny, a flawed sense of identity and common purpose that being a worker was once to be able to supply, and so on. In short, behind the rise or resurgence of CP is the

[3]Robert Blauner, *Racial Oppression in America* (New York, Harper & Row, 1973), p. 52 (italics in original).

[4]William M. Dobriner, *Class in Suburbia* (Englewood Cliffs, N.J., Prentice-Hall, 1963); Herbert Gans, *The Urban Villagers* (New York, Free Press, 1962); *see* also Gans's *The Levittowners* (New York, Pantheon, 1967).

[5]Michael Novak, a liberal Catholic intellectual of Slovak origin, regards ethnicity "as something larger than self." See *The Rise of the Unmeltable Ethnic* (New York, Macmillan, 1971).

current anomie in American society — more specifically, a rising crime and delinquency rate, an energy crisis, rising inflation, a crisis in political leadership both at home and abroad, and findings that suggest a general loss of confidence in the American Dream. It is this development that must be understood alongside the postwar assertion of rights by many previously "omitted" or "left-out" groups — blacks, Hispanics, and others — which has spawned defensive counterclaims and countermobilization on the part of white ethnic groups who feel most directly threatened by the demands of the previously "omitted." Finally, government, the newly and vastly enlarged welfare state, has become the center of decision making concerning everything from housing through schooling to abortion that profoundly touches the interests of all groups. The government's apparent willingness to deal with groups of citizens on the strength of their ethnic backgrounds has strengthened interest group resolve to organize or mobilize along racial or cultural lines.[6]

We are no longer a nation of "closet ethnics"; many are busy searching through the ancestral tree in search of some special ethnic identity. The upshot of this phenomenon has been nowhere more apparent than on television. First, there was Archie Bunker, who was certainly no closet bigot, then came "Sanford and Son," Chico, Rhoda, Kojak, Florida, the Jeffersons, Horshack, the Montefuscos, and so on.

It is important, therefore, to recognize that today's resurgent ethnicity suggests the past experiences of oppressed minorities as merely the starting point of a political and economic strategy calculated to cash in on today's rapidly changing political situation, particularly the role played by the federal government. The common elements fashioning today's CP are the crucial considerations of deprivation, powerlessness, alienation, frustration, and the like. In the not too distant past, such conditions were viewed largely in terms of an individual-personal

---

[6]It seems that those groups who have been historically subject to discrimination, largely on the basis of race, have taken this negative situation and transformed it into a powerful weapon of positive action. Blacks, Hispanics, and others are declaring that ethnicity is "beautiful," not just aesthetically but politically. The force of this is seen insofar as "we the people" of the Constitution is reinterpreted to mean "we the peoples" or definable groups.

162   *Pluralism in Education*

discontent, and help was sought from relatives and friends. But today individual-personal discontent has been replaced with collective-political discontent, and ethnic groups seek significant power to harness the sources of discontent and to establish a political and economic base under the emotive slogan of CP.

What is significant about this "retribalization" is that in the CP advocated today, the older view that interest should guide reason in social decision making and such interest was determined by economic position has dramatically shifted to the view that interest should guide social decision making, but the economic and social interests of the members of a cultural, racial, or national group are paramount. In other words, curiously, *the interest-defined group of today is behaving as an ethnic group, whereas in the past the ethnic group behaved as an interest group.*

What needs clarifying here is that in the earlier Americanization movement culturally diverse groups were perjoratively "labeled" ethnics by the older established Americans who claimed a cultural superiority. European immigrants were told explicitly and implicitly how much they differed from the host or dominant culture. Such a labeling rarely accommodated ethnic identification and human dignity marching hand in hand. It was a process of cultural debasement and gross prejudice.

In the shift from a group being "labeled" ethnic to a group asserting its ethnicity is the fact that today's ethnics themselves elect to make certain criteria count in establishing differences, but today the criteria are not necessarily culture, language, religion, and nationality; rather they are of the ascriptive sort, and should be recognized as such. Ethnicity appeals to and is fast taking hold among many Americans who know they cannot shake or be rid of certain identifying characteristics such as skin color or sex. Thus, the phenomenon of "retribalization" is indicative of more than a resurgent ethnicity; something larger is taking place. It is caught, in part, by what we have been referring to, namely, "retribalization" — the return to ascriptive rather than achieved characteristics as determinants of social stratification. Moreover, as Daniel Bell put it, "Ethnicity has become more salient than class because it can combine an interest with an affective tie. . . . "[7] Apparently, the strategic efficacy of ethnicity is seen as a major focus for the mobilization of a group's interest. It is recognized as an effective strategy for asserting claims against the dominant institutions of society, for any oppressed group has a good chance of changing the system if it is able to raise the communal consciousness of its individual members.

Hence, ethnicity, and the ideology of CP that rationalizes it, has considerable utility in the minds of many today. CP is defended on the grounds that cultural diversity is good insofar as a society is enriched by a varied population because such groups extend the range of interests and human interaction. Secondly, CP enhances the right of the individual to be different; such individuality challenges sameness and blandness. Hence, any conflicts that appear to disrupt the existing social order are to be seen as meaningful attempts to reorder society. The socially significant aspect of CP as ideology is the degree to which it is claimed to be an attempt to redefine, or better, the social order in terms of reaching a new, changed social consensus.

The conclusion we can draw with regard to the question, Why the rise of CP? is given, at least in part, by the recognition that CP is a fashionable ideology that supports cultural diversity, including ethnicity, as a basis for group mobilization, and legitimizes demands made by cultural and ethnic groups.

ETHNIC COMMUNALITY, CP, AND CULTURAL DEMOCRACY

We turn now to what was implicit in the foregoing — the argument that ethnic communality is a clear case of CP and CP is "cultural democracy" at its best. The Kallen argument was supportive of pluralism in an America which reveled in ethnic communality, and he proclaimed that ethnicity is the basis for democratic association. In short, ethnic communality is considered to be a necessary condition for CP, and, historically, the

---

[7]See Nathan Glazer and Daniel Moynihan, "Why Ethnicity," *Commentary,* 58 (October): 36, 1974.

struggle to eliminate racial and religious prejudice and discrimination from American life has marched step-by-step with
the glorification of ethnic communality. The relationship of
"cultural democracy" — a society in which all groups maintain
their communal identity and are rewarded for so doing — and
ethnic identity is programmatively interwoven. Green, it will
be recalled, previously argued that CP, as a social ideal,

> ... involves a belief in freedom of association. Secondly, it
> contains the belief that there is no single way of life which
> can without question claim to be best; thirdly, it implies the
> belief that a humane society must afford room for many com-
> peting ways of life. And, finally, the ideal of pluralism im-
> plies that it is good to have such ways of life in competition
> and in contact and that the differences between them will not
> be endangered but enhanced by the contact between them.[8]

The value commitments itemized by Green suggest what has
been commonly referred to as "cultural democracy." Implied is
a kind of "equality without conformity," or a spirit of "universal brotherhood."

The struggle to eliminate racial and religious discrimination
in American life, i.e. to make incarnate cultural democracy,
involves opportunity for the different ethnic factions to come
together so that, in Green's words, "the differences between
them will not be endangered but enhanced by the contact between them." Perhaps the argument for ethnic communality,
CP, and cultural democracy will be best served if made explicit
as follows:

  (i) If ethnic communality represents CP, then ethnic com-
      munality is cultural democracy.

 (ii) Ethnic communality is CP.
      Therefore,

(iii) Ethnic communality is cultural democracy.

What needs to be teased out of the argument are the following presuppositions:

1. Ethnic communality rests principally on personal choices

---

[8]Thomas F. Green, "Education and Pluralism: Ideal and Reality" (Twenty-Sixth Annual
J. Richard Street Lecture, Syracuse University School of Education, 1966), p. 11.

in primary group relations and private organization affiliations.

2. CP posits the right of self-interest groups of various forms to maintain their communal identity and their own subcultural values.

3. Cultural democracy is the legitimation of group choice of whether to fuse or remain separate in society.

The inevitable vagueness of the key terms of the presuppositions requires a judgment about whether the facts warrant asserting these presuppositions. For example, in any society communality rests in large part in affiliation that is not challenged. The group constrains and restricts its members by intimidation, indoctrination, shame, guilt, and other coercive methods. And with only moderate concern one may point out that even if we accept the truth of the *first presupposition*, don't the democratic values of "cultural democracy" prescribe free choice not only for groups but for individuals? With enough ingenuity we might consider a scene in which an ethnic asserts himself, saying, "I wish not to be a Jew, or a Catholic, or a Protestant, or an Indian; I am a person." He tries then to branch out by moving away from his ethnic enclave, but feels intimidated and subject to feelings of personal guilt and, therefore, rather than continue to experience considerable psychological discontent, he returns to the confines of his ethnic community to remain ethnically enclosed forever. In short, the individual, as he matures and reaches the age when rational decision is feasible, should be allowed to choose freely whether to remain within the boundaries of communality created by his birthright ethnic group, to branch out into multiple interethnic contacts, or even to change affiliation to that of another ethnic group should he wish to do so.

With regard to the *second* and *third presuppositions*, while it is true that CP has the advantage of preserving the distinctiveness of different groups in a society by maximizing the means of maintaining their communal identity, it fails to include any kind of continuing and functional contact among groups. In this regard, CP can be and is a threat to the unity of the society, producing a tendency for groups to constitute a threat to the social order insofar as exclusivist groups exhibit tendencies strong enough to offer a divisive threat.

However, the truth of the first premise is precisely what is at issue here. Does ethnic communality represent CP? Mainstream pluralists generally acknowledge that ethnicity is a basis for group association, but they see its political salience fading rapidly in any country that fosters democratic, individualist participation together with a wide distribution of society's goods and services. Some see a persistent gap between the values of CP, those that Green so clearly enunciated, and an ethnic communality that promotes groupism and conformism, particularly with warring ethnic enclaves. The vulgar extremes to which ethnicity has been taken and the unscrupulous uses to which it has been put to deny children free access to better schools has put the notion that ethnic communality is CP and that it represents cultural democracy seriously in jeopardy. If tolerance is basic to CP and to cultural democracy, it may be that when ethnics talk of tolerance, they mean tolerance not of other individuals but of the groups to which they belong.

The soundness of the argument is, however, less of a preoccupation with those who wish to forcefully assert their position than is its effectiveness. The often preeminent position of effectiveness over soundness considerations is best explained by a search for meaning and direction in the midst of wide-range change and confusion. To be ethnic is to be deprived in some way of mobility and power. In this sense, both mainstream or historically identified ethnics as well as dissidents agree not only on the need for ethnic solidarity but on the legitimacy of ethnic demands. If a widely accepted pluralism stimulates and helps ethnics achieve political and economic gains, then the proposition that ethnicity, CP, and cultural democracy are intimately connected will not be easily denied. But until ethnic communality is considered to be a position wherein individual human beings associate and the group has no reality apart from the individuals who belong to it, ethnic communality will not achieve the collective entity called cultural democracy. Individuals will continue to be denied and, likewise, individual opportunity and fulfillment as the legitimate ends of the cultural democracy. Democracy and public spirit must stem from individual interests and actions; groups and groupism tend to deny these.

CULTURAL PLURALISM AND RELATIVISM

Within the last decade or so, the revitalization of CP has been supported by various passions. First, there is the pluralist account of politics that entails a rivalry between interests. It starts from the premise that members of groups with distinctive interests will tend to act politically in a way conducive to advancing those interests, and it assumes that the more equality of power is approached the more nearly will there be equality of consideration of interests. But, above all, in CP there is the love of self-interest. For many today, it is not necessary to take seriously the claims of others in political and economic matters. States of mind, such as envy, greed, pity, fear, and remorse, may dominate as motivational channels along which the concern for one's own interests may flow. They also provide the incentives for any individual to make up his mind about the alternatives open to him. To demand that people should think things through to explore the "common good" or "common interest" is to ask more than the situation allows. The activity of resurgent ethnicity group interest is paramount, and it need not be informed and sensitized by knowledge of other views.

Second, and this is a corollary of the first point, CP is a device for giving leverage to one's views or demands. It is presupposed that, *ceteris paribus*, any ethnic demand is legitimate and is to be taken seriously. If a person is going to benefit with regard to reaping more of society's goods and services, nothing else save some special characteristic of one or another can be given which relevantly differentiates one claimant from the others, but that characterization cannot be made on the basis of any special *a priori* set of rules or regulations.

The positive side of the legitimacy of all ethnic demands is the assertion that "all claims are valid and no important consideration of claims can be immediately judged." This means that agreement about which claims are to be accepted is not to be had. Thus, conscious, explicit attempts must be made to develop some form of public test to decide between competing group interests. Obviously, such a position invites disagreement about the type of considerations that are to count as deciding in the public arena, and political debate and decision making are tremendously handicapped. On the negative side, not only can no adjudication of demands be dealt with easily, but society is likely to tear itself to pieces in the process. There seems to be no way of allowing all demands as legitimate and devising and regulating a political process so that it leads to a just outcome for everyone.

A third reason for the resurgence of CP is its close, almost inseparable in the minds of many, connection to relativism. In its main outline, relativism takes the form "X is good" and expands it to read "X is approved by ———." For certain cases the word "approved" may give way to some other attitude-designating term, such as "liked," "favored," or "esteemed." Essentially, it is assumed that people's judgments vary, differing from place to place and from time to time. Hence, the statement "X is good," expresses the more expanded sense "X is good, comparatively or relatively speaking." Given any specific judgment of the form, "X is good," there is one and only one sort of reason that is sufficient to justify it, namely, "X is good because the society in which I live agrees that it is or approves of it."

It is commonplace, of course, that "X is good" reduces to "X is considered good in a certain society." It is commonplace insofar as it is believed that things or states of affairs considered good by some people are not considered good by others. Hence, "X is considered good in $society_1$, and considered not good in $society_2$."

Actually, we must distinguish two aspects or elements of relativism. First, there is *cultural relativism* or the view that in different cultures the same action or thing (or same kind of action or thing) is judged differently. And the cause of this divergence is that the people who make the judgments come from different cultures. And second, there is *ethical relativism* or the view that accepts the thesis of cultural relativism and, in addition, contends that in each of the respective cultures the judgments made by the members of that culture are correct.

The differences between the two positions is immensely important and is reflected in the following. Cultural relativism is a causal theory which accounts for the fact of moral disagreements in different cultures in terms of the differences in cultures. In this sense it is empirical theory, for the common argument used to establish this view rests on the evidence of cultural anthropologists and social psychologists showing that ethical and value judgments of different people and societies are different.

This point is of extraordinary importance. The relativism which supports CP is promoted and accepted because it seems a correct position which accounts for certain facts, i.e. that in different cultures the same action or thing is judged differently, and the cause of this divergence is that the people who make the judgments come from different cultures. But the problem arises from a deplorable confusion which mistakes cultural relativism (empirical theory) with ethical relativism (philosophical theory) concerning the grounds which warrant moral claims. Put differently, the confusion centers around the difference between the causes of belief (cultural relativism) and the reasons or arguments which warrant moral claims (ethical relativism). The misunderstanding involved in promoting relativism as supportive of CP can be viewed as resulting from confusing a causal explanation of behavior (cultural relativism) with a justification or moral action in terms of reason (ethical relativism).

Our concern here is with the claim that there is no objectively valid rational way of justifying basic ethical or value judgments one against another. This claim is a tempting one, widely subscribed to, and accounts for the widespread appeal of ethnic demands. It is not, of course, cultural relativism, but ethical relativism that is being considered.

Michael Scriven explained it as follows:

The confusion of *pluralism*, of the proper tolerance for diversity of ideas, with *relativism* — the doctrine that there are no right and wrong answers in ethics or religion — is perhaps the most serious ideological barrier to the implementation of moral education today. . . . Pluralism requires respecting the right to *hold* divergent beliefs; it implies *neither* tolerance of *actions* based on those beliefs *nor* respecting the *content* of the beliefs. Some actions are morally indefensible, even if done "in conscience" — that is, because dictated by our beliefs (e.g., sacrificing one's children to one's gods); and some beliefs are false, even if we respect the right of people to hold them (e.g., the belief that there is a supreme being who requires the sacrificial killing of his follower's children). There is an objectivity of fact — not a perfect objectivity of knowledge — on which ethics must be built, or rot away. It does not justify intolerance, but neither does it justify relativism or a moral education that teaches relativism or implies it.[9]

It is this connection of pluralism with relativism that is the issue here. The point is that Scriven suggests in what he calls "relativism" that no actions are either right or wrong. From this it follows that nothing we do is moral and nothing immoral and that everything is permitted and nothing morally forbidden or obligatory. Moreover, it follows that there are no correct ethical standards, because if there were, then the actions they required would be morally obligatory, and the actions they forbid would be morally prohibited.

Scriven, of course, takes offense at the relativistic doctrine "that there are no right and wrong answers in ethics or religion." He contends that it is simply not the case, arguing that there is "an objectivity of fact . . . on which ethics must be built. . . ." Such an objectivity of fact, for Scriven, "does not justify intolerance, but neither does it justify relativism or a moral education that teaches relativism or implies it."

In general, however, it is helpful to see what Scriven's position suggests for CP. First, CP is a form of pluralism, which Scriven defines as "the proper tolerance for diversity of ideas." Hence, CP can be modified to imply that in any social dispute a diversity of ideas is to be properly tolerated, and relativism —

[9]Michael Scriven, "Cognitive Moral Education," *Phi Delta Kappan, 61* (10, June): 689-694, 1975 (italics in original).

the doctrine that there are no right and wrong answers in ethics or religion (one is tempted to say in *ethnics* or religion) — serves as its rational support. The social interest in this identity of pluralism with relativism is crucial. The notion of relativism is related both to the expression "What's right for you is not always right for me" and "There are no right and wrong answers in anything." Where these intersect, controversy and conflict ensue. The rise of various ethnic groups has been judged by many writers to have aggravated such conflict because of their increasing reliance upon CP as a defense of ethnicity as well as favoring either expression of relativism. Even where we have reason to suppose a group's beliefs and demands regarding these to be bizarre, at least from *our* standpoint, we are uneasy and defensive, upon reflection, to take account of the group's goals as irrational because of the persuasiveness of the view that implies both "What's right for you is not always right for me" and "There are no right and wrong answers in ethics or religion."

This is the heart of the problem. Today's CP has been broadened to suggest that in any social dispute no group need necessarily submit its demands to the judgment of others. That is, demands cast in the mold of ethnicity by pluralists are supported and cushioned by the ready acknowledgment that such demands cannot be circumscribed by objective data. The presumption remains: Ethnicity is more than an enduring fact of American life; it is CP in its most realizable form, and all ethnic demands are *prima facie* legitimate because there is a most intimate connection between CP and relativism.

The above presupposition views the demands of ethnics, in the name of CP, not to be limited by political choices and patterns based on an artificial ordering of priorities made by those in control of society's resources whose policy prevents various groups from gaining the resources they need to compete in society. Not only does ethnicity challenge the established social order, but it seems to rest on an impregnable position. This fact has been noted by Nathan Glazer:

> In short, with regard to the question of whether the new

ethnicity is serious, my conclusion is that we (that is, informed public opinion) have given up the claim to know how to answer it. No matter how extreme or outlandish it may seem to begin with, if the demand is raised, persisted in, finds adherents, it *is* serious, or as serious as anything becomes in this world. There is no universal arbiter who decides which ethnic demands are serious and just and which are not, who honor those of the blacks, Mexican-Americans, Puerto Ricans, American Indians, on the one hand, and rejects those of the Poles, the Irish, and the Italians on the other. Maybe there should be such an arbiter, but we would be deceiving ourselves to believe that there is.[10]

Glazer takes the position that acknowledges not only the seriousness of ethnic demands, but sees its political salience quite clearly. To be ethnic is to be acknowledged as having legitimate and serious demands. We might present this point more succinctly. Ethnic communality as an expression of CP encourages the view that any demand, if cast in the mold of ethnicity, is serious, and legitimate. The argument is as follows:

(i) If a demand is an ethnic one, then that demand is legitimate.

(ii) Demands are made by ethnics.
Therefore,

(iii) Ethnic demands are legitimate.

In this argument, ethnicity is cloaked with an impregnable status giving ethnic demands a legitimacy. With this newly altered status ethnic demands do not allow of a universal or objective scale against which they can be measured. We can state the argument more cogently as follows:

(i) All ethnic demands are legitimate.

(ii) No ethnic demand is illegitimate.

(iii) *Therefore,*
If all ethnic demands are legitimate, then no ethnic demands are to be denied.

(iv) All ethnic demands are legitimate.
Therefore,

[10]Nathan Glazer, "Ethnicity and the Schools," *Commentary,* 58 (September): 58, 1974.

(v) No ethnic demands are to be denied.

If we reflect for a moment on the above argument we can see that the notion of restraint in the pursuit of narrow or group-interested ends is removed. But the argument leaves entirely open what it is that legitimizes an ethnic demand. That is, ethnic demands are not *prima facie* legitimate, they must derive their legitimacy from some argument not previously given. The point is then to ask, Whence the legitimacy?

Much of the force of justifying ethnic demands as legitimate stems from relativism, particularly the claim "What's right for you is not always right for me." Because this claim seems to be true, many of us become convinced of the legitimacy of ethnic demands. But this is an ambiguous claim, and those interpretations of it which are readily acceptable are not those which imply ethical relativism. For instance, one interpretation of "What's right for you is not always right for me" is the following:

> The right action for you is not always the right action for me. This interpretation is often true because two people are often quite different, but there is an inherent ambiguity in this. For example, if you are a good swimmer and I cannot swim, then in the same situation where each sees a child drowning, it is right for you to swim to help the child, but right for me to run off for help. But although what each of us ought to do in this same situation differs, it is still true *that both of us should do our best to help the child.* There is nothing relative about this.[11]

What we must do is avoid confusion concerning the distinction between the *relativism of ethical actions* and the *relativism of ethical standards*.[12] The former assumes that actions are in some situations right and in some situations wrong. The latter assumes that ethical standards are in some situations correct and in some situations incorrect. In the consideration of the drowning child, we see the basic characterization of action relativism, not standard relativism. Both adults in that situation applied the same standard, namely, that both were obliged

---

[11] James W. Cornman and Keith Lehrer, *Philosophical Problems and Arguments: An Introduction* (New York, Macmillan, 1974), p. 432 (italics added).
[12] Cornman and Lehrer, *Philosophical Problems and Arguments*, p. 433.

174 *Pluralism in Education*

to help the child. Thus, and this is crucial, there can be a relativism of right actions without relativism of ethical standards.

Hence, on this interpretation of "What's right for you is not always right for me," action relativism is expressed, ". . . but because ethical relativism concerns standard relativism and because action relativism does not imply standard relativism, this often true claim does not imply ethical relativism."[13]

The claim, then, that "What's right for you is not always right for me" is not the basis of ethnic demands. Rather, it is the claim that *there is no objectively valid way of justifying basic ethical or value judgments*. The common argument used to establish the case for this claim rests on the evidence of cultural anthropologists. While it is true that the same action or thing is judged differently in different cultures, it is a major and unwarranted jump from the description of existing relativism to the claim that no objectively valid rational way of justifying basic ethical or value judgments exists. To prove the validity of this jump, according to William K. Frankena, "One must also prove that people's basic ethical and value judgments would differ and conflict even if they were fully enlightened and shared all the same factual beliefs. It is not enough to show that people's basic ethical and value judgments are different, for such differences might be all due to differences and incompletenesses in their factual beliefs. . . [14]

To make explicit his argument, Frankena offers us the case of one society where members believe that ". . . children should put their parents to death before they get old, whereas we do not. These primitive people may believe this because they think their parents will be better off in the hereafter if they enter it while they are still able-bodied; if this is the case, their ethics and ours are both alike in that they include the precept that children should do the best they can for their parents. The divergence, then, should be in factual, rather than in ethical beliefs."[15]

---

[13]Cornman and Lehrer, *Philosophical Problems and Arguments*, p. 433.
[14]William K. Frankena, *Ethics* (Englewood Cliffs, N.J., Prentice-Hall, 1963), p. 93.
[15]Frankena, *Ethics*, p. 92.

According to Frankena, it is not enough to show that societies espouse different basic ethical and value judgments; one would have to show that such disagreement over judgments ". . . would still be different even if they were fully enlightened, conceptually clear, share the same factual beliefs, and were taking the same point of view.[16] To demonstrate this, it would be necessary to find model cases in which all these conditions are fulfilled and people still disagree. Frankena claims that cultural anthropologists have not shown us such cases, for their cases exhibit differences in conceptual understanding and factual belief.[17]

It is important, therefore, to draw the conclusion that the claim that there is no objectively valid rational way of justifying basic ethical or value judgments one against the other has not been proved. It is, of course, very difficult to show that people's basic ethical and value judgments would not differ if they were fully enlightened. But the burden of proof is on the maker of the claim who contends that such is not the case — a claim implicit in the present-day ethnic's claim that there is no objectively valid rational way of justifying basic ethical disagreements.

The upshot of this is that ethnic demands, like other demands, are not immune to criticism and critique. They may be serious, either politically, economically, psychologically, or socially, but they are not free from the kind of critique and open debate so necessary for decision making to take place. To consider otherwise is to start in motion a devolution of power based on appeasing self-interest groups who cannot be denied by so-called objective or rational means. This may lead to decentralization of political units, a retribalization of politics, and a "refeudalization" of society.

CONCLUSION

Some may contend that the gains made by ethnics and dissidents recently is the price to be paid for group conformism and

---

[16]Frankena, *Ethics*, p. 93.
[17]Frankena, *Ethics*, p. 93.

mobility. CP and the claims made for it — a relatively hetero-
genous society with a high degree of cultural democracy — is a
far more desirable social order than one with a homogenous
sameness. In this sense there seems to be some value in an
ideology that declares ethnicity to be beautiful and provides
identity, solidarity, and legitimacy to groups traditionally subject to discrimination and vilification, largely on the basis of
race or sex.

CP as a vehicle for sustaining and supporting ethnic diversity seems peculiarly fitted to the task of adapting to new conditions in American society. On a positive note, cultural
pluralists will argue that a devolution of power, leading to
decentralization of political units, could lead to community or
local control, a highly regarded bastion of democratic decision
making. Further, CP may develop into a broader movement of
cultural democracy by denying the narrower self-interest ends
of ethnicity in favor of the ideals enunciated by Green, a result
which would be the embodiment of cultural democracy.

Whether such possibilities constitute wishful thinking is the
issue. Our modern, bureaucratic, interdependent national state,
with its great penetration into every citizen's private life in
education, morality, housing, and work, generates the conditions which will either sustain the cultural pluralist's beliefs of
realizing cultural democracy or will make of those beliefs a
hollow mockery. If government, political parties, and the array
of private institutions of American society organize themselves
to deal formally and officially with individuals and groups on
the basis of their ethnic background or some common bond of
ethnicity, then it is worth remembering that such blocs can be
penalized as well as rewarded on the basis of a so-called
common past, race, religion, or "bloodstream." We need only
remember the precedents of European enmities as well as blacks
in the pre- 1954 South and the Japanese-Americans on the West
Coast during World War II. Do we really want government and
the various institutions that have considerable power over our
lives to act on the assumption that a common past, accent,
religion, sex, or life-style generates common, even identical,
interests and responses among individuals? To do so is to deny

our basic individuality, a trait basic to the realization of democracy.

Ethnic groupings are not irrational, but ethnic demands
couched in the language of uncompromising demands may be.
In this regard, it would behoove policy-makers to clarify the
distinction between cultural relativism and ethical relativism.
Above all, it would behoove legislators to recognize CP for
what it is, namely, a vehicle promoting ethnic identity and
goals as well as helping subsume ethnicity under the broader,
more acceptable, rubric of cultural democracy.

Chapter Seven

BILINGUALISM AND PLURALISM: BETWEEN A ROCK AND A HARD PLACE*

I AM pleased to have the opportunity to respond to Professor Pizzillo's[1] paper because the topic he has chosen appeals to, perhaps fascinates, huge audiences, not solely because bilingualism and pluralism are current, but because each offers "the glimpse behind the curtain" in terms of what it is to live a different way of life, to perceive oneself and the world in quite a different way. Each reveals aspects of American life rarely caught except in certain novels or in movies such as *The Godfather* and the Swedish import *The Emigrants*.

In his paper, Pizzillo has set forth a description of the prevalent state of bilingual education and has proposed reasons for directing our attention and effort toward asking some hard questions and making bilingual education a much-needed and vital part of the American educational experience. His general aim, I take it, is to provoke each reader to self-inquiry and to realize that there is no single culture in the United States whose symbols, values, roles, attitudes, or general life-style are acceptable to all. In short, Pizzillo wishes to alert us to a new ethnic consciousness, one that delights in the glory of America's recently rediscovered pluralism.

These are most provocative considerations, demanding our attention and critical judgment. I would like, therefore, in the first part of my response, to offer a critical account of some of Pizzillo's basic ideas, which seem to me intrinsically interesting and, moreover, important for education. In the second part of my response, I will formulate certain criticisms and reserva-

---

*Adapted from *Current Issues in Education* (Glassboro, N.J., John Dewey Society, 1976).

[1]Joseph J. Pizzillo, "Bilingualism in the United States and Its Relationship to Pluralism," *Current Issues in Education*, Vol. 1, No. 1, January 1976.

tions concerning the basic features of Pizzillo's descriptive account. My remarks in this section will be grouped under three headings: "Conceptual and Moral Difficulties," "Cultural Diversity and Cultural Pluralism," and "Instructional Problems."

A CRITICAL ACCOUNT

We have much to learn from Pizzillo's paper. It is readily agreed that it is perhaps impossible to exaggerate the importance of language acquisition in the education of our children. He warns us that bilingual education is not new in the United States, having its roots in America's diversity of an earlier period. The commitment to bilingual education, according to Pizzillo, was choked off by the rising tide of American nationalism that emerged along with World War I. The return or reinstatement of bilingual education came about, at least in part, by the awareness that the educational level of Mexican-Americans, revealed in the data of the 1960 national census, was considerably below the national average. After considerable effort in Congress, the Bilingual Education Act, Title VII of the Elementary Education Act, was passed.

Bilingual education, according to Pizzillo, is demanded and quite fashionable today. Public interest and support continue at high levels. He gives short shrift to glorified versions of remedial reading programs or English-as-a-Second-Language programs, and proposes that increasing the student's competency in two languages, his native tongue and English, employing both as a vehicle for content instruction, is called for. But along with the instructional use of language should go an emphasis on culture. Pizzillo, following Rodriquez, informs us that "language is not just an instrument for communication and learning; it is a set of values. Bilingual education is, then, best viewed as bilingual-bicultural education."

Pizzillo's definition of bilingual education is crucial, for the entire thrust of his argument turns on the acceptance of bilingual education as bilingual-bicultural education. In such a program, there is no merit in learning a new language just for the sake of exercising certain skills. If the bilingual-bicultural education program does anything at all, it is to develop an

integrated personality, enhance a positive self-concept, and promote cultural understanding. If it is eminently successful, the
bicultural individual has developed a high level of proficiency
in two languages, neither preferring one to the other but using
either one in the appropriate situation, and has mastered the
nuances of two distinct cultures.

In a discussion of the target audience of bilingual education
in three states, Pizzillo makes explicit the primary thrust of
bilingual education, which is, of course, the inclusion of a
second language other than English, the official language of
the American school, on an equal footing. His discussion of the
characteristics of existing programs is highly descriptive and
too elaborate to summarize here, but he intends that the reader
will come to appreciate variant forms and possibilities of the
different approaches to bilingual education programs.

One irony is to be considered in connection with the above. I
found myself not so much impressed by the great variations
and possibilities in the existing programs but puzzled by the
cumulative effect arrived at after reading Pizzillo's admittance
that "there is considerable variation among the communities in
which bilingual education programs exist," "bilingual programs range in grade levels from pre-school and kindergarten
through twelfth grade," "the many programs differ considerably in emphasis," "There is little consensus about the
methods to be used in bilingual programs," and "finding qualified bilingual staff has been a problem." With regard to materials, "there is wide diversity among bilingual
programs in terms of material used." Finally we are informed
that "the field of bilingual education is still in a developmental state."

Yet despite the foregoing itemization, Pizzillo tells us that
"schools with bilingual programs can serve as catalysts for the
integration of diverse cultures within a community." He claims
that "this can be accomplished in part by the teacher, with the
community's assistance." Giving the teacher this very important function, Pizzillo considers certain cultural competencies
needed by teachers in bilingual settings. Finally, he proposes
that "On a national basis, generally, bilingualism fosters cul-

tural pluralism in our international society, through maintenance of the lingual-cultural heritages of various groups — a concept which is consistent with the democratic principle of choice, central to the American way of life — principles now rejected in a free society, and associated with the myth of the 'melting pot' tradition."

What is wanted, according to Pizzillo, is a pluralism where not only do the members of society function successfully in one, two, or more languages and cultural styles but where individuals can abide by and function successfully, adhering to different customs and languages and to less crippling language stereotypes than those accepted today. Bilingual education is offered in the hope of promoting a society where groups function without cultural bias and are behaviorally committed to the value that no one race, culture, or language is preferred *prima facie* over another.

The above sketch of Pizzillo's ideas does not do justice to the detail of his treatment, but his main points are, I believe, now evident, and I turn thus to the positive consideration of their import, adding further detail as the need may arise.

First, I should express my agreement with much of what Pizzillo has to say on the topic of bilingual education. Surely the state of language instruction in the United States is vulnerable to the criticisms he offers. In particular, recognition of the functional illiteracy problem of many non-English-speaking children in America should move us to some new ideas to deal with the problem. The fact that children in the United States are living in a society of persons who come from a variety of racial and cultural backgrounds, and that, if individual learning and growth are to be enhanced, each child must be helped to come to terms with the reality of his own significance and must be able to express this sense in behavior, means we need to help children experience their worth both as individuals and as cultural beings. Only if we acknowledge and show respect for cultural differences in values, beliefs, and behaviors that exist among our children will we be able to foster positive and constructive learning.

Second, I applaud the notion that children should use their

mother tongue and be able to relate it to their identities. If we accept rather generally the notion that culture is "the general method by which a group of people organizes its life from the cradle to the grave," we take into account the idea that culture is a method or tool constructed for dealing with common life problems. These problems are, of course, experienced by all groups, and yet there is no universally accepted pattern for handling any of these problems. Different cultural patterns are thus different solutions to the same human problems. Hence, difference does not entail or imply inferiority. It is harmful and destructive for any child to be led, either explicitly or implicitly, to believe that cultural differences are hierarchically arranged with, say, middle-class Anglo-American culture being somewhat better than other cultures in our nation, or that Anglos are better than non-Anglos.

Non-English-speaking children in America need to experience that the language they bring with them to school is valued as an asset to be used and respected. Moreover, English-speaking children need to learn that another language can be a valuable tool for learning, for conceptualizing, and for interpersonal relations. Bilingual education is therefore good because it can help many of our students understand and respect the deep meaning that language has for personal identity and worth, both for themselves and for others.

Finally, I endorse the implicit objective of bilingual education of fostering the core belief that every culture is good and intrinsically worthwhile. I presume that such an aim seeks to empower children who are receptive and flexible in facing culturally diverse values, beliefs, and life-styles.

Having indicated a broad area of agreement, I proceed now to formulate certain criticisms and reservations concerning basic features of Pizzillo's account.

CONCEPTUAL AND MORAL DIFFICULTIES

What mainly is at rock bottom in Pizzillo's paper is the concept of bilingualism. But just what is bilingualism? It is not

clear from Pizzillo's account what it is. But surely its explication is basic to understanding the concept of bilingual-
bicultural education put forth. We would profit from an
ordinary language analysis that reveals customary uses, distinctions, relations, and emphases. However, because of the limitation of time, perhaps it will suffice to recognize that the
concepts of bilingualism and biculturalism are related, but not
identical. We commonly take note of the fact that large minority groups in the United States who are bilingual also have
a culture that is different from the host or dominant Anglo-
American culture. For instance, in the Southwest all the bilingual people speak Spanish or an Indian dialect. Hence, in the
Southwest bilingualism always connotes biculturalism. But it
takes only a moment's reflection to see that some minority
group members, even though bilingual, may not be bicultural.
The literature on American immigrants and their children is
replete with such examples, particularly in the case of the second generation. Many of these have been portrayed as typically
"marginal persons" groping aimlessly and accepting fortui-
tously from either culture. Or, to take another tack, we can see
that a group may indeed be bicultural, as in the example of the
Jew who spends part of his daily life immersed in secondary
relationships involving business with Gentiles, but whose
home life and primary associations are spent wholly with other
Jews. It is not inconceivable to think of a Jew who shares two
cultures, but speaks only English.

Hence, even though interrelated and interdependent, biculturalism and bilingualism are not identical terms. Bilingualism, in its most ordinary employment, means fluency in at
least two languages, including oral communication, the en-
coding and decoding of written symbols, and the correct inflec-
tion and pitch, commonly called the superimposed structure of
a language. Facility in the use of two languages may range
from a minimal competency in either language to a high level
of proficiency in both. Generally speaking, however, the bilingual person tends to be more proficient in one language than the
other even though he or she may have attained a high level of

proficiency in both languages.[2] Biculturalism, on the other hand, refers to the cultural elements that may include language but go beyond language, insofar as it is a functional awareness and participation in two contrasting sociocultures (statuses, roles, values, etc.). Thus for the purpose of clarifying the conceptual difficulty here, if it is only the language fluency that is assessed as bilingual, it is obvious that bilingualism is not biculturalism. Hence, it is possible to attain bilingualism without dual acculturation, and biculturalism can be achieved without bilingualism.

Does our briefly put description of "bilingual" offer us any warrant for asserting more than "having a fluency in two languages"? I doubt it. How, then, does Pizzillo's account move from bilingual education to bilingual-bicultural education? Bilingualism, adapted to groups by Pizzillo, gives the connotation that self-images, emotions, intellects, and different socioeconomic levels of living must be connected to the point of amalgamation of languages with people. This then leads to Pizzillo's conclusion that much more than fluency in two languages is necessary. He proposes, in effect, melting two cultures through the vehicle of language, namely, bilingual-bicultural education.

My major criticism is that Pizzillo's argument for bilingual education turns on a definition of bilingual education that encloses bicultural education. That is, as against those interested in English-as-a-Second-Language or monolingual education, Pizzillo declares that bilingual education should increase the student's competency in both English and, say, Spanish, and both should be used concurrently as media of instruction in any portion of the curriculum except the languages themselves. Thus, for instance, science will be taught in both Spanish and English, or arithmetic in Spanish and social studies in English. But without the least acknowledgement of the

---

[2] I am puzzled about Pizzillo's ignoring the fact that the so-called bilingual may actually have a very low level of development in both languages, thus making the student functionally illiterate in both languages. *See* Guy Pryor, "Evaluation of the Bilingual Project and Hardendale Independent School District, San Antonio, Texas, in the First and Second Grades of Four Elementary Schools During the 1967-68 School Year." Our Lady of the Lake College, San Antonio, Texas, 1968. Mimeographed.

radical differences in context of bilingual education and bicultural education, or the morally crucial variations of the meanings of "bilingual" and "bicultural", Pizzillo's discussion glides easily and resoundingly from the notion of bilingual education to that of bilingual-bicultural education.

There is a sense in which it would be hard to find a better example of the danger of naively defining a term in educational discourse in order to win acceptance of the program offered. In brief, Pizzillo has not offered us a reportive definition of bilingual education, but has stipulated its use to include biculturalism. Moreover, something of importance is taking place in this "move." Pizzillo's definition raises much more than instructional concerns; practical and moral issues are posed. My major point is that it would be foolish to challenge the accuracy or form of Pizzillo's definition of bicultural education. Rather, as Israel Scheffler tells us,[3] what needs to be examined and justified is the program (in its moral and practical aspects) called for by the definition.

I assume Pizzillo's point to be that a program that is bilingual without also being bicultural restricts a child's learning, and demeans him as well. Such a program denies the deep psychological and social meaning of language and is merely a "bridge model" of bilingual education which, if successful, has the effect of phasing out the non-English language as soon as possible. Thus Pizzillo's programmatic definition of bilingual education rules out the teaching of a second language that stresses only skills (TESOL: Teaching of English to Speakers of Other Languages) and any other of the so-called "bridge" models.

Rather than take issue with the definition, it would be of interest to find out what evidence exists concerning the efficacy of Pizzillo's bilingual education versus the bridge models. Is one program more productive of students capable of getting and holding onto jobs, not just menial ones, but jobs with a future? What of the financial cost? The *Lau vs. Nichols* decision mandating bilingual education programs and their suc-

---

[3]Israel Scheffler, *The Language of Education* (Springfield, Thomas, 1960), *see* especially Chapter 1.

cessful establishment is a wide gap to fill.[4] It will require trained teachers in bilingual education and new curriculum material. According to Pizzillo, there is a dearth of both. Which type of bilingual program can best accommodate large-scale in-service work by the universities? At what cost? Many state legislatures will be involved, since the programs require a larger percentage of school money to come from state funds. The implementation of bilingual programs by school districts and universities will, to a great extent, be dependent on how the legislators assess the cost and efficacy of the various versions of bilingual education programs. State legislators and school district officials will have to review carefully the hard data on this matter. In any event, a decision that has such great importance is not to be decided by a programmatic definition of bilingual education, but on the basis of accurate and reasoned judgments. Important questions of practical import require critical and careful judgment, not merely solution by definitional fiat.

However, I suspect that Pizillo's definition of bilingual education hides another important point, namely, a value question. His definition commits us to the value that a bilingual education that fails to deal with the attitudes, theories, and values of another socioculture cannot produce a "truly" bicultural individual. If this is what Pizzillo intends, then a question needs to be asked. Clearly Pizzillo regards bilingual education as an instrument or process necessary for producing the valued bicultural individual. The question becomes, Is this valid? Is the bicultural individual best produced by a bilingual education program? It seems that we have here something akin to earlier views of pedagogy that considered mathematics to be the best means of producing someone knowledgeable about logic. In other works, we taught math in order to teach students logic. Today we know that there is something dreadfully wrong with

---

[4]In this case, the Supreme Court upheld a class action suit filed by Kinney K. Lau, a minor, through Mrs. Kam Wai Lau, his Guardian and Litem, to compel the San Francisco Unified School District to provide all non-English-speaking Chinese students with bilingual compensatory education in the English language. Associate Justice Douglas wrote that short opinion in which Associate Justices Brennan, Marshall, Powell, and Rehnquist joined. Concurring opinions were written by Associate Justices Steward and Blackmun, with Chief Justice Berger joining with both concurring opinions.

teaching A explicitly in order to arrive at students learning B implicitly. If this analogy holds, then perhaps the claim should become that "true bilingualism is better attained when the individual becomes bicultural, rather than the claim that bilingualism produces biculturalism. However, the answer to this question remains unclear.

But perhaps Pizzillo's breaking down of the distinction between bilingual and bicultural into bilingual-bicultural education aims to commit us to the position that although the relationship between the two terms is not necessarily a natural, commonplace one, it *should* be. He may be warning us that while it is possible to be bicultural to some extent without knowing the language of the second culture, "complete" biculturalism cannot be achieved without high levels of proficiency in the languages of both cultures. The valued bicultural student envisioned by Pizzillo has a firsthand knowledge of, and acquaintance with, the roles that she is expected to play in the two sociocultures. Not only does she know how to play these roles, but she is well-versed in and has some emotional commitment to the value systems of both cultures. She knows not only the spoken language of both cultures, but knows the "silent language" in playing these roles. Moreover, she neither intrinsically prefers one socioculture to the other, but rather uses either system in the appropriate situation.

No one could guess, from Pizzillo's account, that there is any problem of arguing from facts to values, since he is quite forthright in pronouncing his values and makes little effort to avoid giving the impression that these values are proper and thoroughly democratic. Indeed, at one point, after telling us that the curriculum and the orientation of teacher training must be reorganized so that "the English-speaking Anglo-oriented perspective is shared with other viewpoints and ideas," he declares that "bilingual education allows people to live in and be part of two cultures." Yet he never explains how the basic justification of his programmatic definition of bilingual education can yield all the value judgments he offers nor, alternatively, what their warrant is. It is objected, in other words, that such claims as "bilingual education would seem pedagogically sound. Educators stress the importance of allowing the individual to begin and maintain his schooling in his first language" make the case for Pizzillo's bilingual education. We must not take it for granted that there is no need to differentiate between a bilingual education program that is taught as a worry-free activity in a purely academic setting and one which is taught as a technique for those whose survival depends on learning another language. For the non-English-speaking student, the latter may be the case; for the Anglo-American student, the former may be found. For the sake of greater clarity and moral integrity, it would have been helpful if Pizzillo had addressed himself to this problem.

CULTURAL DIVERSITY AND CULTURAL PLURALISM

In this section I wish to consider Pizzillo's effort to persuade us of the importance of bilingual education because of its intimate connection to and significance for pluralism (that is, cultural pluralism). Hence, he has not only offered a rationale for bilingual education that claims pedagogical soundness and the stamp of moral authority, but he has given us pluralism as its social significance. There are danger signals, however, in that this position may be either socially naive and/or logically confused.

Social naiveté is exhibited by Pizzillo insofar as his piece is largely ahistorical. From a not too distant historical perspective, foreign language instruction in general and bilingual education in particular has been tied to a deep class bias in the United States. For generations the children of immigrants tried to rid themselves of the stigma of employing a second language, particularly with an accent. Speaking a second language was a mark of class, either denoting a recently arrived or nonacculturated immigrant family — thus, generally speaking, marking a lower class person — or it was a quality distinguishing the elite, the wealthy, the indolent rich or refined minority, whose survival did not depend upon learning a second language, but whose rank demanded it. This class acquired a second language as a mark of status or wealth, and it reflected leisure time learning. But in either instance, ability to speak a second language was considered a class symbol in America,

ither of the class below or the class above, and in many re-
pects the symbol was to be avoided.

There are, of course, numerous exceptions to the above gen-
ralization. Mainly the exceptions have come from religious
ommunities where the learning of a second language — He-
rew, German, French, and the like — was considered essential
n the moral training of children. But, actually, few adults have
ad a strong desire to become bilingual, no less bicultural. For
nany Americans, it would seem, to be asked to become bilin-
ual would be no less an affront than to be asked to become
isexual. It seems to be the case that many American parents,
or one reason or another, refuse to expend the time or energy
eeded to acquire bilingualism, although they would like their
children to develop a speaking facility in a second or even a
hird language, but remain Anglo-Americans who know
another language or two.

My claim is that Pizzillo is socially naive insofar as he fails to
ake account of this long-standing cultural bias. He does take
ains to argue that bilingual children are advantaged, and the
ntire effort of his paper stems in one way or another from an
effort to give significance to the bicultural individual. If
we recall that biculturalism refers to the cultural elements
that *may* include language but go beyond language, then a program of bicultural education may be more easily accepted by
parents than a program of bilingual education. Naiveté is thus
replaced with the more sophisticated judgment that bilingualism is better attained when the individual becomes bicultural.

Logical confusion is exhibited by Pizzillo in a common but
deplorable confusion that mistakes cultural diversity for cultural pluralism. Pizzillo, failing to analyze the lack of identity
here, simply equates the two. Implicitly he accepts and values
the notion of diverse cultures living side by side, each en-
hancing the other, yet each assured of its own worth and value
as well as its integrity. As has been pointed out in detail in
preceding chapters, the two terms — cultural diversity and
cultural pluralism — are not identical, and it is misleading in
the extreme to equate them.

But what of cultural pluralism? Varying degrees of confusion surround the concept since its inception by Horace M. Kallen in the second decade of the present century.[5] As early as 1915 Kallen predicted the realization of cultural pluralism in the United States as —

> . . . a federal republic; its substance a democracy of nationalities, cooperating voluntarily and autonomously through common institutions in the enterprise of selfrealization thróugh the perfection of men according to their kind. The common language of the commonwealth, the language of its great tradition, would be English, but each nationality would have for its emotional and involuntary life its own peculiar dialect or speech, its own individual and inevitable esthetic and intellectual forms. The political and economic life of the commonwealth is a single unit and serves as the foundation and background for the realization of the distinctive individuality of each *natio* [sic] that encompasses it and of the pooling of these in a harmony above them all. Thus "American civilization" may come to mean the perfection of the cooperative harmonies of "European civilization" — the waste, the squalor and the distress of Europe being eliminated — a multiplicity in a unity, an orchestration of mankind.[6]

What is crucial in such a statement is the notion of cultural *pluralism* as respectful of the dominance of core culture embodied in the English language, values, and tradition. Diversity and its acceptance has been exhibited in the ethnic cruisines, Columbus Day, and in religious toleration, but the respect tended to those who diverged from the WASP ideal was minimal at best and nonexistent at worst. Cultural *pluralism*, in effect, remained more a myth of American society than a concept which has supported its institutions and practices. The myth assumed that American society would be able to fulfill democratic goals by absorbing differences. But the fact is that American society did not tolerate cultural diversity and insisted on a pervasive sameness by.all who wished to share in its resources. Moreover,

---

[5]Early in 1915 there appeared in the pages of *The Nation* a series of two articles by Kallen under the title "Democracy *Versus* the Melting Pot." Reprinted in Horace M. Kallen, *Culture and Democracy in the United States* (New York, Boni and Liveright, 1924).

[6]Kallen, *Culture and Democracy in the United States*, p. 124.

even those who were willing to abandon their cultural back-grounds to gain their share of the "good life" were often denied entrance into society. Thus there were those for whom the price was *never* too high, those for whom the price was always too high, and there were those who were never allowed to even know or pay the price.

The re-emergence of the concept of cultural pluralism in recent years is perhaps testimony that the older myth is no longer accepted today. Today's cultural pluralism, however, is decidedly different from that of its predecessor. What is different is the emphasis on *cultural* pluralism, and its fundamental posture is that individuals and groups can function successfully and democratically if they believe that no one race, culture, or language is preferred over another. In short, *cultural* pluralism assumes the following:

1. There must be a rejection of any position that assumes that some people are better than others, that homogeneity is better than heterogeneity, and that some culture forms (language, values, etc.) are better than others.
2. There must be rejection of the model of the "preferred American American" — the WASP — and adoption of a view which encourages and supports diversity in language, life-styles, religions, and any other cultural characteristics.

Thus there is an important difference between yesteryear's cultural *pluralism* and today's *cultural* pluralism. The former was found wanting because it was used to create an illusion of respect for cultural diversity and equality of opportunity. Non-whites and others did not receive the rewards of society and were held responsible for their failure. Today's *cultural* pluralism, on the other hand, demands that Native Americans, blacks, women, Hispanics, Jews, and any group feeling different or which dares to be different have access to the resources, privileges, and power of American society. A corollary of this view includes the rejection of concepts, institutions, and actions that reward individuals or groups on the basis of race, culture, sex, class, and national orgin.

It would, perhaps, be helpful to suggest a kind of formula for seeing the relationship between *cultural* pluralism and cultural diversity. This relationship may be put in this way:

1. CP (*cultural* pluralism) is desirable as an end.

2. In present-day society, CD (cultural diversity) as a social ideal is the best way of achieving CP.

3. Therefore, do whatever CD involves.

In short, the new *cultural* pluralism is a response to a changed situation; one that is not satisfied with a mere acknowledgement of diversity of cultures in American society. The fact is that the United States has included citizens of diverse cultures; it is also a fact that many groups have been disenfranchised or "made invisible" for generations. *Cultural* pluralism recognizes and celebrates America's diversity but goes further to demand a state of equal coexistence in a mutually supportive relationship within the framework of each person securing his own identity and willing to extend to others the same respect and rights that he expects to enjoy himself.

Hence, the concept of *cultural* pluralism suggests a movement of affection and identity, enriched perhaps by the subtle, provocative ways in which one differs from others, and reinforced by a strong attachment to one's diversity. The concept, in other words, makes a great deal of cultural diversity and is a force for asserting claims against the institutions of society, for any oppressed group has the best chance of changing the system if it raises the communal consciousness of its individual members.

The new emphasis on *cultural* pluralism does not require renaming it, but it does give direction to those who, for many reasons, experienced deprivation, powerlessness, alienation, and frustration. Consequently, *cultural* pluralism may now be seen to read as *cultural socioeconomic pluralism*. It demands political and social policies which would result in a more equal distribution of the goods, prerogatives, and services of American society.

The major political and social policy reflective of *cultural* pluralism in education has been the development and implementation of bilingual-bicultural programs, both in the public schools and in teacher education programs. Implicit in the arguments of Pizzillo and others linking bilingual education with bicultural education is the belief that these programs will somehow "foster cultural pluralism in our intercultural society. . . . "

According to Pizzillo, "Ideally, bilingual education is intended to produce a balanced bilingualism-biculturalism within the learner, whereby he has the ability to function equally well in the two linguistic and cultural contexts."

Pizzillo's programmatic definition of bilingual-bicultural education makes the assumption of the transferability of bicultural skills into effective participation in society. Moreover, a bilingual education program aims to enable each student to retain and develop his cultural identity while he becomes versed in the language and values of mainstream America. Hence, for Pizzillo, the product of bilingual education is biculturalism: the ability to function competently and comfortably in the culture of the student's family as well as the culture represented by the majority of Americans.

The common assumption of *cultural* pluralists is that *cultural* pluralism is achievable through programs of bilingual-bicultural education. Non-English-speaking students studying and interacting with English-speaking children, will somehow work this out. In effect, the assumption is that *cultural* pluralism is to be had through schooling that influences people's attitudes and behavior, so much so that institutions are eventually changed. But isn't this too naive a view? Doesn't our experience suggest the limitations of schooling in this and other regards? Cultural parity among diverse groups is not likely to be achieved in public education alone. The extent to which entrenched institutions other than the school are reluctant to grant cultural parity will determine whether or not some sort of meaningful *cultural* pluralism can be achieved.

INSTRUCTIONAL QUESTIONS

To this point, I have attempted to question broad-ranging aspects relating to bilingual education. There is, in addition, another area of practical import to consider, namely, instructional matters.

The primary thrust of bilingual education is, of course, the inclusion on equal footing of a second language other than English in the school. On the surface this would seem to be an innocent enough objective. But when the educational personnel of a school district attempts to implement this objective, it may be that there are certain problems and implications which have to be considered. For example, is it the case that teaching a person in his native language is an irrelevancy? Although Pizzillo tells us that such a practice is "pedagogically sound," isn't love, compassion, understanding, dignity, and respect what is really necessary in teaching, in whatever language? Although bilingual education programs do indeed attempt this, is this "good teaching" syndrome necessarily excluded from other forms of language education programs? It may be, I suspect, but I do not think Pizzillo has sufficiently made the case for it. We are left with little or no idea about such an important consideration.

More specifically, however, Pizzillo never tells us if the second language is going to be used to move the student faster into adequate proficiency in English so as to ensure the non-English-speaking student normal progress in schooling. We are unsure whether or not the English-speaking student will be graded in terms of developing equal proficiency in both languages. Is it the case that the non-English-speaking and English-speaking student will be expected to develop equal proficiency in both languages? If so, to what levels will they be raised? These are questions that must be encountered and answered if anyone is going to take bilingual education seriously.

What is perhaps even more important for the educator is the instructional question of bilingual education itself. That is, what does it mean when we say that students will be taught in two languages? If we take the Hispanic communities in the United States as our example, we readily see that there are strong language clashes within the general language area, so that Puerto Ricans in New York City, Cubans in Miami, and Texas-Mexicans in El Paso find their own language differences quite exaggerated. Pizzillo, following Steiner, claims that, "Chicanos are developing an authentic third language which is neither Spanish nor English, and which has developed so far as to be creating its own literature." Thus quite innocently we come to the vexing question, What counts as two languages? The question of what counts as a language is indeed important, but an instructional question of major concern is, Are we talking about bilingual or trilingual education? Is the Chicano's first language (Tex-Mex) to be retaught as a second language to attain literacy and to establish a base of language on which English proficiency can be developed? Or is the Chicano to become literate in Tex-Mex only? Is literacy demanded in at least two languages? If so, then the Chicano student might need to become trilingual, speaking Tex-Mex and becoming literate in both standard Spanish and English.

Another question that has to be raised is what aspects of the bilingual education program are to be taught in which language? Are the sciences better taught in English than, say, in Spanish? Is the highly technical vocabulary of science more infused with English words than Spanish words? If so, then is it easier for the Spanish child to read "science" because of the rather easily identified English science words, or does the reverse hold true? Would the use of Spanish entail awkward and difficult translations of technical terms — for example, how to translate into Spanish the term *technology*? What of history and mathematics? What is the evidence in this regard?

This is not the place to explore all the questions facing the bilingual education teacher, but in particular it seems necessary to raise one final consideration. Consider the problem of teaching students such sophisticated concepts as "slavery," "exploitation," "colonialism," or "authority." These concepts are abstract, and ordinarily young children lack the rich content derived from personal experience to grasp their meanings and use. Acceptance of Pizzillo's stance on bilingual education would impose on the teacher the moral choice of teaching the concept of authority in terms of, say, the Mexican-American who considers authority to be embedded in the paternalistic, autocratic family and the offspring's role to be that of an obedient, respectful son or daughter in an intensely cooperative family relationship, or, on the other hand, teaching the concept of authority of America's counterculture which views authority as suspect, contaminated, corrupt, and regards authority relationships as neo-anarchists. A teacher should not be *in* authority, nor even, in R.S. Peter's distinction, be *an* authority.[7] At best the teacher is a friend, his job is to expose his frailties in the interests of mind expansion, eliminating the artificial boundaries between teacher and student imposed by wrongheaded notions of authority.

The problem is a major one. The teacher is not merely giving cognitive knowledge to his or her students, rather, teaching involves value stances. One may talk about authority, but in the second case above, openness and vulnerability are dispositional traits, not cognitive beliefs, and they are the prime requirements of teaching. It seems imperative to recognize that teaching, wherever it occurs, generally has conjoined cognitive, affective, and behavioral involvements. It has basic and pervasive effects whose causes are not located merely in propositional knowledge about a concept such as "authority." The way one teaches the concept of authority, the constraints on teaching, helps shape the way children learn and use the concept.

In any event, apart from the problem just posed, the fundamental question of practical consideration is this: What of teaching the same concept in two languages? Would not such an instructional practice double the cost in terms of energies and resources without the attainment of substantial gains? How sensible would be such a practice in terms of the student, providing, of course, that the teacher is capable of "pulling it off"? Is a double performance never or always, or just possibly, a waste?

There are the kinds of instructional questions that need extensive probing if we are to clarify our ideas about bilingual education.

---

[7]R.S. Peters, *Ethics and Education* (Glenview, Illinois, Scott, Foresman and Co., 1966), *see* especially Chapter 8.

CONCLUSION

What must be the general conclusion from what has been said thus far? To my mind, the inescapable one that stands out is the absolute necessity to recognize that we have been toying with the tip of the iceberg — trying to avoid it and feeling assured that nothing else exists to threaten us. Bilingual education programs, of whatever stripe and purpose, merely represent the tip of a problem that goes much deeper. At bottom is the recognition by many Americans that the traditional curriculum and language training are not appropriate today. We should take more than passing notice of the fact that what is wanted by non-English-speaking Americans is a greater share of the wealth and power of American society, an according of respect and dignity by groups historically considered to be "superior," and a social order that guarantees the end to humiliation and denial of elementary human rights. It is tragic that the United States has, in the past, offered its allegiance not to fairness and justice to all but to self-interest, prejudice, and Anglo-conformism.[8]

This is not the place to illustrate in detail, nor do I command the rhetoric to speak of, the long history of injustice suffered by America's racial minorities and women, but I am deeply aware that these groups will no longer peaceably accept the existing distribution of power, domestic or international, and the

---

[8]A very recent exception to this is the requirement, under amendments to the Voting Rights Act, that 464 counties in 27 states, including every county in Texas, will have to protect the voting rights of non-English-speaking citizens by conducting elections in more than one language.

This requirement, according to the Justice Department, applies in Autumn 1975 and to all future elections in the affected counties, even on local matters such as bond issues. This means that parts of more than half the states will now have to offer their voters special assistance — through ballots printed in languages other than English or through other means — to ensure that all have an equal chance to participate in the electoral process.

As defined by the Voting Rights Act, minority groups entitled to this assistance are American Indians, Asian Americans, Alaska natives, and persons of Spanish background. Spanish, the primary language of large groups throughout the Southwest, Florida, and New York, is expected to be the language that will figure more prominently in future bilingual elections.

political-socioeconomic realities that flow from it. School-oriented individuals must expect that the terminology of the social and behavioral sciences, e.g. culturally deprived, will no longer protect their actions from criticism and attack. But the long-suffering groups should be aware of the fact that schooling has little to say, in the final analysis, about the problems of man and society that really matter. Bilingual education programs, no matter how honest and well-intentioned, cannot rectify the distribution of power in favor of minorities, nor can it be used to change domestic policies.

If the majority of Americans come to be preoccupied with questions of human dignity, worth, and justice for all, then the schools might have an invaluable civilizing influence on such society. If, as is more likely, such questions are regarded with disdain, then our minorities and women will have to look elsewhere for enlightenment and help.

INDEX

A

Accommodation politics, 19, 22, 45
Addams, Jane, 41
Allport, Gordon, 109
Anglo-American tradition, 126
Authority, 196
A-w/o-B procedure, 136, 137

B

Bell, Daniel, 163
Biculturalism, 184
Bilingual Education Act, 179
Black Muslims, 145
Blacks, xxi, 4, 15, 19, 22, 33, 46, 50, 63, 65, 77, 122, 139-140, 144, 161, 179
Blauner, Robert, 159
Brown, Thomas M., 108

C

Caesarism, 109
Cajuns, 50
Canada, 139, 140, 143
Catholics, 14, 33, 63, 108, 143, 152
Civil Rights Movement, 38
Clark, Lorenne, M.G., 52
Coalitions, 103
Colonialism, 160
Common interest, 47, 76, 167
Community, 67, 74, 84, 135-136, 148-155, 163-167
Consciousness raising, 11, 163
Cornman, James W., 173, 174
Crisis of identity, 13-14, 15, 18-19
Cuber, John, 130
Cuisine, 31, 48
Cultural imperialism, 74, 78
Curriculum, 23-24, 73, 75
Curriculum, hidden, 116
Curry, Richard O., 108

D

Dahl, R.A., 102
Dahrendorf, Ralf, 17
de Crèvecoeur, J. Hector, 28
Democracy, cultural, 7, 67, 122, 138, 139, 164, 165, 167, 177
Democracy, participatory, x
Democratic Party, 19
Deschooling, 118
Desegregation, xvi
Dewey, John, 23, 148
Differences, 5
Discontent, 17-18, 162
Discrimination/prejudice, 27, 64, 82, 84, 139
Dobriner, William M., 160

E

"Easy riders", 44
Education, compensatory, 140
English-as-a-second-language, 179, 184
English democratic tradition, 126
Ennis, Robert H., 95
Ether, John, 123, 126
Ethnic demands, 168, 172-176
Ethnic identity, 13-14
Ethnic studies, 73, 74, 77
Ethnicity, viii, x, xii, xvi, xx, xxi, 3, 10, 12-20, 21-22, 27, 32-35, 38, 49
Ethnicity, resurgent, 12-20, 161, 162, 167
Ethnics, new, 15-16
Explanation, 105

F

Factions, 101
Federalist Papers, 101
Frankena, William K., 174
Freedom of association, 7
Freire, Paulo, 115

199